SWITZERLAND

100 Locals Tell You Where to Go, What to Hike, & How to Fit In

ISBN-13: 978-1508869399

CONTENTS

ABOUT THIS BOOK

This book is for people who want to see another side of Switzerland.

To stroll past the main attractions, yes, but also to find the hidden-away mountain path leading to a quiet glacial lake with a view of the Jungfrau peak (page 83). To learn that the world's first dining in the dark restaurant—with a blind waitstaff and a light-free eating experience—is in Zürich. Or to discover places like Thun (page 68)—a lesser-known lakeside town whose charm and beauty rivals the more popular Lucerne.

In other words, this book is for people who want to get under the skin of another culture. Who want to rent apartments and live in local neighborhoods. Who want to eat in tiny restaurants without English menus. Who want to deepen their experience of this wild, beautiful country.

Think of this as a supplement to your traditional guidebooks. Use those for their handy place histories, lists of local hotels (if that's your style), restaurant pricing charts, and basic language lessons. And then use this to go deeper—to find the most colorful neighborhood markets, the most delicious restaurants in the city center, and that pretty forested hiking trail that leads to a chalet-laden car-free ski town.

Now, a little orientation:

This book is split into 100 interviews with people who live all over Switzerland. Many have lived in their cities and towns for decades. Some were born and raised in the region. Others are expats who have fallen in love with their new country. And all of them love talking about the best their towns have to offer.

Below each person's name, you'll see a short bio designed to help you understand his or her background. If you are passionate about food, look for someone whose short bio includes "foodie" or "chef." If you're a culture lover, look for a culture lover. If you love to hike, look for hikers. And so on.

ABOUT THIS BOOK

Many of the interviewees are also tour guides, artists, business owners, or bloggers. Watch for web addresses below their interviews if you'd like to learn more about their art, blogs, businesses, or tours.

Finally, a few notes about Switzerland and the book:

On hiking: Hiking trails in Switzerland are extremely well marked. So if someone recommends hiking from Wengen to Kleine Scheidegg, just look for the yellow signs marking the way. Many of the interviewees don't give detailed trail directions and this is why. It's easy to find your way.

On mountain huts: A few interviewees suggest spending the night in a mountain hut. You can find contact information for the huts at *myswitzerland.com*. Just choose Accommodation > Other in the navigation, check the box marked Alpine Huts, and choose your region on the map.

On language: There are some common German suffixes that will help you understand what you're reading both while reading this book and while in Switzerland. The most important of these are: *weg*, which means "way" (and thus a *wander-weg* is a walkway and a *bergweg* is a mountain way); *brücke*, which means bridge (thus Kappelbrücke means Chapel Bridge); and *see*, which means lake (thus Thunersee is Lake Thun and Brienzersee is Lake Brienz). Similarly, in French, you'll often notice the word *pont*, which means bridge.

On websites: While American websites often end in .com, Swiss websites often end in .ch. You'll notice many URLs throughout this book with that ending. There's no need to add a .com to these—just type them in as you see them.

Finally, you'll notice this book doesn't have photos or maps. This is for length and printing reasons. That said, most tourist offices in Switzerland offer free maps and you can find photos of each featured place at *gigigriffis.com/switzerland*.

Now, then, into the book...

ON TRAVELING LIKE A LOCAL

Like many well-loved places, Switzerland has two faces.

There's the face that most tourists see, full of well-known lakeside cities, crowded chocolate shops, imposing clock towers, and pricey mountain railroads.

Some of these things are worth seeing and experiencing (as many of my interviewees will tell you). They're world-famous and beloved for a reason.

But they aren't the whole story of Switzerland.

There's another face, another story—one that the locals live every day—full of hidden-away hiking trails, alp cheese purchased directly from dairies on the mountainside, shopping centers in old aqueducts, and thrilling high-mountain sled runs.

For me, the goal of any travel is to experience both sides of the story—to see the major sights, certainly, but also to slip into the culture, to try to understand it. I want to feel—even if I am only there for a few days—like I am truly living in that place, exploring its more hidden corners.

I'm sure many of you feel the same. Which is, of course, the whole point of this book.

In over 15 years of short-term international trips, two years of traveling full-time, mostly in Europe, and one year as an expat here in Switzerland, I've come up with a routine that makes me feel more like a local. And the most important truth behind this routine is simply this: **the best way to live like a local is to ask locals.**

Which is why, for those of us who don't have a local friend to show us around, I've collected these interviews and written this book.

Before you dive into the interviews, though, here are five more ways to experience Switzerland (or any country, really) in a fresh, authentic, local-centric way:

1. Travel slowly. Spend some real time in a place. It would take a lifetime to see everything this lovely little country has to offer. But staying for a week or more in one place is a good start.

2. Rent apartments, preferably in a neighborhood full of local people. (Not sure how to find the right neighborhood? I've asked locals to tell us in the interviews you'll find in this book. Not sure how to find apartments? My personal starting point is Airbnb. And if you sign up at *airbnb.com/c/ggriffis?s=8* they'll give you a credit for your first trip.)

3. Shop at fresh markets, small butcher shops, and neighborhood bakeries. This is how the locals eat, so it's also where you'll find the most authentic local food experience.

4. Make friends with people who live there. Ask people about their lives, their thoughts, and their cultures. Expats and locals are both incredibly fascinating and every conversation will teach you a lot.

5. Try to fit in. In Switzerland, this means being relentlessly polite and considerate—letting people off the train before you attempt to board, stepping to the side before consulting your map, keeping the noise level low after 10 p.m., and always saying hello (in English, German, French, or Romansch, as you like) when you pass someone on a hiking trail.

It is these principles and this type of travel that I've molded the questions in this book around. I hope they make your experience of Switzerland as rich as mine has been.

AN INTRO TO SWISS FOOD

Surprisingly, when it comes to food in Switzerland, the main specialties are the same everywhere.

When you interview 100 people in Italy (as I did a year ago), you find that food is *very* regional there. 100 people give 100 different answers to the question "What dishes should we try while in your town?" But when you ask that same question in Switzerland, the answers are surprisingly similar—from the French part to the German part to the obscure corners of Romansch country.

Sure, there are still regional specialties (and you'll see some of them mentioned in the interviews later in the book) and even the overall Swiss specialties have their own twists in different regions. But overall, the Swiss must-eats are the same, whether you're in Zürich or Zermatt.

So, what are these country-wide specialties? Well...

Fondue
Fondue is a pot of melted cheese cooked with wine or other alcohol and served with bread and veggies for dipping. Different regions feature different cheeses and alcohols (in Geneva and Gruyères, for example, the local fondue—called moitie-moitie—is a mix of gruyère and vacherin fribourgois cheeses and the popular Mauler fondue is made with sparkling wine), but the basic concept is the same everywhere.

There are also non-traditional fondues popular with some locals. Around Lake Geneva, the most beloved is tomato fondue, which is eaten with potatoes and cooked with tomato sauce instead of wine. And in the Bernese Oberland, there's fondue chinoise—a meat fondue that comes with pickles, onions, rice, fries, and sauces.

Raclette
Olly Norris (page 253) put it best when he said, "[Raclette] is a cow's milk-based semi-firm cheese that comes in a wheel. The name is derived from the French verb racler, meaning 'to

scrape,' and refers to the way that this cheese is served: melted and then scraped onto your plate, often accompanied by local dried meat, potatoes, and salad. It is not for everyone, but you can't say you've experienced the Alps until you've tried raclette."

Raclette originated in the Verbier area (where Olly's based) but is beloved all over the country.

Rösti
Rösti is the Swiss take on hash browns. It's often served with a fried egg on top (or maybe a little liver), but local restaurants put their own various spins on it. Personally, I've seen rösti served with everything from mushrooms in a cream sauce to bacon and tomato sauce to finely prepared pork.

Cheese
When it comes to Swiss cheese, Beverley Wood (page 93) says it best: "Cheese is *the thing* here in the Swiss Alps. Typically, the farmers take the cows up to pasture early- to mid-June and stay there for 100 days. As summer continues, the cows are moved to higher and higher pastures and milked twice a day. The farmer makes cheese once a day. At the end of summer, the cheese is divided amongst the farmers based on how much milk each cow (from each farmer) produced. The wooden structures seen all over the mountains are where the farmers stay in summer and also where they store the cheese.

In late September, the cows return to the valleys and there are little festivals (called *chästeilet*—which literally means dividing or sharing of the cheese) held to celebrate. During those events, you can sample the cheese and enjoy the popular chäsbrot (grilled cheese on local brown bread sometimes with a shot of schnapps on the bread!). When the cows come back down to the valleys with flowered headdresses, this means that the herd is intact and it was a successful summer."

You'll have heard of the famous gruyère cheese, but other popular forms include alpkäse (cheese from the high Alps) and vacherin fribourgeois (from the Lake Geneva area).

AN INTRO TO SWISS FOOD

For a detailed look at Swiss cheese, see page 46 for an interview with a man whose title is literally "Master of Cheese."

Other Cheese Dishes
Other popular cheese dishes include chäsbratl (melted cheese on a slice of bread), macaronis du chalet (macaroni with cottage cheese), käseschnitte (cheese toast), and beignet de vinzel (cheese fritters).

Meats
In the meat category, Switzerland is known for good steaks and a variety of dried meats and sausages. Some of the dishes I heard about over and over again? Bernerplatte (a typical Bernese platter featuring bacon, sausages, sauerkraut, dried beans, and potatoes), Walliserteller (a plate of wafer-thin sliced dried meats and cheeses with little pickles and small silver onions often served with rye bread), grilled veal sausages, assiette valaisanne (Valais meat platter), and planchette (a spread of local meats and cheeses from Lake Geneva).

Some of the dried meats and sausages you'll see on a typical platter include landjaeger, bündnerfleisch, mostbröckli, and speck.

Wild game is also widespread in the fall (hunting season). You'll find locally hunted rehschnitzel (venison) and gemspfeffer (local mountain goat meat, wine-marinated and served as a stew) just about everywhere. In French-speaking Switzerland, look for the a la chasse menu, which features various wild autumnal fare (deer, wild boar, pheasant, mushrooms, etc.).

Also popular are cordon bleu, frikadelle (meatloaf), hörndli und ghackets (macaroni with minced meat), and züri gschnätzelts (slices of veal with mushrooms and cream, served with rösti).

If you're anywhere near a lake, perch, trout, pike, bondelle, and whitefish are likely to be the fare of choice. As Florence Vehier of Neuchâtel says, "Everybody here is fond of filets de perche, even though the fish no longer come from our lake (there are too few left)."

Other Specialties
Finally, other interviewee favorites and popular national dishes include kartoffelstock (mashed potatoes with vegetables), älplermakkaronen (alpine macaroni), and glühwein (very strong mulled wine with liquor, served in winter). There are also some special festival foods that show up from time to time, including grilled sausages, roasted chestnuts, and candied almonds.

Drinks
The best summary of the Swiss drink menu comes from Margo Cummings (page 100) in Spiez, who says, "Switzerland produces some fine wines, which are made in such small batches that they are not available for export (but are quite tasty and drinkable if you snag one while you're here). Every canton has its own favorite locally brewed beer and schnapps. Ovomaltine is a vitamin- and mineral-enriched chocolate powder mixed with warm or cold milk and is a beloved breakfast beverage. And the Swiss national soft drinks are Rivela (available in five different flavors) and Sinalco (available in orange and cola flavors)."

Ticino
While still Swiss in the sense that everything is clean, well organized, and on time, Ticino is an outlier when it comes to food, serving up a mix of northern Italian fare and Swiss specialties. You'll still find fondue and raclette in Ticino, but you'll also find pizza, pasta, gnocchi, polenta e spezzatino (cornmeal and red meat), salametti (local sausages), BBQ pork ribs, risotto, minestrone soup, filetto di cavallo (horse filet), Tichinese Merlot (red and white), and nocino (a walnut liquor enjoyed as an after-dinner digestivo).

TIPS FOR BUDGET TRAVELERS

It's no secret that Switzerland is an expensive place to visit.

That said, like anywhere in the world, Switzerland can be done extravagantly or on a budget. Here are a few local suggestions for stretching your dollars here in the Alps:

Transportation

1. If you're staying awhile, **consider a half-tax card.** These cards, which cost about 175 francs, cut almost all your train fares in half. For a short stay with a couple train rides, you probably won't need it. But if you're on the trains every day, it could save you a lot. So do the train ticket math before you come (you can find fare prices at *sbb.ch*) and keep the half-tax in mind.

2. Consider **buying a bike**, which could save you a lot on public transport, especially if you're staying awhile.

3. **Ask at the train station about special deals or discounts.** Or check online at *sbb.ch*.

4. **Consider a rideshare**. The Swiss trains are lovely, but sometimes it's cheaper to grab a ride through one of the many rideshare websites out there.

Food

5. **Cook your own food**. With average entrees costing around 25 francs, you'll save tons if you cook at home, even just for a few meals. You can also buy bread, cheese, and wine at the local supermarkets and picnic alongside one of Switzerland's lovely lakes, lookout points, hiking trails, or rivers. There are free BBQ areas and benches scattered along trails, lakes, and parks. And there's no better place for dinner with a view.

6. **Have your main meal at lunch.** Most restaurants have special lunch menus at about half the price of dinner.

TIPS FOR BUDGET TRAVELERS

7. Mixed drinks are expensive, so **stick to beer and wine.** And buy your beer from the Denner grocery store—it's the cheapest place around.

8. **Check out the restaurants in the Coop and Migros** supermarket chains for reasonably priced food.

9. **Swiss tap water is safe to drink**—as is the water provided by fountains along the hiking trails. So there's no need to pay extra for bottled water.

Accommodations

10. **Try Airbnb instead of a hotel.** Not only is it often less expensive, but you'll also have a kitchen.

11. **Consider camping.** Swiss campgrounds tend to have rather nice facilities (often including cabins, kitchens, and laundry rooms, and sometimes including dorms) and cost less than most other accommodations.

12. **Check out Switzerland's youth hostels.** Like all things Swiss, these tend to be very nice (though they're still more expensive than hostels elsewhere in the world).

13. **Travel in the off-season.** Prices for both housing and activities tend to drop in the spring and fall—and both can be quite lovely.

Activities

14. **Get outside.** Switzerland is, of course, all about the outdoors. People come here because it's heart-achingly beautiful...and most of that beauty is free. So, go for a hike. Enjoy a picnic. Take a stroll along the valley floor. The scenery doesn't cost a dime.

15. If you are in a large group, **split the cost of a mountain guide** and ask him or her to show you some of the most beautiful, challenging, or hidden hikes in the area.

THE INTERVIEWS:
PLAN BY INTEREST

THE GREAT OUTDOORS

Martin Schürmann
Professional Mountain Guide.

About Martin

I grew up, went to school, and did my apprenticeship in the Bernese Oberland, where (as luck would have it) the outdoor industry was huge and growing all the time. These days, I am a licensed mountain guide, a ski instructor, a BASE jumper, and a hunter. I also do helicopter rescue work at the official Rescue Station in Lauterbrunnen (*mountainrescue.ch*).

Before I became a mountain guide, I was a ski instructor, a mountain bike expert, and a guide for canyoning and bungee jumping. My degree is in electromechanics, but after an apprenticeship in 1997, I realized I didn't want to leave the mountains for a career in the city—so I stayed and built my work around the place and the sports that I love.

It's really difficult to become a mountain guide. It took me three years, but that was my biggest dream. So in 1999, I began my training, which, over several years, involved intensive avalanche courses, ski training, ice climbing, rock climbing, alpine mountain climbing, etc. In 2003, I officially became a mountain guide—just like my grandfather was.

Walks For Beginning Hikers

The easiest and most popular hike is from Wengen to Kleine Scheidegg. This walk has beautiful scenery with the Jungfrau peak constantly in the foreground. Another similar hike is from Grütschalp to Mürren with the Jungfrau, Mönch, and Eiger peaks in a panorama to your left. Finally, I'd add the hike from First (pronounced "fearsht") to Gross Scheidegg.

These three hikes are for everyone. They're relaxing, nice, and not too difficult. Which also means they're the most popular and you'll see plenty of other people on the trails.

For more intermediate hikers, we have hundreds of trails. In the Jungfrau region, you can hike a different route every day going hut to hut or village to village. You can even walk all the way from Mürren to Kandersteg going hut to hut.

Walks For Advanced Hikers

The trek from Schynige Platte to First is nice and you can join an organized hiking group if you like. From Isenfluh to Lauberhornhutte to Saxeten is also really nice—and you can take a public bus back. And one particularly famous route is the Eiger Trail, which runs from Eigergletscher (the Eiger Glacier) to Alpiglen.

Then there's Schilthorn—the 9,700-foot peak above Mürren. You can take the cable car up and walk down. Or you can walk from Mürren up to the top [editor's note: this is my personal favorite hike, also mentioned on page 82].

For advanced hikers who are interested in transitioning into climbing, there's the *via ferrata* (a protected climbing route that doesn't require full climbing gear or experience) from Mürren to Gimmelwald, which I created because I wanted to expose people to the next level—something not too extreme but a bit more than hiking. If you want to do high alpine treks or climbing, this is a good start. You'll need good shoes, a harness, and a via ferrata set (two carabiners).

Outside the Bernese Oberland

Zermatt, Saas-fee, and Engelberg are the most well known hiking areas. Graubünden and Ticino are super nice as well. And in Canton Valais, there are so many long hikes, you could walk forever. You could do the Mont Blanc route, which takes you on an eight-day tour of Switzerland, Italy, and France. Or the Jungfrau Massive, which takes you around the Jungfrau. The bottom line is the possibilities in Switzerland are endless.

Summits For Beginning Mountaineers

Here in Switzerland, we talk about the 4,000-meter peaks. These are important and they vary in difficulty. The easiest is Breithorn in Zermatt. Then there are the Hohberghorn and Allalinhorn peaks near Saas-Fee. If you're a little more intermediate, Weissmies is a good choice. If you summit that one, you can start thinking about doing more difficult peaks.

Here in the Bernese Oberland, the Mönch is the first one we summit with clients. Jungfrau is a bit more high altitude; to do it, you have to sleep overnight in a hut about 12,000 feet above sea level.

Whatever peak you do, if you aren't experienced, you'll need to hire a mountain guide.

Summits for Experienced Mountaineers
This valley—the Lauterbrunnen Valley—is the valley of north faces. You can climb the Mönch north face, the Eiger north face, Breithorn, Grosshorn, Jungfrau...and, outside the region, the Zermatt north face. Those are the most famous, technical, and difficult climbs. This part of the world—Canton Bern, Canton Valais, and Chamonix in France—is one of the biggest draws for alpinists. You have so many options.

Martin's Favorite Mountain Experience
For me, the most impressive experience was climbing the Eiger north face. I climbed it twice and the first time I stopped at a place called the "death bivouac"—and that spot is where you really realize how impressive it is. You realize the tourists below can't even see you, you're so small. If you keep going at that point, it's impressive. I have big respect for the guys who checked the route and climbed it first in 1938.

Long Treks for Distance Hikers
In this region, the Aletschgletscher—the longest glacier in Europe—offers a two- to 10-day hut-to-hut trek on the glacier with 4,000-meter peaks. The main trek (the famous one) takes two days. But you can extend it.

Staying Safe in the Swiss Mountains
Equipment is very important. Start with your shoes. You need a shoe with a good profile that fits your feet well. Clothes should

THE GREAT OUTDOORS

be functional. Don't wear jeans; if they get wet, they take way too long to dry.

Of course, you'll also need a backpack, your map, and water (though you don't need a lot, as we have tons of huts and water along many trails). Know where you're going. Inform yourself before you start. Have a goal. Make a plan. If you want to stay in a hut, reserve it beforehand. If you can't make it, call them. Those are the most important things.

Make sure someone knows where you're going. Tell them "If I don't call you by X time, I'm in trouble. This is where I'll be." This is important. Take a cell phone with you.

Keep in mind that if you do need rescue, the rescue team will need to know where to find you. So you should have a map and a plan. Knowing what trail you're on, what town you're near, where you were headed, and where you were coming from is important in a rescue situation.

Check the weather before you go. The weather here isn't accurate two or three days ahead of time, so double check the forecast before you go hike. You really don't want to get stuck in a storm in the mountains. If you are going to be gaining altitude, make sure to bring the proper clothes. The temperature difference can be shocking. Finally, make sure your travel insurance covers mountain rescue, especially if you are doing high alpine hikes.

Hiking Etiquette
First of all, if you walk past someone on the trail, say hello. It costs nothing and if you get in trouble, that person may be the one who has to help.

If you have a dog and will be passing cows, keep the dog leashed. The momma cows might see your dog as a threat to their babies. So keep your dog close. Walk through quickly (but don't let your dog run). We also have a lot of wildlife here—

18

mountain goats, deer, foxes, marmots—so make sure to respect that.

Carry your trash out. Clean up after yourself. If you brought it in, you bring it out. If it is biodegradable, throw it off the path. And don't poo next to the paths (I can't believe I even have to say that, but I do). If you open a gate, shut it behind you.

Trail Markers

The normal trails are marked with red and white. You'll see the red and white trail markers painted on rocks or trees along the way. You can usually see these even if there's snow. If you see a trail marked with blue and white, it's an alpine hike and may cross snow or glaciers. These are higher risk.

Similarly, if you see a sign that says *wanderweg* (literally "walk way"), that's an easy, walkable hike that is checked often and kept clear for hikers. A *bergweg* (mountain way) sign means a more technical hike and a trail that isn't checked or cleared. There may be snow, rock falls, floods, or mud.

If you're not sure about the difficulty of a hike or whether the trail is being kept up, the best thing to do is ask someone or hire a guide. We have hiking guides for normal trails and mountain guides for high alpine hikes and summits.

Our hiking trails range in difficulty from T1 to T5, in which T stands for technical. There are guidebooks with detailed information about these. The important thing to know is that if you plan a T5 hike, you need to be very sure-footed.

Legal Concerns

In the national parks (which are well marked as such), there is no wild camping. Outside the parks, generally camping is allowed. If you want to camp in the wild, ask the local people or the tourist office for information or look it up before you go.

When to Hike & Trek in Switzerland

Hiking season is usually from May to November. Some trails

may be closed in May—especially north faces—because of the snow. But usually you can start hiking in May, particularly on the sunny side of the slopes. November is the same.

High alpine season starts from mid-June and runs through mid-September. The actual dates depend on the snow conditions. Most of the alpine huts are open during those months. You can reserve a spot in one for a meal and a bed, so you don't even need to carry food for overnight hikes if you plan that way.

There are also winter routes for some of the alpine huts—but you'll have to carry your own food and melt snow for water.

Final Tips & Other Notes

If a sign says the hike is one hour, overestimate. You might take 1.25 hours or 1.5 hours. The hours on the signs are just an average (and keep in mind that that average is set by Swiss people used to living at altitude and hiking often). Your speed will depend on you, your fitness level, how often you stop, how many photos you take, etc. It's best to estimate more time until you're familiar with the trails.

If you are hiking to a destination (a town, a cable car station, etc.), check the connections before you go and make sure you can make the last cable car. You don't want to be late and get stuck walking down a dangerous trail in the dark. When you're doing this, it's also important to give yourself extra time and check your progress along the way. If you get half-way and it took you an extra hour, assume the next part of the trail will take even longer (because you're probably higher up and more tired). Make a new plan if you have to. Finally, if you will be sleeping at high altitude, you won't sleep very well. If you do a two-day hike above 3,000 meters, that second day can feel twice as hard as the first. Most people don't realize this until they experience it.

Find Martin at www.be-je.ch.

THE GREAT OUTDOORS

Dave Storey
Kayaker. Entrepreneur.

About Dave

I'm originally from Manchester but moved to Switzerland five years ago to be a ski instructor. After teaching kayaking in the U.K., it was always my dream to set up my own school, share my love of the sport, and get myself out on the water more often. So, after a couple years of preparation, hard work, ups, and downs, we (my wife and I) set up a kayak school. In 2015, we'll see our third summer running tours and coaching courses throughout Switzerland and abroad.

In addition to kayaking, I spend my free time with my little son, Timo, who keeps me from overworking too much, along with my very understanding wife. My wife and I also love skiing.

Where to Kayak

Paddling on Lake Brienz is one of the highlights of any trip...It's probably my favorite place to kayak in Switzerland. (Despite being on the lake all summer, I never get bored of it). Lake Brienz is calm and quiet with incredible mountain scenery and, of course, that beautiful turquoise glacial lake color.

Outside the Interlaken area (where my business is based), another favorite place is in the Urnersee on Lake Lucerne. Dramatic doesn't even begin to describe the huge cliffs that tower above you. It's also renowned for its wind, which can come out of nowhere and make it a serious place sometimes. Doing a guided trip here is definitely recommended.

My third choice would be the Lago di Lugano in Ticino, which is an area with great food, beautiful scenery, and a distinctly Italian flavor. It always feels like a holiday down here.

Hidden Gems for Kayakers

Going kayaking here is already a bit off the beaten track, especially in Interlaken where there are so many things to do and see. That said, sneaking just a few miles away from the hustle and bustle of town, Lake Brienz offers secret little beaches and BBQ spots, stunning cliffs, and· views that the majority of tourists simply don't see.

For those who'd like to try their skills on a river instead of a lake, the obvious classic is the Vorderrhein (II-III) in Graubünden. It's known as the Swiss Grand Canyon. If you aren't a seasoned river kayaker, I recommend taking a course. You can do white water training on the lake and then tackle an easy river like the Aare from Thun to Bern. Another easy way to get a river experience is, of course, to go rafting. Here in Interlaken, we have the Lütschine, which is an exciting ride.

Kayak Etiquette & Legalities
When paddling away from the shore, you're required to have a buoyancy aid with you. And on the lake you have to stay out of the way of *kursschiff* (ferries) and fishing vessels (make sure to give these an especially wide berth, as they might have lines or fishing nets around them; you will recognize them by the white ball on a post above the vessel). Also, stay outside areas with yellow buoys. They are either nature reserves or swimming areas and if caught you're liable for a 400-franc fine.

Safety Tips
Always wear a buoyancy aid, get proper training (know how to rescue each other and yourself), and always take note of the water temperature and be prepared in case of a swim (at a 50-degree water temperature more than 30 minutes inside means game over). Don't go out in strong winds (it can be difficult to control your kayak). And if you can't self-rescue, always stay within swimming distance of the shore.

When to Kayak in Switzerland
You can actually kayak all year, as long as you have warm clothes and a dry suit in winter. Kayaking is one of those activities that is still nice in most conditions. It always offers something different and we've had some great reviews from

people who've been out in pouring rain. Rain makes for a really special atmosphere and, as long as you're dressed for it, it's no problem.

After Kayaking...

If you're in Interlaken, I recommend staying outside the center. Matten (a pretty little village and definitely one of the livelier spots in town) is a good place. Bönigen (where we're based) is quiet and pretty and right on the lakeside. And Neuhaus—at the other end of town—gets the evening sun.

As for things to do, in Bönigen, there's an unofficial beach that has stunning views and is a great place to have a BBQ and take time out from a busy travel schedule. On the other side of town, there's a good kebab shop at the Interlaken West train station by the crossing. Other good food options include the Three Tells Irish pub (at Hauptstrasse 49 in Matten), Little Thai (at Hauptstrasse 17 in Matten), and Onkel Tom's Hutte at Dorfstrasse 194 in Grindelwald (this place is really great!). For drinks, try Avocado (at Dorfstrasse 158 in Grindelwald) and the new Haarigekuh brewery (at Kammistrasse 11 in Interlaken).

If it's raining hard, Trümmelbach and Giessbach falls are amazing. For a cheap way to see the mountains, the Harder Kulm has a beautiful panorama of the Jungfrau region and the two lakes at a fraction of the cost of Jungfraujoch (the highest train station in Europe).

Find Dave at hightide.ch.

Lisa Hutchins
Air Sports Expert. Entrepreneur.

About Lisa

Honestly, I arrived in Lauterbrunnen not knowing what or where it was. I had flown from my then-home in Australia to paraglide with a friend for a month. A year later, I was back. And almost four years later, I'm still here.

THE GREAT OUTDOORS

I am a rookie paraglider, myself, and I work with most aspects of air sports here in Lauterbrunnen. I have a BASE jumping gear store called Valley BASE Gear, which serves the needs of the many jumpers who come to this BASE mecca every year. And I also work with Airtime Paragliding, which offers tandem flights—a beautiful way to see the mountains and valley.

Where to Paraglide in Switzerland
I am based in Lauterbrunnen, which has a cable car right next to the paragliding and BASE landing area, giving you access to over 2,500 feet of altitude in 10 minutes (not bad, right?). Fiesch, in the Valais Canton, is the Swiss paragliding mecca. And for huge cross-country flights, the best place to take off is Niesen (above Spiez). That said, Switzerland—and the Alps in general—is bursting with flying spots and paragliding is still a small and friendly enough community to simply rock up to a landing area and ask.

Where to Skydive in Switzerland
Skydiving can be learned anywhere, so really the world is your oyster. Jump tickets (the amount you pay every time you get on the plane) vary greatly all over the world. Just be aware that skydiving is not the cheapest sport—you pay every time you get on that plane.

As for specific spots, some of the top places are Reichenbach (a lovely place in the Bernese Oberland), Wilderswil (where you can jump from a helicopter over some spectacular views), and Paracentro Locarno.

Where to BASE Jump (or Watch BASE) in Switzerland
There are BASE jumps everywhere, though there are certainly spots where BASE jumping is more accepted. Here in Lauter-brunnen, for example, it is legal, accepted, and growing. It's also a place where it's easy to watch the jumpers. Just take a walk along the valley floor, especially in summer.

Outside the Lauterbrunnen Valley, Walenstadt (particularly the jump called Sputnik), St. Gallen, Kandersteg (great for wing suits), Gastern Valley, and Fisistock are all solid choices.

Lisa's Favorite Air Sports Spot

Here in Lauterbrunnen the concentration of air sports is awe-inspiring. We have paragliders—from experienced tandem pilots flying travelers across the valley to acro pilots (advanced acrobatic flyers seeming to defy the laws of physics). We have speed-flyers (known in winter as speed-riders on skis)—a new sport pioneered in the air above the valley with a smaller, faster paragliding wing. And, of course, we have BASE jumpers jumping the cliffs with or without the flying squirrel suits (wing suits). This is something most people will never get to see. Ever. And yet here you can sit and watch them all day.

The access to launching and landing areas via cable car or train is, in true Swiss style, efficient and surprisingly affordable, so whether you are a pro wanting to practice some moves or just want to give flying a try, it is all here. Accessible. Affordable. Breathtakingly beautiful.

Air Sport Safety

Working in tandem paragliding, the most common question from clients is "is it safe?" People want to be told that it is entirely safe, that nothing will ever happen to them, that they are making the right choice to go flying. I tend to ask them if they arrived by car. Yes? Well, you've just done the most dangerous part of your day then!

Any sport that involves leaving the ground and then rejoining it has the chance of injury or accident, just as hurtling along tarmac at 80 miles per hour in a metal box has risks. The key is to mitigate those risks, which is what every pilot (and hopefully, car driver) does.

So, go for a tandem flight, but don't go with your friend who has never flown before (that would be crazy). BASE jump off a

THE GREAT OUTDOORS

cliff, but don't jump after only 10 skydives and "learning" BASE on YouTube (also crazy).

Air Sport Etiquette

In Lauterbrunnen, you need to know about the grass. This valley is all about the cows and the grass is grown in summer to feed the cows through the winter. So any grass more than a foot high should not be used for landing. The farmers put out windsocks to indicate which field they would prefer people to land in, so watch for those if you are flying solo.

Now, each place will have its own rules, so outside the valley may have some different etiquette. Often there is a delicate balance struck between pilots, jumpers, and locals. By simply chatting with the pilots to ask about local etiquette, you can avoid annoying anyone and disrupting the balance.

Legal Requirements for Air Sports

For solo air sports, you'll need to have a paragliding license and a special third-party insurance for aircrafts (which covers hang gliders, paragliders, and parachutes). If you're taking classes or riding tandem, your pilot probably has it covered.

When to Fly

The best time for big lift and long flights is from mid-March to mid-July. A great time to learn is autumn or winter, when the conditions are calmer and the valley winds weak.

Sky Diving Courses in or near Switzerland

Personally, I work closely with SkyHigh, a drop zone in Eschbach, Germany, where many of my friends—sky divers and BASE jumpers alike—go to jump. It is a family drop zone with a bunkhouse to sleep in (or you can camp!), a café, a skydive school, a wing suit school, and a gear shop. There are kids, dogs, and sky divers running round, slack-lining in between loads, and generally having a lovely time. It's also only two hours away from Lauterbrunnen in the flatlands, which makes a nice change from the mountains sometimes.

Paragliding Courses

Ikarus, Chillout, and Bumblebee flight schools, all located in Interlaken, are good, solid choices.

Final Notes & Other Tips

To non-flyers: if you only ever do this once, do it here. Taking off towards the Eiger, Mönch, and Jungfrau peaks and flying the waterfalls and sheer cliffs of the Lauterbrunnen valley is not something easily forgotten. Ever.

Find Lisa at valleybasegear.com and airtime-paragliding.ch.

John Klemme
Cyclist. Swiss Cycling Tour Company Owner.

About John

I grew up in Iowa on a dairy farm. My dad bought me my first road bike when I was 12 and took my on a weeklong cycling event across the state. I've associated cycling with travel and vacation ever since.

I went to the University of Iowa and did a junior year abroad in France. Leaving the USA for a long period of time was life-changing. When I was in my early 20s, my only goal was to return to Europe to work and live. I managed to accomplish that by getting a Masters in Teaching English. One of my first jobs was at a Swiss boarding school. And once in Switzerland, I didn't want to leave.

Although I enjoyed teaching, I got a bit burned-out. And since I had my summers off, I started running bicycle tours across Switzerland. That was 11 years ago. The business became successful enough to stop teaching and bicycle tours are what I focus on full-time now.

Swiss Cycling for Beginners

Switzerland has nine national routes that crisscross the country.

THE GREAT OUTDOORS

There are also a large number of regional routes and mountain biking routes. So, really, there's something for everyone.

A good beginner route is National Route #5, also called the Mittelland Route. It begins around Yverdon and follows the Aare River for the most part (and thus is very flat). You'll see lots of families on this route and it goes through a lot of interesting villages and countryside. For the most part, you're following a dedicated bicycle path, so there's not a lot of motor traffic.

Switzerland for Intermediate Cyclists

I encourage more experienced riders to try National Route #9, also known as the Lakes Route. There's more uphill but nothing too extreme. You'll also see landscapes that are more typically Swiss...mountains, waterfalls, lakes. The route passes through many of the most well known cities and towns in Switzerland, including Gstaad, Interlaken, and Lucerne.

Swiss Cycling for Experts

There are lots of possibilities, of course. But if you're on a road bike, I recommend Route #4, also known as the Alpine Route. As the name suggests, there's a lot of uphill. It follows paved roads for its entire length.

John's Personal Favorite Cycling Spots

I like to bike in Appenzell. It's very pristine, with manicured meadows and houses tidy with blooming flowers. I also really like the Swiss Jura Mountains, which follow the Swiss-French border from Geneva to Basel. It's probably the least densely populated region of Switzerland and there's just so much countryside to take in.

Cycling Safety in Switzerland

Everyone in Switzerland has a bicycle. Perhaps they don't ride every day, but they all understand and respect cyclists. When foreigners come to bike in Switzerland, they don't realize this and it sometimes causes problems. For example, many American cyclists yield to cars no matter what and this causes some confusion and frustration because the drivers here expect cyclists to act like cars. So, if you've got the right-of-way, take it. If you're entering a roundabout, do it.

Cycling Etiquette in Switzerland
Many cyclists here have bells on their bikes. Even roadies often have bells. This isn't just to warn pedestrians but is also helpful when passing other cyclists to let them know you're there.

When to Cycle in Switzerland
You always have to be prepared for rain and, if you're in the mountains, cold. But really, anytime from April to end of September is good. March and October can be good as well, although a bit riskier.

Final Notes & Other Tips
Switzerland has nine national routes and over 50 regional routes. All of these routes are maintained, signposted, and mapped, making this a great place for cyclists. Additionally, the train system is the best in the world and you can always travel with your bike for a small extra fee [editor's note: make sure to pay the fee *before* you get on the train to avoid fines]. And finally, know that it's not all mountains here. Don't be intimidated.

Find John at bikeswitzerland.com.

Ramon Hunziker
Pro Mountain Biker.

About Ramon
I grow up in Thun and still live there today. I started riding bikes with my dad and brother when I was 13. First, I rode cross-country, then I switched to downhill and 4X racing, where I competed for a few years. For the last seven years, I have been competing in free-ride and slope-style competitions.
I also like to ski, surf, or ride my motocross.

29

THE GREAT OUTDOORS

A few years ago, my brother and I started a company to promote the sport of mountain biking. We organize contests (such as Swatch Rocked Air) and shows and build parks, pump tracks, and downhill trails.

For Beginning Bikers

If you like to ride Enduro (a form of off-road motorcycling), Switzerland is a paradise. You can ride on all the hiking trails and they are all over the country. Get a supertrail map and enjoy (*supertrail-map.com*).

If you like dirt jumping (riding bikes on jump ramps) go to the Dirt Park in Steffisburg (on Sonnenfeldstrasse). It is a public park built by the Flying Metal Crew. There's something for riders at any level.

If you are into downhill riding, you'll find a cool beginner trail from Sunnbüel to Kandersteg. Other good downhill areas include Crans-Montana, Bellwald, Anzere, Kandersteg, and Chatel (my personal favorite, which is five minutes across the French border). You can also find good parks in the Valais Canton, Crans-Montana, Les Portes du Soleil, and Bellwald.

Ramon's Favorite Rides

For dirt jumping, I love the Dirt Park in Steffisburg. For downhill, I enjoy riding in Portes du Soleil. I also love searching for freeride lines in the Alps (and you can see what I find on the Red Bull website; just search my name).

Biking Safety

A helmet is a must. Kneepads and a back-protector are also important. If you want to be a bit more protected, you can get body armor.

Biking Etiquette

Just ride smart. If you are riding down and hikers or mountain bikers are coming up a trail, slow down and pass with care.

Final Notes & Other Tips

Switzerland is a mountain biking paradise. Sometimes it is not easy to find the best trails. Go to the local bike shop or ask other bikers. They'd love to show you around. You can also go to *traildevils.ch* and ask about specific trails in the forum.

Find Ramon at flyingmetal.ch.

Ulo Gersch
Ski Expert. Inventor. Entrepreneur.

About Ulo

I've been doing snow sports since I was a small child. Born in the ski town of Wengen, skiing was quite simply in my blood. I started skiing almost before I could walk. (And I'm 75 now, so that's a long history of snow sports.)

Back then, my parents were running a snow sports shop (which has been since passed down to my brother and now his son) and growing up I was really interested in the workshop and the equipment, particularly ski bindings, because at that time they were very bad and there were a lot of accidents.

It was this curiosity and innovative mindset—along with my 10 years of experience as a ski instructor and mountain guide—that eventually led me to a career as an inventor in the snow sports industry.

These days, I'm working on snowshoes that you can walk and climb in and also ski downhill in. I call them Crossblades. I'm also working on a project where the skis are linked in front and back so that they always remain perfectly parallel, making the same angles. We call it the synchronized ski system because everything is balanced—and the goal here is safety. The skis cannot cross, separate, or catch an edge.

My company was also the first to put an indoor ski carpet in Switzerland. We didn't invent that, but we brought it to the

THE GREAT OUTDOORS

Swiss Alps. It's the perfect place to test our projects and demonstrate them for PR purposes. It's also loved by athletes doing serious ski training, because indoor skiing isn't a slave to the mountain conditions or sunlight hours and doesn't require hours of travel to get onto the slopes.

Swiss Skiing for Beginners

What is the best place for beginners? I should, of course, say Wengen. But I discovered (during my time as a ski instructor) that areas with less height are actually better for beginners because being a little lower can feel less scary (even though the beginner slopes up high are really the same as the ones down low). If you'd like to start low, the Simmental (Gstaad) is not as steep or high as the Jungfrau area. It's less intimidating.

Some people don't mind the height and if that's the case, the Jungfrau region (Wengen, Mürren, Grindelwald) is a good area for beginners. Adelboden is also a good choice.

Swiss Skiing for Experts

For those who prefer steep slopes, you'll find them almost everywhere in Switzerland, including at the Eigergletscher or Schilthorn in the Jungfrau region. That said, Zermatt deserves a particular mention, as does Verbier, which has become high class and glitzy—a place for kings and queens.

In general, for steep terrain, you want to be in the real Alps and the high areas. Beginners will stay lower.

Ulo's Favorite Slopes

Of course, I like Wengen and the Jungfrau region a lot because I have such a strong connection here, having grown up on the mountain. But as I get older, I find that I prefer February and March skiing (when there's more sun), so my favorite places are places that are at their best in spring.

THE GREAT OUTDOORS

One such place is Mürren/Schilthorn, where you can get incredibly high up on the mountain (altitude is a big consideration in the sunnier days of spring).

Another favorite is Lötschental. Take the train to Goppenstein and go left into the valley. From there, you can catch a bus to a place called Wiler and get a cable car up the mountain. There are some really beautiful slopes up there, most are really steep, and the big advantage is that the cable car goes all the way to 11,500 feet above sea level. The reason I like this place is that it's not elite; it's full of local families.

Finally, of course, you have Graubünden. The area around St. Moritz is fantastic. There's so much there...you can change up the landscape and slopes every day.

Ski Safety
For beginners, places like Wengen are a safe option because skiers can get to the slopes by train. Chair and ski lifts are much more dangerous than trains, so when you're just starting out, picking an area with good train connections is a good idea.

Ski Etiquette
The International Ski Federation (FIS) has established ski rules that apply everywhere. Check out *fis-ski.com* to brush up.

Ski Season in Switzerland
Usually, ski season kicks off around Christmas and, in most places, ends the week after Easter (depending on snow conditions and when Easter falls). Personally, I like spring skiing because there's so much more sun. The only problem is that the snow can get soft and you have to head to higher altitudes and get up earlier in the mornings.

Find Ulo at inventra.ch.

THE GREAT OUTDOORS

Marco Bruni
Professional Snowboarder.

About Marco

I grew up on Lake Zürich in a town called Stäfa. After my schooling, I did some traveling and then moved to Ticino. I've been windsurfing, surfing, snowboarding, and skateboarding since I was a kid.

I was a coach for 20 years. For 12 of them, I was a national coach for the Swiss National Freestyle Team, and the last two years I coached Louri Podladtschikov privately and exclusively in a project to win the Olympic games, which we did.

Professionally, I'm still managing action sport athletes (mostly snowboarders). And I'm opening a sports class for snowboarders and skaters in Zürich in 2015, which will allow kids aged 12 to 15 to go to school for sports and arts.

In my free time, my favorite things to do are travel, surf, and snowboard. And when I'm not doing sports, I love cooking and gardening.

For Beginners

There are many ski resorts that I know very well, but I spend most of my time in Engadin in St. Moritz, which is where I got my start. Aside from my home slopes, I recommend Laax, which is the mecca of snowboarding. You can also pick a random small ski resort and take your family out in the snow. Switzerland has 300 resorts to choose from.

For Intermediate & Expert Snowboarders

Laax has perfect infrastructure, with good schools, great teachers, and easy slopes. It's the perfect way for anybody to progress. For expert freeriding, I highly recommend the valley of Engadin's Diavolezza and Corvatsch mountains. You'll find every type of difficult terrain up there.

THE GREAT OUTDOORS

Marco's Personal Favorite Spots
I love Engadin, Diavolezza, and Corvatsch (the last two are peaks, the first a mountain valley).

Safety Tips
Pick a day with soft snow. That's the most important thing. Everything is easier. Turning is easier. It's better when you fall. You fall soft. If you can pick a day with soft snow or in the spring when it just snowed, that is such a big advantage.

Snowboard Etiquette
The slopes are busy, so respect other skiers and snowboarders. If you really are a beginner, remember not to sit in the middle of the slope to keep yourself and others safe.

Legal Rules
The basic rules on the mountain are always on a signpost at the bottom of the hill. You can also check with your instructor or the tourist office.

The Best Times to Snowboard in Switzerland
You can start snowboarding in Saas-fee as early as July, with the glacier and the snow park there. But typically in seasonal places, resorts open the last week of November and close at the end of April.

FOOD & WINE

Chef Andreas Caminada
Chef Patron at Schloss Schauenstein.

About Chef Caminada

For the last 10 years, I've been the chef and leaseholder of the Schloss Schauenstein Hotel and Restaurant in Fürstenau. The restaurant (which is in a historic castle) holds three Michelin stars and 19 Gault Millau points. I'm also proud of the fact that we're on the S. Pellegrino list of The World's 50 Best Restaurants, which is a very special kind of honor.

I was born and raised here in the canton of Graubünden and am very attached to my home. Like most people here, I'm a down-to-earth sort of guy. I do my own thing in the kitchen. My cooking philosophy is inspired by French cuisine but retains a local touch with ingredients sourced from the sunniest valleys in Graubünden.

My aim is to serve a modern, light cuisine that makes optimum use of top-quality products. But the most important thing is giving guests an all-round experience that goes way beyond what's on the plate.

Swiss Must-Trys

When it comes to food, we have a lot to offer. But let's start with the classics:

Switzerland means cheese, so a cheese fondue or raclette is a must. The best places to enjoy a good fondue are the mountains of Valais, the Bernese Oberland, or Graubünden.

Fondue is made using regional cheeses and tastes different every time you eat it. First, because the cattle spend the summers up in the lush alpine meadows and, second, because the mix of cheeses used varies widely.

FOOD & WINE

Don't forget to try the regional cheeses as well; with a good glass of wine, they are the perfect way to round off a meal.

Something else you have to try is Swiss wine. Hardly any other country makes such intensive and varied use of its vineyards. You can't go wrong with a lovely, fruity white from the French-speaking part of the country or a Pinot Noir from the Bündner Herrschaft in the canton of Graubünden.

Hidden Foodie Gems for Savvy Travelers

Let's take one specialty from each language region. A well-made risotto (a creamy rice dish) from Ticino, the Italian-speaking part of Switzerland, is always good. The rice should still be slightly firm when you bite it and is usually best in one of the traditional grottos (simple taverns in hidden-away places).

In the French-speaking cantons, I'd go for raisiniée. This is made by slowly simmering pear or apple juice over an open wood fire for days until it turns into a sticky, thick syrup. Serve it with crème fraîche or ice cream and it's a showstopper.

A decent rösti (the Swiss version of hash browns) belongs on any list of dishes you simply have to try in German-speaking Switzerland. Around Bern, a traditional rösti is nice and crispy, but the one served with sliced veal and mushrooms in cream sauce at the world-famous Kronenhalle (at Rämistrasse 4 in Zürich) is as good as it gets. This traditional establishment has been a popular haunt of the great and the good for a century and has the most unbelievable collection of art you'll ever see in a restaurant.

One of the specialties in Graubünden is capuns. These are made of spaetzle dough with sausage and bacon wrapped in chard, but ultimately the filling is up to the chef. They do very good capuns at the Hotel Gasthaus Krone (at Via Cumünela 2 in La Punt Chamues-ch near St. Moritz).

As good as our everyday local cuisine can be, you should also make time to visit to a top-level restaurant. Switzerland has the densest network of Michelin stars in the world.

FOOD & WINE

A Travel Itinerary for Foodies
The best idea is to cross the country visiting each of the language regions in turn. In French-speaking Switzerland, consider starting in Crissier at Benoit Violier's three-star restaurant (at Rue d'Yverdon 1). It doesn't get much better than that.

Lucerne should also be one of the stops on your journey. The city has lots of tourist attractions, including its hallmark, the wooden Chapel Bridge. One of the regional specialties there is chügelipastete, a puff-pastry shell filled with diced veal and mushrooms in a creamy sauce. Try it at a restaurant or as a take-away from one of the city's bakeries.

Consider ending your journey in Graubünden with its breathtaking mountain scenery. The best way to travel and take in the scenery is with the Rhaetian Railway. The various routes take in some of the most spectacular views in the entire region, as well as cosmopolitan centers like St. Moritz.

Great Restaurants Around Switzerland
The list is long, but if you're planning to discover Switzerland's best places to eat and you're starting off in the French-speaking part of the country, your first stop should be Benoit Violier's Hotel de Ville in Crissier (mentioned above). Moving closer to German-speaking Switzerland, I think immediately of the Parkhotel Vitznau (at Seestrasse 18 in Vitznau).

Once we get to Zürich and the surrounding area, there's the Wirtschaft zum Wiesengrund (at Kleindorfstrasse 61 in Uetikon), the Kronenhalle (at Rämistrasse 4 in Zürich), and the Grand Hotel Dolder (at Kurhausstrasse 65 in Zürich), which has a long and fascinating history.

In Graubünden itself, there's the Hotel Gasthaus Krone in La Punt Chamues-ch (mentioned above).

These are all restaurants that serve well-made, honest food with fresh, seasonal products. But these really are just a few off-the-cuff tips, and there many, many more very fine restaurants that I could recommend. My advice, then, is to get hold of the Michelin Guide for Switzerland, which lists all the country's best places to eat. It's available at any good bookshop and is published annually.

Connecting With the Culture

The Swiss can be a little introverted, but at heart, we're friendly and hospitable. Having four national languages makes us pretty unusual, and encourages tolerance, cosmopolitanism, and an understanding of other cultures. However, having said that, I wouldn't recommend drinking Coca Cola with fondue (we never would).

Simple Tips For Experiencing Swiss Food

The easiest thing to do is grab yourself a good piece of bread, some bündnerfleisch (air-dried beef), and a decent glass of wine and watch the sun go down over the Alps, an experience guaranteed to be unforgettably authentic and beautiful.

Find Chef Caminada at andreascaminada.com and schauenstein.ch.

Greg Witt
Owner, Alpenwild Hiking/Walking/Food Tours.

About Greg

I first visited Switzerland in 1970 as a teenager from California backpacking through Europe—back when the dollar was king. Frommer's Europe on $5 a Day was my bible and my diet consisted of yogurt and French bread. When I arrived in Zermatt in view of the Matterhorn, I knew my destiny. I returned repeatedly, hiked thousands of miles, and climbed many of the peaks in the Alps and, in 1986, started my travel company.

Even though living and traveling in Switzerland is old hat for me, I still get excited on arrival and have this sense of wonder and amazement in each new encounter. In the years since my

FOOD & WINE

first trip, both my budget and tastes have improved. I now live about four months of the year in Switzerland where my company, Alpenwild, is the leading tour operator doing hiking and walking tours in the Alps.

Our clients come primarily for the hiking, but the cuisine is generally a close second on their list of priorities. So we place a strong focus on food as part of our overall experience. We prepare elaborate picnic lunches to enjoy on the trail and include all trail snacks—and it's never just apples and granola bars. We're talking magrets de canard (pan-grilled duck breast), smoked salmon, pate, the finest cheese, and the best Swiss chocolate (I'm a Lindt Lindor gianduja dark man).

We are an adventure tour operator and so we encourage our guests to be adventurous in their food choices, too—from rabbit pate to air-dried chamois (a local goat-antelope), horse tartare, sheep cheese, and lemon-thyme sorbet. It's always a highlight to uncover a new culinary delight—and it happens almost daily.

Although our brand is still hiking and walking in the Alps, we've expanded to include some food and wine tours. We visit Alpine dairies, premier chocolate manufacturers, farms, vine-yards, wineries, and herb growers. And we also offer custom private tours for cheese-makers, chocolate aficionados, and oenophiles.

Swiss Must-Trys

For first timers, cheese fondue is obligatory—even if cliché. For the Swiss, it's traditionally a winter comfort food and always a social experience; no one eats fondue alone.

Fondue has its origins in 18th-century Switzerland as a way for farm families to stretch their limited resources during the winter months. With some remaining cheese, stale bread, and a dash of wine, the family could gather around the hearth and enjoy a simple meal together.

FOOD & WINE

Even though there are regional variations, you can find great fondue throughout Switzerland. There is no standard or official recipe, but it's typically a blend of two cheeses. The most common blend is half gruyère and half vacherin fribourgeois. In the canton of Valais, they favor raclette as one of the two cheeses, while in the canton of Bern it's emmentaler and in eastern Switzerland's Appenzell Alps it's appenzeller cheese.

I love it all, but my heart and my nose favor the appenzeller rendition. I walk into a restaurant where the intense, spicy aroma of melting Appenzeller wafts from the kitchen and I'm mesmerized.

Next up, you've got rösti, which is considered the national dish of Switzerland. Rösti is similar to hash browns and often includes cheese. The Swiss are very particular about potatoes. They have a saying: "The bigger the potato, the dumber the farmer"—meaning it takes a smart, expert Swiss farmer to grow the good-tasting small potatoes used to make rösti. You'll find rösti served throughout Switzerland, though it's most popular in the German-speaking regions and particularly in Canton Bern.

Many restaurants in the Bernese Oberland have several different versions of rösti on the menu, often served with a fried egg on top or with sliced tomatoes or ham or bacon in the mix. I've had my best, most authentic rösti experiences at some of these places.

Another food every first-time visitor will see at virtually every breakfast in every hotel in Switzerland is muesli—locally known as birchermüesli. Many first-time visitors think it's just cold oatmeal and avoid it, but it's a wonderful way to start the day. The ingredients include rolled oats, shredded apples, nuts, berries, milk, and yogurt or fruit juice. And for the Swiss it's not just for breakfast anymore—it's often a quick lunch, snack, or light evening dish. Every gasthaus (tavern), inn, or hotel has its own version. I enjoy them all but have a slight preference for the variety in the Bernese Oberland with berries.

41

FOOD & WINE

Finally, while not exactly a dish (I've always considered it more a food group of its own), chocolate as we know it was really invented in Switzerland. And the Swiss have the highest per capita consumption of chocolate in the world. I won't say much about it here since Americans are already familiar with Swiss brands like Lindt and Toblerone. But when in Switzerland you'll want to get acquainted with Nestlé's premier brand, Cailler, which is not found in the U.S. It's one of the few chocolate brands made with fresh milk, rather than powdered. Also, watch for Läderach, a chocolatier with shops throughout Switzerland that you mustn't miss.

Hidden Foodie Gems for Savvy Travelers

The first thing that comes to mind is cholera. Don't let name scare you away. Cholera is a savory pie or tart made with potato, onion, bacon, and apple—similar to (but much tastier than) a Cornish pasty. It originated in the Upper Rhône valley of Goms (in the Valais Canton) and I've never seen it served outside of that relatively remote region. Its name and origins came from a cholera outbreak in 1836 when trade was cut off and this isolated valley had to subsist on the foods in their own cellars and pantries. It's absolutely delectable and always made with the local ingredients on hand.

Next up, capuns. You'll find these dumplings almost exclusively in the Engadin Valley around St. Moritz in the canton of Graubünden. They are made from spätzle dough and locally dried meat wrapped in a chard leaf. Then they are cooked in a broth-filled baking dish and topped with an Alp cheese.

Then there's wood-fired raclette. I see home raclette grills at Bed Bath & Beyond and Williams-Sonoma, but for the authentic experience head to Valais. Many small restaurants in traditional Alpine villages have an open wood-fired oven where they place the half-wheel of raclette cheese in a cradle in front of the fire. Raclette is a great melting cheese and as it melts in front of the fire the cheese becomes more flavorful and absorbs the smokiness of the burning wood along with a slight crust. At just the right moment, the racleur scrapes off a portion of the melted cheese and slaps it onto a small plate along with a pearl onion and a small pickle, ready to serve. By the way, raclette, the name of the cheese, comes from the French word meaning "to scrape." The dish is common to the Haute-Savoy region of France and to the Valais region of Switzerland just across the border. But Raclette AOC cheese is produced only in Switzerland.

Finally, a few wonderful miscellaneous items:
- Air-dried meats from Valais (similar to prosciutto);
- Meringues in Gruyère served with double crème and fresh raspberries (double crème has a 48 - 60% fat content compared to traditional whipping cream's 35 - 36% fat content);
- Vacherin mont d'or, which is widely recognized as one of the finest cheeses in the world and is made from August 15 to March 15. It contains 45-50% milk-fat and is best enjoyed warm and spooned over potatoes with a dash of salt and pepper;
- Älplermagronen (the Swiss farm lunch version of macaroni and cheese, which often includes bacon);
- Croûte au fromage (a thick slice of bread with a little wine and gobs of melted gruyère placed under a broiler—the ultimate comfort food);
- Bünder gerstensuppe (barley and air-dried beef soup that originated in the canton of Graubünden);
- Summer sausage (a good smoky beef or pork sausage from Bern. Along with some appenzeller cheese and a Cailler Frigor dark chocolate bar, this is the best possible trail snack for a hike in the Swiss Alps).

A Travel Itinerary for Foodies

Switzerland is a small country—about half the size of West Virginia—so it's easy to get from one region to another and see a lot in a trip. Valais is one of the great culinary regions of Europe, on par with Tuscany. The Engadin in southeastern Switzerland has been influenced by the many cultures that have crisscrossed the region and boasts wonderful local specialties. The milk from the cows in Gruyère, in the lush pre-

FOOD & WINE

alpine hills of the Fribourg Canton, works its way into the finest cheese, double crème, and chocolate.

You'll find great restaurants in Zürich, Geneva, Lugano, and Basel, but don't overlook smaller towns with agricultural roots or trade-route tradition—Appenzell, Chur, Scuol, and Locarno. And, of course, you'll find great international cuisine at resorts that cater to the international market—Zermatt, St. Moritz, Davos, and Verbier.

A Taste of History & Culture

Swiss food is rooted in survival. For Alpine farmers, existence depended on getting enough fat in their diet to keep them alive through the winter. So they became proficient in developing means of producing and preserving foods that would enable them to survive the winter—cheese, sausage, and potatoes. Even today, in some alpine villages that's the foundation of their diet.

The remoteness and isolation of alpine villages also demanded self-sufficiency. Add to that 230 years of military and political neutrality and two world wars in which Switzerland remained neutral and rather isolated and you have a country that developed the ability and skills to be economically and agriculturally self-sufficient.

Even though Alpine villages were remote and isolated, Alpine passes and valleys were well-traveled trade routes. Most north-south trade in Europe—from Germany or France to the Mediterranean—ended up passing through the Alps. So Switzerland was always well connected and integrated with the culinary traditions of other European countries. And with four different language regions (German, French, Italian, and Romansch), the Swiss are very adept at picking up and sharing culinary traditions and styles among themselves.

With all that in mind, it's easy to understand why the largest food company in the world (Nestlé) is Swiss and why many food processing and handling innovations (chocolate conching, meringues, stock cubes, aluminum foil, and cellophane, for example) are all Swiss inventions.

Additionally, with a steady flow of pilgrims and merchants traveling through alpine valleys and passes, hospitality became an important industry in Switzerland. In fact, it's safe to say that the Swiss invented the hotel and hospitality industry as we know it today, which also includes great hotel restaurants. They developed the hospitality industry into an esteemed career track and have universities and hotel schools that produce some of the top hotel managers and hospitality executives for hotels around the world. Cesar Ritz, whose name is synonymous with elegant accommodations, came from a small alpine valley in Switzerland and went on to create his namesake hotel in Paris (hiring Escoffier as his head chef). And today, Switzerland has more Michelin stars per capita than any country in the world.

Connecting With the Culture

In Switzerland, meals are meant to be a relaxing social experience, so fast food, gulping down a quick lunch, or rushing through a dinner is definitely not Swiss. American casual dining restaurants survive by turning a table two or three times a night—a thing that's unheard of in Switzerland, where you come to a restaurant and expect to stay two or three hours. It's considered rude for a waiter to bring you the check until you ask for it. When you're in Switzerland, get used to a more leisurely pace of service.

Tipping is not expected in Swiss restaurants. The Swiss avoid ostentation and while a small amount (a few extra francs) is fine, lavish tipping (15+%) is considered boorish and even insulting. Employers are expected to pay a livable wage to waiters and restaurant staff and providing a high standard of service is an essential part of the job.

Simple Tips For Experiencing Swiss Food

I think there is a tendency among Americans to avoid hotel restaurants. There is no reason to do that in Switzerland, since the best restaurants—especially in smaller towns—are almost always connected with a hotel.

Find Greg at alpenwild.com.

Niklaus Stadelmann
Master of Cheese.

About Niklaus

I was born into a farming family with 15 siblings in the town of Meierskappel in 1945. Even as a child, I worked on the farm at home, getting to know the origin and production of milk as a basis for cheese-maker training. At the age of 16, I started a three-year apprenticeship program in cheese making, working in three different Emmentaler cheese factories.

Back then, the dairies weren't really mechanized, so there was a lot of manual labor. The individual cheeses weighed 160 – 240 pounds and were stored overhead. So you can imagine the physical labor.

In spring 1964, I graduated and started working in dairies. In 1969, I passed my exams at Dairy School Sursee and was appointed Master Cheesemaker.

After that, I ran a cheese factory with my wife for 10 years before taking over the Käserei Stofel (Stofel Dairy) in Unterwasser. Milk was and is our passion. For 20 years, we've specialized in cow's milk, goat's milk, and sheep's milk. Then, 10 years ago, I handed the business over to my son, Thomas, who continues to run it to this day.

Finally, eight years ago, my wife and I founded the Käse-akademie Schweiz GmbH (Swiss Cheese Academy), where we offer workshops in cheese making, as well as cheese pairings (with wine, beer, etc.).

FOOD & WINE

Swiss Cheese Basics
My first suggestion is to try a Swiss cheese or two (like Columbia Cheese in New York City) before you leave home. This will get your palette used to our cheeses, which are ripened naturally and produced without additives.

So, what's the process without additives? First, we start with cow's milk, obtained from healthy cows twice a day. Then we use a coagulation enzyme called Lab2, which is required for the production of cheese. Then we use salt (NaCl), submerging freshly produced cheeses in salt water for hours. The cheeses are also regularly rubbed with salt water throughout the ripening process.

When you're tasting cheese (or anything, really), it's important to use all your senses. Take the time to really look at, smell, taste, and—yes—even listen during your cheese tasting experience. And cheese tasting should also always be done in the right order—from mildest to strongest.

Warm Cheese Dishes
First, there's fondue, which is a dish where several kinds of cheese are melted in wine and scooped up with small pieces of bread on a fondue fork. Next: raclette, which is melted on a grill or griddle fire and eaten with potatoes and a variety of mixed pickles and fruit. Then, there's käsesuppe (cheese soup), which is eaten with a spoon and is similar to fondue, only much more diluted. This is an excellent starter before a meal.

Cold Cheese Dishes
One thing that's important to note is that "cold" cheese should be served at room temperature. This means that cheese stored in the fridge should be taken out early enough to warm up. The rule is one hour per 100 grams, which means a 200-gram chunk should be taken out of the fridge two hours before serving.

Cold (room temperature) cheese dishes include käseplatten (a platter to share), käseteller (a plate for one), and käseportion (a snack-sized piece of cheese).

FOOD & WINE

In Switzerland, there are a number of dairies designed for tourism and connected to some sort of tasting/gastronomy facility. In other dairy farms, hygiene regulations are very strict and visitors require a great effort (so if you want to visit a dairy, your best bet is a tour in one of the tourism-ready ones).

The Hidden Gems of Swiss Cheese
For cheese connoisseurs, I recommend the Toggenburg region, which is a center of excellence in Swiss cheese-making. In this area, almost all Swiss cheeses are produced commercially. The Käseakademie Schweiz (Swiss Cheese Academy) is located here as well.

Unique Cheese Experiences
There are some cheeses in Switzerland that are forgotten or ancient (or both). The world-famous Slow Food Association promotes and protects products, including the almost-forgotten bloderkäse (a slightly sour tasting cheese) and schlip-ferkäse (a slippery cheese with herbs and seasonings).

Then there is a group of sour-milk cheeses, which were actually the indigenous forms of cheese, rarely seen outside their regions. These include the bloderkäse (mentioned above) from the high altitudes of the Toggenburg region. It's a very healthy cheese, high in protein, easily digested, and containing almost no fat.

A Cheesy Itinerary
If you are planning a cheese-themed trip, Switzerland's discovery trails are ideal (cheese-themed trails include Chemin du Gruyère: The Swiss Chocolate and Cheese Trail and the Emmen Valley Cheese Trail). I know I'm biased, but I think a visit to our Käseakademie Schweiz (Swiss Cheese Academy) is also a good choice for the cheese-lover.

Tips for the Best Cheese-Tasting Experience
Remember: cheese must be at room temperature. In Switzerland, we have a large selection of local breads, which can

be eaten with our cheese to great effect. You can also pair cheese with fruit (which should be mature and sweet), sweet jams, and fruit juices. And if you're tasting at a dairy, ask the farmer for fresh milk, which always pairs well with cheese. As for cheese and chocolate, the darker the chocolate, the better the pairing will taste.

Final Notes & Other Tips

Our cheese variety in Switzerland is huge and includes cheeses made with cow, goat, sheep, and buffalo milk. We have creamy cheeses in many forms (with or without herbs or spices), soft cheeses with edible *weissschimmel* (white mold) or *geschmierter* (lubricated) rinds, semi-hard cheeses, hard cheeses (including emmentaler and gruyère), and extra hard cheeses (like sbrinz, hobelkäse, and alpkäse).

Find Niklaus at kaeseakademie.ch and his son's dairy at bergmilch.ch.

M. Rohr
Third-Generation Chocolatier.

About M

I'm a third-generation chocolatier, so chocolate has been part of my life since I was six months old. I run three chocolate shops in and around Geneva. In my free time, I love spending time with my family, dabbling in photography, and riding my bike.

About Swiss Chocolate

The reason that Swiss milk chocolate is the best in the world is because of the special alpine milk we have in Switzerland. (In fact, the Swiss created milk chocolate.) All major innovations in chocolate production have been made here in Switzerland. And our annual per capita consumption is 12 kilograms (the highest in the world).

FOOD & WINE

What to Try (The Basics)
In Geneva, try the specialties of Chocolaterie Arn (located at Place du Bourg-de-Four 1), La Bonbonnière (at Rue de Rive 11), Marc-Andre Cartier (at 8A Chemin Vandelle à Versoix), and Poncioni (at Rue Micheli-du-Crest 1). In Bougy-Villars, on Lake Geneva, I enjoy Tristan. In Crans-Montana, David L'instant Chocolat (at Avenue de la Gare 6) is not to be missed.

Unique, Strange, or Unusual Chocolates
In my shops, you'll find les poubelles genevoises (made specially for the Geneva International Museum of Reformation and filled with crispy praline) and les petits calvin (our own invention, filled with smooth chocolate and cream ganache). And in most of the chocolate shops in Geneva, you find pavé glacé or pavé de Genève (dark chocolate with hazelnuts, cognac, and saffron). You can also experience chocolate production itself at Maison Cailler in Broc.

How to Eat Chocolate in Switzerland
Never keep chocolate in the fridge; chocolate should be kept at 65° Fahrenheit and protected from daylight. It is best to taste at 70° F. When eating dark and very dark chocolate, pair with an old Porto or Cognac. White chocolate is very nice with red wine.

Find M Rohr at rohr.ch.

Ashley Isaacs Ganz
Owner, Artisans of Leisure.

About Ashley
Originally from the Philadelphia area, I started my travel company, Artisans of Leisure, in 2003 after spending a few years living overseas (Australia, Japan, and England) and traveling extensively.

FOOD & WINE

When I travel, I'm always interested in experiencing the most authentic local culture and cuisine. I started my company because I wanted to offer tours that would appeal to travelers like me—who want to go beyond the most famous attractions and delve deeper into local culture through the cuisine, market visits, and other cultural and culinary experiences. That's why Artisans of Leisure specializes in private, customized international tours in 60+ countries. We consider enjoying local food, wine, etc. to be a highlight of any international trip.

Swiss Must-Trys
Start with lots of cheese, especially raclette (cheese melted and served with potatoes, meat, and pickled veggies), fondue (dipping cheese), and älplermagronen (Swiss macaroni and cheese with potatoes, onions, and applesauce).

From there, move onto rösti (the Swiss version of hash browns), Chasselas and other Swiss wines, and veal dishes. Make sure to try some contemporary cuisine at a fine dining restaurant (of which there are many in Switzerland). Seek out the Luxemburgerli macaroons from Sprüngli. And try some Swiss chocolate from the nearest specialty chocolate shop.

Hidden Foodie Gems for Savvy Travelers
Some particular favorites include:
- Grilled sausages at Vorderer Sternen restaurant at Theaterstrasse 22 in Zürich...especially St. Galler kalbsbratwurst (veal sausage), which is a specialty of the town of St. Gallen;
- Fried perch from Lake Geneva;
- Laeckerli sweets in Basel;
- Marzipan-like Mandelbärli bears from Bern;
- Chestnut products, polenta, and risotto from Ticino;
- Cured and dried meats from many regions;
- Micro-brew beer from all over the country;
- Kirschtorte (which is similar to Germany's Black Forest Cake and is originally from Zug but available everywhere);

- Pizzoccheri (thick buckwheat noodles cooked with cabbage, potatoes, and lots of cheese) from the eastern Graubünden region, particularly in the areas that border Italy;
- The Engadiner nusstorte (a delicious tart filled with a caramel walnut mixture popular around St. Moritz);
- Zopf (or zupfe)—a braided bread, similar to challah, particularly good around Bern (you might see it studded with bits of cured pork, also known as speck, in a version called speckzopf).

A Travel Itinerary for Foodies

The Lake Geneva region is home to many of the country's best restaurants and offers easy access to towns like Gruyères, which is famous for cheese and chocolate, the Jura region (for more amazing cheese), and the Lavaux, a beautiful, historic wine region on the edge of the lake.

Switzerland also allows easy access to great cuisines just across its borders in the Alsace region in France and the Lakes District of northern Italy.

A Taste of History & Culture

Regional variety in Switzerland reflects the German, French, Italian, and Romansh traditions. In recent years, immigrants from other parts of Europe, as well as Africa, Asia, and the Middle East, have imported their own culinary traditions. In general, Swiss food has become much more sophisticated and international while still maintaining its strong traditions.

Simple Tips For Experiencing Swiss Food

Keep an open mind and follow the locals.

Find Ashley at artisansofleisure.com.

FOR HISTORY BUFFS

Professor Clive Church
Emeritus Professor of European Studies.

About Professor Church

I started my academic life as a historian of France and did my research on the formation of the bureaucracy during the later revolutionary era. That research eventually turned into a book called Revolution and Red Tape in the early 1980s. Over the next 20+ years, I taught at Trinity College Dublin, Lancaster, and finally Kent, from where I retired in 2003. In the last two, I moved into European Studies and became more of a political scientist. So I taught a lot of European history, including that of France and Italy, not to mention the Philosophy of History. And, more recently, I taught contemporary European politics and European Integration. As a result, I have published books on Continuity and Change in Contemporary Europe, The Penguin Guide to the European Treaties, and Understanding the European Constitution, along with many articles.

Before Revolution and Red Tape was published, however, I started work on a history of the European revolutions of 1830, having realized that that nobody had ever written one. And it was doing this that brought me into contact with Switzerland for the first time.

In 1971, I was living with my family in a little village outside Bologna working on my new project and knowing vaguely that there had been disturbances in Switzerland in 1830. I asked my long-suffering wife if she would mind my going off to Lausanne for a couple of days to suss things out, leaving her with our two small girls. Luckily she agreed. (If she had not, things might have been very different for me.)

So there I was, wandering the center of Lausanne one evening, wondering whether to start in the University Library or the cantonal archives. As the former was a large, florid, and imposing building, I thought I would start next day in the more modest setting of the cantonal archives. It was lucky that I did

FOR HISTORY BUFFS

because I met a couple working on Swiss history and they took me under their wing. So I was allowed to listen to Professor Jean-Claude Biaudet, the University's specia-list on the Swiss Regeneration, lecturing on Switzerland in 1830. Not only did I do a fortnight's work in a couple of hours, but I found it all absolutely fascinating, especially when I started reading the records of the Vaudois authorities for the time. Watching the development of a revolutionary movement was a real insight.

Hence, not only did I go on to finish a chapter on Switzerland, which appeared in Europe in 1830 a few years later, but I did work on the Ticino as well as Vaud. More importantly, I decided to start a history of Switzerland, nobody having written one in English since about 1950 and there not having been any up-to-date translations of histories by Swiss writers. In this, I suppose I was responding to market opportunity. I started work and my family and I spent several highly enjoyable periods in Switzerland thanks to my friends' hospitality.

Back in England, the fact that people knew I was working on Switzerland meant that academics in European Studies began to ask me about EFTA, in which Switzerland was then an active member. So I began to organize conferences and start interviewing Swiss academics and diplomats. This coincided with my move into politics. At the end of the 1980s, I complet-ed this by working on the then-emerging Swiss Green party. And I found Swiss politics just as interesting as its history.

With my history project set aside, I went on to write two books, The Politics and Government of Switzerland and an edited volume on Switzerland and the European Union. These were quite well received. And they taught me a lot. Moreover, because the market failed to throw up anyone else, I thus became the go-to person for all things Swiss, writing on elections, recent political developments, EU relations, Switzerland and the UK, and its political culture.

When I retired, I decided to go back to the history of Switz-erland, my feeling being that its history would move at a slower pace than the frenetic field of European integration. Thanks to the Swiss National Science Fund I was able to spend some time in the University of Fribourg working on a book (co-written with Randy Head) that was eventually published by CUP as A Concise History of Switzerland. Doing this again taught me a lot, revealing aspects of the country I had not been aware of, and helping to explain how many present day phenomena came about.

I am now working on a new book on political change in Switzerland since the 1990s. I have been—and indeed remain—happy to accept such commissions partly because I still find the country so interesting and appealing and partly because I admire its very unusual political system and the effective way things run. The fact that it is still so little known and so often misconstrued also drives me on. So when people ask me why I work on Switzerland, it is only partly a joke when I reply "someone has to."

Where to Go (The Basics)

You ask where history buffs should visit on their first trip to Switzerland—and this is a difficult question, because Switzerland is anything but a conventional western European state developing around a monarchical center. It grew up in a variety of places and at a variety of times. It did not really become a single country till 1848. And it remains a highly decentralized federation.

Not only does it have four different language areas, but it encompasses three geographical zones that are all different: the Jura Hills to the northwest, the central Plain or Mittelland, and the Alps to the south. And part of it is beyond the Alps, even further south.

Religious divisions still have an impact too. All of these variations matter, as do villages, smaller towns, and the half dozen or so big cities: Zürich, Bern, Basel, Geneva, Lausanne, and St. Gallen. Anyone trying to come to terms with Swiss history needs to see a selection of these.

FOR HISTORY BUFFS

Thus, you could visit Bern because it was so important in the middle ages and is now the capital. It is also beautiful, sits in a partly French-speaking canton, and has an interesting historical museum. You could also visit Aargau, which is said to be the most typical canton because of its make-up. Its capital, Aarau, is a typical smaller town of the Mittelland.

Zürich is the biggest and most industrial city. It also hosts the revised and controversial National History Museum. A trip to somewhere like La Chaux-de-Fonds is a good introduction to the dark valleys of the Neuchâtel Jura, often known as Swiss Siberia because of the fantastically low temperatures recorded there, which can be lower than those in the high mountains. Finally, Glarus is a good introduction to the pre-Alps, as are many of the small places in the Graubünden.

Hidden Gems for History Lovers

I think Bellinzona—with its three castles—is wonderful, especially if you go there on the old Gotthard railway line (which will be ignored once the base tunnel line opens in a couple years) where you can laugh at Swiss holiday-goers trapped in miles of blockages in their cars.

The Gotthard was the key to mediaeval Swiss development. Associated with this is the Rütli meadow on the shores of the Lake of the Four Forest cantons (Lucerne) where the mythical founding of Switzerland took place and where General Guisan rallied his officers and national morale during the last war.

If you interest is in more recent history, consider the Grossmünster in Zürich where Zwingli preached. Or go to Cully in Vaud and see the Liberty tree planted in 1798. Or go anywhere in the mountains and look for the concealed hangers and artillery erected to help the country resist possible Nazi invasion between 1940 and 1944.

FOR HISTORY BUFFS

Favorite Sites

I love the ruined castle of Habsburg in the village of the same name in the Aargau. It was from this so-called hawk's nest that the Imperial family, so long a threat to Switzerland, took its name. It is remarkably atmospheric and commands marvelous views.

Somewhere I would like to see more of is Schloss Waldegg in Solothurn. This is a huge, almost Versailles-like palace built by one of the great patrician families who fatally dominated the country in the 17th and 18th centuries.

Finally, I love going up the Rhine from the tiny settlement of Gottlieben in Thurgau to the marvelous city of Schaffhausen with its magnificent castle. There, you can go in and out of Germany, as well as seeing (and tasting) the local vineyards.

(Speaking of going in and out, drive along the shores of Lake Morat and see how you go in and out of cantons because of the odd way they developed in early modern times.)

Recommended Reading

There is a good introductory chapter in Jonathan Steinberg's Why Switzerland?, a third edition of which is due out in 2015. This will be a very up-to-date assessment of a whole range of aspects of Switzerland.

For Swiss history before 1900, it is also worth looking at J. Murray Luck's History of Switzerland. Like many others, Luck stops telling a story in the late 19th century, though, and offers mere descriptions afterward. Leo Schelbert's Historical Dictionary of Switzerland also answers a lot of basic historical questions.

In Switzerland you can also buy a little book by Joelle Kuntz called Switzerland: How an Alpine Pass Became a Nation. If you like cartoons, you can try Gregoire Nappey's Swiss History in a Nutshell. Pro Helvetia still produces a useful Outline History of Switzerland. And, of course, there is a voluminous amount of writings in the national languages.

FOR HISTORY BUFFS

Notes on Swiss Culture

I am not sure I am the right person to talk about culture with a capital C, but two things do occur to me:

One is that my experience of Switzerland is that it is a very friendly country and not the intrusive, censorious society described by others.

The other is that the idea of Switzerland as unchanging and wholly at odds with Europe is quite wrong. In fact, over the last 20 years, the country has changed radically, both socially and politically. Moreover, many of these changes—like immigration and the rise of populism—have been European in nature. The country is, in fact, an integral part of Europe, even if it is not a member of the EU. Balancing the tensions between this Europeanization and the desire to maintain, or restore, past independence is a major feature of today's Switzerland and one that I watch with fascination. And the rate of change means that Swiss history did not end in 1848; it is still going on.

Find Professor Church's books at Amazon.com.

THE INTERVIEWS:
PLAN BY PLACE

BERN & THE BERNESE OBERLAND

BERN

A capitol bursting with architecture, markets, festivals, & character.

FIND WI-FI HERE: Starbucks, Wartsaal Kaffee, & the local library.

LANGUAGE: German   **CANTON:** Bern

Patrick Bolzli
Tour Guide. Musician. Traveler.

About Patrick
I was born and raised in Bern and have been here 34 years and counting. I am a software developer but use my free time to play in several orchestras (trumpet, cornet, flugelhorn) and to host free walking tours. I also travel as often as I can.

What to Do In Bern (The Basics)
The old town was founded in 1191 and is a UNESCO World Heritage Site today. Explore the 11 fountains from the 16th century with their beautiful statues, the minster (the tallest church in Switzerland), and the clock tower (with its astronomical clockwork and moving figures). Watch the bears at the bear park (a sort of mini zoo near the center). Have a coffee in front of the parliament building. Visit the Einstein exhibition in the history museum. And enjoy the sunset from Rosengarten (rose garden).

If you come in the summer, bring your swimsuit and join the locals for a refreshing swim in the crystal clear (but chilly) water of the Aare River.

And nightlife in Bern might not be the most exciting in Switzerland, but there are a lot of small bars, theaters, and the like hidden in the cellars of the old town. It's very fun to explore them.

Hidden Gems for Seasoned Travelers

For something special, take a stroll through the Matte quarter—the old working-class area from medieval times. Or take in a concert at Reitschule (the old riding school), the most controversial place in town, which began with an illegal occupation in the '80s and is currently a graffiti-covered building that strikes some as art and others as an eye-sore.

Day Trips

As Switzerland is pretty small, you can reach all the bigger cities (Zürich, Geneva, Basel, Lucerne) in less than two hours. Thun, a beautiful city on a lake, known as the "gate to the Bernese Oberland," is only 20 minutes away.

Another good option is a visit to the region of Emmental with its hilly landscape. Come learn how the famous cheese is made.

Where to Hike

Climb Gurten—the mountain in Bern's backyard—and enjoy a fantastic view of the city and the Alps. Or visit the "glass fountain" in the middle of Bremgartenwald (Bremgarten forest). According to an old legend, its water has healing powers!

What to Eat & Drink

Aside from the typical Swiss specialties you've read about on page 8, there is also the haselnusslebkuchen—a special type of gingerbread made with hazelnut.

Where to Eat & Drink (Favorite Restaurants & Bars)

Kornhauskeller (at Kornhausplatz 18) is a beautiful restaurant and bar in the basement of the old granary. The Rock Garden restaurant and bar (at Christoffelunterführung 2) is right in the middle of the remaining foundations of the old city walls. Turnhalle Bar (at Speichergasse 4) offers live music in a former gym hall only a few minutes from the train station. And, finally, Altes Tramdepot (located next to the bear park) has great food and is famous for its home-brewed beer.

How to Fit In

Yes, Switzerland is an expensive place, but we don't like people to mention it all the time. In general, it's a good idea not to talk about money. And don't ever say (or try to say) *grüezi*. Bernese people would never use that term. Use *grüessech* (pronounced groo-sah) instead.

How to Meet Locals & Make Friends

Most Swiss are a bit shy. The best way to start a friendship is to approach us; don't wait until we make the first move.

Best Places to Take a Photo

Try the Rosengarten (rose garden). You get a perfect view over the old town, especially during the blue hour before sunset... Another good option is Gurten. There is a train to take you up.

Find Patrick at freewalkingtoursbern.ch.

Tatiana Warkentin
Typist. Blogger. Traveler. Expat.

About Tatiana

I am originally from Canada and now live in Bern with my husband. I work as an assistant typist in the English Language Typing Pool at the Universal Postal Union (a special department of the UN).

What to Do In Bern (The Basics)

Bern is an incredibly pretty city. There's something interesting to see everywhere you look. I highly recommend checking out the Rose Garden, which always has something in bloom and has the most amazing view of the city. The Bear Pit (where you'll see actual bears wandering around) is a cool place with a really interesting history not far from the Rose Garden. And you should also check out the Zytlogge (clock tower) and the apartment that Einstein used to call home while he worked for the Patent Office.

Hidden Gems for Seasoned Travelers

Go one or two streets over from the tourist areas to explore the small funky shops and cool (and cheaper) places to eat.

Berne is a little weird and that's delightful. In addition to our baby-eating statue (yes, that's a thing), in the Natural History Museum, we have a 200-year-old taxidermied St. Bernard named Barry who is considered a folk hero. We also have the skeleton of an elephant that the Bernese shot with a cannon after it killed its trainer.

Day Trips

Everyone should head out to Thun, which is just a short train ride from Bern. It's located on Lake Thun (Thunersee) and is home to a pretty cool castle. You can take boat trips, go hiking, or just explore the town. The people who live there are on the younger side as well, so it has a pretty great bar and club scene in the evening.

Where to Hike

Mount Gurten has some great hiking trails. Just take the funicular to the top and hike your way down. Or vice versa. It is almost 3,000 feet high and the summit yields views of Bern, the Jura Mountains, and the Alps.

How to Fit In

Switzerland is small, so a lot of the social norms are built on the idea of not being annoying to others. So being loud and getting in people's way is seriously frowned upon.

Best Places to Take a Photo

We have a fountain with a statue of a baby-eating giant on top. I'm not kidding. I take everyone there for a photo. Also, if you make your way to the cathedral, there are some amazing photo ops and great river views in the courtyard.

Find Tatiana at dubioushausfrau.com.

Sandra Denier
Marketer. Sports Enthusiast. Blogger.

About Sandra

I am 33 and have always lived in Bern. I work in marketing and communication and, in my free time, I love sports and hanging out with friends and family. Another big hobby of mine is my blog, Baerner Meitschi (which means Bernese girls in Bernese dialect). As its name implies, Baerner Meitschi focuses on restaurants, bars, and free time or cultural activities in Bern.

What to Do In Bern (The Basics)

If you are visiting Bern for the first time, the iPod Audio Guide at the Bern Tourism Office (at Bahnhofplatz 10a) is an excellent introduction to what Bern has to offer. You should also take a tour of Bern's old town and visit The House of Parliament, the clock tower, the cathedral, and the Bear Park.

Bern's old town was added to the list of UNESCO World Heritage Sites in 1983 as an excellent example of an advanced and coherent city core whose original character has remained intact. It is surrounded by the Aare Loop (where the river loops around the city) and features a stunning view of the Alps.

Other special features of Bern include its 100+ fountains and its arcades (protected shopping streets), which make it possible to shop at your leisure, even it rains.

Hidden Gems for Seasoned Travelers

I love the Rose Garden, which is a lovely place to while away your time and enjoy a fantastic view over Bern. Another of my favorite hidden gems is the open-air market in the heart of town from 8:30 a.m. to noon on Tuesdays and Saturdays.

The Matte district is also special. Even though it is actually part of the old town, it is cut off from the rest because it lies directly on the banks of the Aare River. There are many rumors and stories about the Matte. For a long time, it was well known for its bathhouses, some of which were also running brothels (which was why the Matte got the color black in 1798, when colors were given to different city quarters). The young male residents developed a special dialect/secret language called Matte-English. Today the language is almost lost.

Where to Stay
Real life in Bern takes place in its 32 neighborhoods. Some of the liveliest parts of town are the Laenggasse, the Lorraine, and the Breitenrain (where I live).

Day Trips
If you like action and you're visiting in summer, you must river raft down the Aare. The trip takes about four hours from Thun to Bern. Speaking of Thun...it's just a 20-minute train ride from Bern and is also worth a visit. While there, take a cruise on Lake Thun for some exquisitely beautiful views of the Bernese Alps.

And to experience said Alps close-up, take a day trip to Gstaad or Adelboden. Or head to the Top of Europe (Europe's highest train station, also known as Jungfraujoch), which is a good three-hour train ride from Bern (each way). Part of the way up, you'll take a scenic cogwheel train.

Where to Hike
Bern is paradise for outdoor activities. You can hike or jog along the Aare for as long as you like. Or, for more strenuous physical exercise, walk up the Gurten (Bern's 2,815-foot mountain). Another lovely area is the Bremgarten Forest, where there is a network of well-marked jogging trails.

BERN & THE BERNESE OBERLAND

What to Eat & Drink

A nice place to have the classics (fondue and raclette) in Bern is Restaurant Lötschberg (at Zeughausgasse 16), where the atmosphere is relaxed and informal.

Jumi's cheese and meat, which is sold at the market every Saturday, is famous in Bern. Other Bernese goodies available at the market include homemade licorice and toffee.

The most delicious desserts in town can be found at the cozy restaurant Apfelgold (at Bonstettenstrasse 2). And I recommend the home-ground coffee at Adrianos (at Theaterplatz 2) and the famous Bernese beer Baerner Müntschi (which means Bernese kisses) produced by Felsenau Brewery.

Where to Eat & Drink (Favorite Restaurants & Bars)

The coziest coffee house in the old town is Café Einstein (at Kramgasse 49 and Münstergasse 44), which becomes a bar in the evenings.

The Weincafé Klösterli (at Klösterlistutz 16) offers an enormous selection of wines and their absolute hit is the Entrecote Café de Klösterli. Small snacks are also served during the day.

Bern's most centrally located bar is in the Hotel Schweizerhof (at Bahnhofplatz 11) directly across from the train station. You can order delicious drinks in the lobby and in the summer you can go up to the Sky Terrace for a fantastic view of Bern.

Budget Tips

A budget-friendly place to have dinner is Wartsaal Kaffee (mentioned above). Every Monday evening so-called *studentenfutter* (student food) is served, which means a main course and a beverage costs just 15 francs.

Going to the movies is cheapest on Mondays. And in Bern the outdoor swimming pools are free of charge; I particularly recommend the Marzili and the Lorraine pools, which are both situated directly on the Aare. Finally, you can rent bicycles free for four hours at Bern Rollt (*bernrollt.ch*). And after four hours? It's only one franc per hour per bike.

How to Fit In
On the whole, it is customary in Switzerland to tip. We Swiss do not particularly appreciate when foreigners try to speak Swiss German. Your best bet is to speak high German or just stick to English. And we Bernese are offended if somebody mistakenly thinks Zürich is the capital of Switzerland.

How to Meet Locals & Make Friends
Bern is not as international as Zürich or Geneva, but downtown does liven up on Thursday when the stores are open 'til 9 p.m. and the bars stay open for after-work parties.

Best Places to Take a Photo
My favorites are the Rose Garden, Bern's 18 bridges (including the Kornhaus, Nydegg, and Kirchenfeld bridges), and the beautiful terrace at The Bellevue Palace Hotel.

Final Notes & Other Tips
For music lovers, the annual open air Gurten Festival (*gurtenfestival.ch*) on the top of the Gurten is a must. Combined with the music, the view from Bern's own mountain over the city always makes for a magical atmosphere.

For sport lovers, the Postfinance Arena is worth mentioning because it is one of the largest hockey stadiums in Europe and home to the legendary SC Bern (Bern's ice hockey club). The Grand Prix Bern is a very famous racing festival that takes place every year in May. They call its course the most beautiful 10 miles in the world.

Find Sandra at baerner-meitschi.ch.

THUN

An authentic, picturesqure, little-known local favorite on a lake.

FIND WI-FI HERE: All hotels & most restaurants.

LANGUAGE: German   **CANTON:** Bern

Patrick Löffel
Sports Enthusiast. Mountain Biker. Hiker. Snowboarder.

About Patrick
I was born and raised around Thun and still live here. Even though I've traveled the world, I always want to come back home. At the moment, I am studying social work in Bern and when I'm not studying, I like biking (X-country, freeride, and downhill), hiking, snowboarding, and mountaineering.

What to Do In Thun (The Basics)
Thun is a little town with a beautiful old town and a fantastic location at the lake with an amazing view of the Alps. Check out the old town with the castle, shops, and cafés/bars. Take a bus up to Goldiwil/Heiligenschwendi and walk around the countryside. Or visit the Schadaupark where the lake ends and take a swim there in the summer.

Hidden Gems for Seasoned Travelers
Walk up to Rabeflue (the trails are well-marked and the tourist office has maps). It only takes about 45 - 60 minutes to get almost 1,000 feet up and you'll have some nice forest land-scapes and a view over the city toward Bern.

Where to Stay
I'd stay at Schwert Thun (*schwert-thun.net*).

68

Day Trips

If you are feeling lazy and have the money, take the trains, cable cars, and/or funiculars to Jungfraujoch (the highest train station in Europe), Schilthorn (a mountaintop lookout point over Mürren), Niesen (a mountain overlooking Lake Thun), Stockhorn (also overlooking the lake), and Niederhorn (on the other side of the lake). If you're feeling sporty, you can hike at least partway up each of those (all the way up all except the Jungfraujoch).

A trip into the Emmental region is also nice. It doesn't really matter where you go, you'll be walking past farming villages and giant farmhouses.

Where to Hike

Start with Kiental or Gasteretal. Most of the valleys here have trails leading to other valleys. Choose your hike based on what you like, how fit you are, and whether there is snow.

Where to Eat & Drink (Favorite Restaurants & Bars)

For good Swiss food, try the restaurant at Schwert Thun (located at Untere Hauptgasse 8) or Konzepthalle 6 (at Scheibenstrasse 6). For good Italian, check out Sottoriva (at Freienhofgasse 12). As for bars, my favorites are Mokka (best concerts in town) at Allmendstrasse 14, La Cueva at Untere Hauptgasse 32, and Mundwerk at Obere Hauptgasse 49.

Budget Tips

For affordable activities, check out the Alternative Cultural Center (akut-thun.ch), which hosts concerts and events and is pay-what-you-can for drinks (they are supported by the city).

How to Fit In

I don't think anyone will steal your suitcase on a train; just leave it at the entrance where there's space or put it on the top racks instead of keeping it with you when you sit.

How to Meet Locals & Make Friends
Just talk to people. Cultural events are always a good place for that, as you already have an interest in common.

Best Places to Take a Photo
The Rabeflue hike (mentioned above) is excellent. The Rathausplatz (where the city hall is) is perfect in the daytime or evening. And Schadaupark is good if it is nice and sunny.

Final Notes & Other Tips
Stay longer! I always try to stay as long as possible in one place rather than moving around every day. The longer you stay, the better you know the place. I recommend at least a week.

Marc van der Heijden
Whiskey Expert. Hiker. Entrepreneur.

About Marc
I was born in Thun and six years ago (after living in Zürich for 13 years) I returned to my roots and opened a boutique liquor store with my partner, John. Our claim to fame is that we've got the largest choice of spirituous beverages in Switzerland. In our free time, we love to go hiking with our dog.

What to Do In Thun (The Basics)
The historic center of Thun is very small but absolutely worth seeing. And, of course, the landscape is the most beautiful thing about living in this area.

Hidden Gems for Seasoned Travelers
In summertime, you can rent a rubber boat and float on the river Aare from Thun all the way down to Bern (approximately three hours) and take the train back.

Where to Stay
I suggest staying in old town Thun, in the villages around the lake, or in the villages up in the mountains (rather than the touristic hot spot Interlaken).

Day Trips
For mountain landscapes, head up to Mount Niesen by rack railway or take the cable car to Stockhorn or Beatenberg. Or, to enjoy lovely Lake Thun, book a tour by boat (ask for the schedule of the only steamboat, Blüemlisalp).

Where to Hike
If you don't suffer from a fear of heights and aren't traveling with small children, go from Kandersteg to Öschinensee by cable car and hike up to Heuberg, then take the other trail down. You'll never forget the breathtaking views.

What & Where to Eat & Drink
For Swiss food, go to Zu Metzgern (at Untere Hauptgasse 2) or Füürgässli (at Obere Hauptgasse 54) by the river. Then, try Aesszimmer (literally "dining room") in the old town (at Obere Hauptgasse 55). They have a small choice of excellent, always-fresh, seasonal dishes and they're always packed.

Next, I recommend Schwert ("sword") at Untere Hauptgasse 8. It's a traditional and cozy place run by a young and dynamic team (and with very nice rooms, by the way).

Finally, try Am Fluss ("at the river")—a stylish sushi and grill place with a wonderful outdoor section (at Mühleplatz 9).

You should also try our local wines from around Lake Thun. Insider tip: Try to find the very limited white wine, Lumi, made from red grapes from Seftigen.

How to Meet Locals & Make Friends
We might be a bit reserved and shy, but we're actually very nice and sociable. It helps if you take the initiative and start talking to locals.

BERN & THE BERNESE OBERLAND

Where to Take a Photo
Walk on the left side of the river to the lake, take the ferry to the other side and walk back. Anywhere along this route will be stunning.

Final Notes & Other Tips
If you're looking for a special whisky, rum, grappa, or any local spirit or wine, we'll gladly recommend something. So please stop by and visit!

Find Marc, John, and their shop at vanderheijden.ch.

INTERLAKEN

Switzerland's adventure sports hub.

FIND WI-FI HERE: The center of Interlaken (there's a free city connection) & The Three Tells Pub in Matten.

LANGUAGE: German   **CANTON:** Bern

Julie Paterson
Tour Leader. Outdoor Enthusiast. Entrepreneur.

About Julie
I am a Kiwi nomad who has been spending the summers in Switzerland for nearly 20 years now. My "other" summer (the northern hemisphere's winter) I spend leading tours to exotic destinations like Morocco, Egypt, India, or Africa.

When I'm in Switzerland, I work in adventure tourism in Interlaken, a lively summer tourist town, for a company that organizes rafting, canyoning, bungee jumping, and other crazy adventures. For the rest of the year, I run my own company taking women-only tours to all sorts of destinations, from Morocco to India and anything in between.

When I have free time, I head for the hills, mountain biking, hiking, sea kayaking—really, doing anything that involves nature and exercise.

What to Do In Interlaken (The Basics)
I definitely recommend hiking: It's so easy to find your way around the Swiss mountains, the trails are great and well sign-posted, and there are restaurants or huts all over the place so you don't have to carry a lot.

73

Another favorite activity is canyoning: It is something you can't do everywhere in the world and there are different levels to suit everyone. Also, it's interactive and you feel like you have personally achieved something at the end of your trip.

For something less active (if you want it to be), go to Gimmelwald. Stay the night or even just for lunch. It's a classic Swiss mountain village, complete with cows, geraniums, and a stack of huge, glacier-covered mountains to stare at while you eat. It's breathtaking.

Finally, hire a mountain bike and ride from Interlaken up to Lauterbrunnen. Its nice to travel the slow road, to be off the trains, and to smell the forest, hear the river, be in the moment, and take in the scenery as the mountains open up before you.

Hidden Gems for Seasoned Travelers
Grab an e-bike and ride up the mountain to Beatenberg from Interlaken, across to Sigriswil, and along the lake back to Interlaken. It's a nice workout and will take you through gorgeous towns and great scenery on an interestingly narrow, winding road.

Go on an overnight hike. Leave your main luggage at your accommodation, take just what you need for the night (drink bottle, snacks, money, camera) in a daypack, and go stay at one of the many mountain huts in the area. You can buy food at the hut and blankets are provided, so you don't need anything really. Nothing beats a night under a starry sky high up in the mountains. [Editor's note: for most alpine huts, you'll need to book ahead, so plan a bit before you go.]

Where to Stay
Spend a night or two in Interlaken and get your fill of adventures. Then head up to Gimmelwald or even to a mountain hut for a night in the mountains.

BERN & THE BERNESE OBERLAND

Where to Hike
In addition to Gimmelwald, I'd recommend taking the train from Wilderswil to Kleine Scheidegg and hiking from Kleine Scheidegg to First and then on to Grindelwald. You will be walking toward stunning mountain views all day. Take a good lunch, as this is at least a five-hour excursion.

Another nice hike, which takes a couple hours one-way, is from Grindelwald to the Bäregghütte (hut). Take the cable car to Pfingstegg and hike to the hut. Have lunch in front of the glacier or, better still, stay the night and enjoy the serenity of the mountains.

What to Eat & Drink
The area is also known for its meringues with cream. And if you're staying put for the night, get yourself a coffee with some schnapps in it. These have different names, from pflümlischumli to kaffeefertig, and they can all be a nice nightcap.

Where to Eat & Drink (Favorite Restaurants & Bars)
Switzerland is not known for its culinary delights and figuring out where to take my foreign friends for dinner is always a dilemma. That said, I do frequent The Three Tells, an Irish pub with outside seating (at Hauptstrasse 49 in Matten, a suburb of Interlaken). It's great for an evening beer in the sun.

Another personal favorite is The Ox, which has good food and good service (address: Marktgasse 10). And my third pick would be Das Bierhaus (at Postgasse 3) for a great selection of beers, ciders, and other drinks.

Budget Tips
You only live once. Pay the credit card bill off when you get home and enjoy! (Okay, okay, if you really want some tips, note that one of the cheapest restaurants in town is Hooters, which is more of a family restaurant here in Interlaken because of the prices, rather than a sleazy bar like in the US.)

How to Meet Locals & Make Friends
Go to the metro bar at Balmer's (at Hauptstrasse 23 in Matten) where locals are looking to meet.

Best Places to Take a Photo
Hike up the Harder Kulm. This is the closest hike to Interlaken and offers great views over both lakes and the Eiger, Mönch, and Jungfrau peaks.

Final Notes & Other Tips
You'll find something to do for everyone and, in the evening, when the sun is setting over the mountains, there is no better place to be than the big park in the middle of town watching the Jungfrau's glaciers glow pink as the sun goes down.

Find Julie at venusadventures.travel and alpinraft.com.

Phil Hausammann
Outdoor Enthusiast. Business Owner.

About Phil
I am originally from the eastern part of Switzerland, but I've lived in Interlaken for 11 years. I am part owner of Jet Boat Interlaken. And in my free time, I enjoy getting outside in the Bernese Oberland—kayaking, sailing, and paragliding.

What to Do In Interlaken (The Basics)
Get out and about. That is, after all, what Interlaken is famous for. Get on the water (jet boat, kayak), into the air (paraglide, hang-glide), or into the mountains (hike, mountain bike).

Hidden Gems for Seasoned Travelers
Head into the mountains and hike to one of the Swiss mountain huts (where you can stay overnight in the Alps). Go sailing on Lake Thun or sea kayaking (a really beautiful experience) on Lake Brienz. [Editor's note: see page 21 for a full kayaking inter-

view.] Or take advantage of one of Interlaken's various BBQ areas, where you can enjoy the famous Alp-glow as the sun goes down over a glass of wine. It's a real treat for the soul.

Where to Stay
The beauty of a little mountain town like Interlaken is that wherever you stay, you aren't far from anything. That said, stay in Matten if you want to mingle with the young folks and enjoy a pint after a successful day on the lake or the mountain. Or, if beautiful views and upper-class hotels are your thing, the middle of Interlaken is the place to be.

Day Trips
I personally really like Bern, the capitol of Switzerland, which is a beautiful little city to explore.

Where to Hike
One of my favorite hikes is from Schynige Platte to First (pronounced "fearsht"). Take the train up from Wilderswil and walk to First. The hike is about six hours and offers beautiful views over the lakes and mountains. It's not too steep and you can enjoy a ride with the famous First-Flyer, a long zip line at the top of the mountain. And from the bottom of the zip line, you can either take a cable car or hike down to Grindelwald and catch a train back to Interlaken.

Where to Eat & Drink (Favorite Restaurants & Bars)
The Three Tells in Matten (at Hauptstrasse 49) is a great Irish pub with nice pub food and live music. The Hüsi Bierhaus (at Postgasse 3 in Interlaken) has a great selection of beers and there's always someone to chat with. Goldener Anker (at Marktgasse 57) has great food, nice people, and, now and then, some fantastic live music (it's a real Interlaken institution). And Restaurant Laterne (at Obere Bönigstrasse) is the place to be for real Swiss food.

How to Meet Locals & Make Friends
Start chatting with people and don't get irritated if it takes a

little while for us to open up. That's just the way we are, a bit reserved at first and friendly in the end.

Best Places to Take a Photo

Höhenmatte (the big open green space in the middle of Interlaken), the lakes (Thunersee and Brienzersee), the mountains (anywhere really), and Harder Kulm (Interlaken's home mountain).

Find Phil at jetboat.ch.

LAUTERBRUNNEN

Incredible views, 72 waterfalls, outdoor sports, & small town charm.

FIND WI-FI HERE: Airtime Café & the Horner Pub.

LANGUAGE: German

CANTON: Bern

Gigi Griffis
Alpine Hiker. Foodie. Wine Snob. Guidebook Author.

About Gigi

Well, hi there. I'm the author of this unconventional little guidebook. Nice to meet you. After almost two years of full-time travel, mostly in Europe, I convinced the Swiss to give me a residence permit and made Lauterbrunnen my home base. I love it for its wonderful and varying natural landscapes, its clean water and fresh air, its international community, and, most of all, how it makes me feel. It's the only place in the world that I've ever felt like I was truly coming home.

For fun, I spend as much time as I can outside. I love hiking, picnics, sleeping under the stars, and just sitting somewhere outside taking this place in. It never gets old. Other than that, I love reading, writing (obviously), cooking, conversation, traveling (also obviously), and fine wines.

For a living, I write these 100 Locals guidebooks, as well as magazine articles, blog posts, and the occasional website.

What to Do In Lauterbrunnen (The Basics)

This area is all about the outdoors. Go hiking, have a picnic, sleep under the stars (wild camping is generally allowed here), or take one of the very reliable trains or cable cars to the various lookout points and ski towns (in summer or winter).

The area also has lots of skydiving, white water rafting, paragliding, canyoning, bungee jumping, and other extreme sports activities. If you only do one, I recommend paragliding. There's just something unreal about floating gently from a ski town out across the valley, past the cliffs, and down to the valley floor. It's magical—and way less scary than you think.

Hidden Gems for Seasoned Travelers

One of the most unique and interesting things to do here is watch the BASE jumpers. If you aren't familiar with BASE, the story is this: experienced sky divers (you have to have hundreds of skydives before you can BASE jump) jump off the cliffs, fall for a few seconds, and then pull a parachute and float to the valley floor.

There are two types of BASE: wing suit, which makes the jumpers look like flying squirrels as they glide across the valley with a massive wing-span, and tracking suit, which is a special suit that fills with air and allows them to fly away from the cliffs just a little. Wing suit flying is more technical and dangerous.

To watch jumpers from the valley floor, simply walk from Lauterbrunnen toward Stechelberg on the main path. About 20 or 30 minutes into your walk, you'll come across a farm with an alpkäse (Alp cheese) sign and usually a black and white dog out front. Just past this farm on the right is one of the most popular places where jumpers come off the cliffs, so stop and look up here. If you hit the path that turns off to the left with signs for Trümmelbach Falls, you've gone a tiny bit too far.

If you are really adventurous and want to watch the jumpers from the top of the cliffs, you'll need to meet some BASE jumpers and get invited on one of their hikes. The best place to do this is the Horner Pub. If you do get invited along for a hike, you'll need to bring a climbing harness. Most of those hikes are steep and sketchy and one wrong move could be fatal. (So, for the faint of heart, I recommend watching from the ground, which is, honestly, cooler anyway.)

When you're done watching the jumpers, another really interesting and not well-known spot is just above Kleine Scheidegg on the way to the Eiger Glacier. About five or 10 minutes from the Kleine Scheidegg train station, you'll find a pretty alpine lake. And beside the lake there's a mini lake with three metal benches in it. These benches face the three major peaks and there's a button just outside the water that makes the mini lake bubble, so you can sit on the benches with the cold water bubbling around your feet after a long hike. I've never seen anything else like it.

Where to Stay

In Lauterbrunnen (which is very small), my only suggestion is not to stay close to the church. The church bells are extremely loud and go off all the time. Anywhere else in town is really lovely.

If you don't want to stay in the valley, I'm a big fan of Mürren, at the top of the cliffs. The panoramic views are unbeatable and the car-free town is utterly charming.

Day Trips

As I said, my favorite of the little ski towns above us is Mürren. It's exactly what I imagined a Swiss ski town to be, full of chalets and flowers and sweeping views. Go on a clear day and have a hot chocolate in one of the cliffside restaurants (my favorites for views are from the Edelweiss Restaurant, with its tall windows, and the little restaurant by the cable car station, which has a shady wooden balcony).

For views, I'm also a huge fan of Kleine Scheidegg (I love to hike up there for brunch) and Männlichen (whose panorama literally brings me to tears, it's so beautiful).

Slightly farther away, I absolutely adore Thun. It's the big town on Lake Thun (Thunersee) and the view from its castle (built at the top of the hill) is really special. The castle itself has been converted into a museum full of old black and white photos of the area, other artifacts, and local history. And the town is beautiful with lakeside views, swans, and wooden bridges full of flowers. (In my personal opinion, it's a prettier, less-touristy version of the more popular Lucerne).

Where to Hike

My absolute favorite hike starts in Mürren and ends at the top of Schilthorn—a nearly-10,000-foot mountain to the south. It takes about four to five hours and will take you through every type of scenery you can imagine—from fields of wildflowers to scary, narrow ridges to views above the tree line.

For the best route, ignore the signs for Schilthorn (they lead to a far less beautiful trail). Instead, start from the cable car station and follow the signs for rotstocshutte. After an hour or so of hiking, you'll start seeing signs for Bryndli—follow those. Once you are near Bryndli, you'll finally start seeing signs for Birg, Schiltalp, and then Schilthorn; follow them to Schilthorn.

Keep in mind that this route is not for a faint of heart, the unfit, or those with a fear of heights. I wouldn't call it super dangerous, but there are portions of the hike with steep, daunting drop-offs and you may have to cross a rock fall or two.

If you want to make this tough hike even tougher and more daunting, add the steep two-hour trek from Lauterbrunnen to Mürren instead of starting from Mürren.

A few other difficult but wonderful hikes include:

Lauterbrunnen to Kleine Scheidegg: For the most interesting route, start at the trail that begins at the bottom of Trümmelbach Falls. To get there, walk along the main road. When you see the signs for Trümmelbach, pass them and turn left at the next driveway. You'll see yellow hiking signs at the end of the driveway pointing you to the trail behind the farm. Hiking time: about three hours one-way. Train return available. Elevation change: 4,154 feet.

BERN & THE BERNESE OBERLAND

Stechelberg to Oberhornsee: This hike will take you through steep, heavily forested paths (think twining ivy, thick trees, and soft, green moss everywhere) up above the tree line to a pretty little alpine lake (Oberhornsee). About ¾ of the way up, you'll reach a quaint little hotel and restaurant, which is a nice place to stop for a drink, some amazing views, and a much-deserved rest on your way to the lake. The lake itself is glacial. Jump in if you dare. Hiking time: about three to four hours one way. No return bus/train. Elevation change: 4,100+ feet.

Wilderswil to Schynige Platte: Again, this hike will take you through a variety of landscapes—from thick forest to cow-filled meadows to rocky passes. The difference between this one and the two I mention above? About ¾ of the way up, you'll get a sweeping view of Lake Thun. And if you hike just a tiny bit past the train station at the top, you'll get another sweeping view of Lake Brienz. Both are really beautiful. Hiking time: about four hours one-way. Return train available. Elevation change: 4,800+ feet. Tip: For this hike, bring extra water. There's really nowhere to refill along the way.

For something easier, try:

The walk along the valley floor from Lauterbrunnen to Stechelberg. The views are wonderful, with cliffs and waterfalls on either side, fields all around you, mountains in the distance, and a river occasionally winding its way alongside the path. Walking time: 1.5 hours. Bus return available.

The walk from Grütschalp to Mürren. With very little elevation change and a well-kept path, this is an easy hike. And the views to your left are a panorama of the region's most famous peaks. Walking time: one hour. Train return available.

The walk from Wengen to Kleine Scheidegg. This hike is more moderate. There is some elevation gain and a few steep spots, but it's much less steep than any of the difficult hikes I mentioned and doesn't take you along cliffs or ridges. Instead, you'll enjoy fields of wildflowers and close-up views of the famous Jungfrau, Mönch, and Eiger. Hiking time: about 1.5 hours. Train return available.

What to Eat & Drink

I'm something of a food snob, and I'm not a fan of most of the heavy cuisine here (sorry, Switzerland). That said, there are a few standouts, starting with the alpkäse (alpine cheese). The best cheese comes from the farms up in the mountains, so take lots of change with you when you go hiking (usually, there are prices on the cheese and you leave the money in a box) and watch for käse signs along the trails.

Speaking of cheese, if you want something really special and you're planning a trip to Bern, make sure to go on a market day and look for Bruni the cheese-seller. He has amazing cheeses and knows everything about them (seriously, down to the names of the individual cows). My favorite was the cheese made with (wait for it) pine needles.

Another standout is the wine at Rebbau Spiez in Spiez (about half an hour away by train). On a sunny day, it's lovely to wander the vineyards and buy a bottle or two for your next alpine picnic.

If you're in the mood for a Swiss classic, the best place to try rösti in town is the Hotel Oberland, where they serve a version called the Trucker Rösti with bacon and red sauce. It's fantastic (though expensive), especially after a long day of hiking.

Where to Eat & Drink (Favorite Restaurants & Bars)

Here in town, the best (and fanciest) place to eat is the Hotel Oberland. (I recommend the Trucker Rösti and the Merlot.)

If you're looking for something more budget-friendly, the Horner Pub serves cheap and good pub food. I'm a particular fan of their chicken sandwich (which is covered in an amazing garlic sauce) and the chicken curry.

For brunch, I like to hike or take the train up to Kleine Scheidegg and eat on the patio at the Eiger Nordwand restaurant. The mountaintop views are amazing and the big breakfast is simple but wonderful, especially after a hike.

For a light lunch or a snack, I like the savory pies at Airtime Café. They're cheap(ish), small, and delicious.

And if you're tired of the heavy traditional Swiss fare, head to Interlaken, where the Hotel Victoria-Jungfrau's ESPA spa restaurant serves up light, delicious food. I'm a big fan of the salmon wrap with a glass of Prosecco. In Matten (one of the towns connected to Interlaken), you'll find a lovely little hole-in-the-wall Thai restaurant called Little Thai (at Hauptstrasse 19). Everyone who lives here knows about it—it's that good.

One place to avoid? The Base Point. I'm sad to report that the manager has a history of sexual harassment and has been caught slipping things into women's drinks. Ladies, steer clear.

Budget Tips
Specific accommodation ideas for the budget traveler include Camping Jungfrau Holiday Park (I love their clean, simple cabins and how they are just outside town in the valley), Hotel Horner (which is very clean and budget-friendly but can get loud in the summer, since it's over the pub), and Chalet im Rohr (which is a guesthouse in an old chalet but is right across from the church, so you'll have to deal with the church bells).

How to Fit In
Remember that this town and the towns around it are very small. If you're traveling in a large group, make space for people to pass you on the sidewalk. If you want to stop and take a photo, step off to the side. If you want to look up and take in the cliffs and waterfalls (and who wouldn't?), pause and step to the side. Make space for other people who might be running or walking or trying to get to work.

The other really important thing is not to crowd people. The Swiss (and most of us expats) like their personal space. If you bump into someone (or smash their toes or kick their shins), say you're sorry. If there's a lot of space on the train platform or the grocery line, don't stand close to the person in front of you. I feel like this should be a no-brainer, but I get kicked and stepped on all the time.

How to Meet Locals & Make Friends
This is a very international town with a big tourism industry, so you're likely to meet lots of other travelers and people who have moved here from all over Europe (some who come for a year or two and many who come and stay). Everyone is really friendly and easy to talk to, so just strike up a conversation on the train or at the Horner Pub.

Best Places to Take a Photo
For the iconic Lauterbrunnen shot (with our cute little church in the foreground and the waterfall-laden valley behind it), go to the Airtime Café in the center of town, then cross the street on the crosswalk (a few steps down from the café) and follow the little road for a minute or two until you reach a bench. Sit on the bench and the iconic view is spread out before you.

Another favorite is halfway between Lauterbrunnen and Stechelberg on the valley floor. If you're here in spring, this area is alive with wildflower fields and you can see snow-capped peaks in the distance.

Finally, halfway between Kleine Scheidegg and Männlichen—two towns high above us on the Wengen side of the valley—if you turn and look toward Kleine Scheidegg, you'll get a really imposing and majestic view of the Eiger peak, which is almost always snowy and gorgeous.

Final Notes & Other Tips
Keep in mind that you cannot buy tickets on the train (they'll fine you) and the conductor will be appalled if you put your

feet on the seats. Dogs travel free in carriers or half-price out. If you want a little more space on the trains, walk all the way to the front car. Everyone else tries to smash themselves into the middle cars, so you're likely to have a little more room.

Stay away from the cows. They may look sweet, but they aren't. If you're hiking and there are cows on the path, walk around, giving them a wide berth. If you're hiking with a small dog and have to pass some cows, pick the dog up. If you're hiking with a large dog, leash her.

The locals (and us honorary locals) drink the running water that goes into the troughs you'll find along many of our hiking trails. We also drink directly from many of the streams, which are extremely clean. I've never—not once—gotten sick from it. So, while it, like everything, is at your own risk, I wouldn't hesitate to fill up a water bottle along your hike.

If you're coming to Lauterbrunnen from Interlaken by train, make sure you board the train in sectors A or B (the front of the train). This train actually splits in half during the journey with half going to Lauterbrunnen and half going to Grindelwald. If you're running behind or accidentally get on the back, though, don't panic. There are two stops before the train splits (Wilderswil and Zweilütschinen) and you can move to the front of the train at either stop.

Finally, note that many things are closed or have reduced hours on Sundays, including the grocery store. Shop on Saturday for your Sunday needs. And if you desperately need groceries on Sunday, head to Camping Jungfrau Holiday Park, where you'll find a small (and more expensive) convenience store that is open more often and for longer hours.

Find Gigi at gigigriffis.com.

MÜRREN

Fresh air, happy people, an alpine panorama, & car-free living.

FIND WI-FI HERE: The Alpine Sports Centre.

LANGUAGE: German   **CANTON:** Bern

Anne-Marie Goetschi
Hiker. Cyclist. Tourism Professional.

About Anne-Marie

I came to Mürren 28 years ago to work in the tourism industry, running Berghaus Sonnenberg, Hotel Belmont (now Eiger Guesthouse), Hotel Alpenruh, and Hotel Jungfrau, each for several years. Currently, I work up here three days a week as a product manager and spend the rest of my time with my husband outside the Alps.

In my spare time, I do a lot of hiking (mostly in the Bernese Oberland, though I know Switzerland's other mountain regions well) and cycling.

What to Do In Mürren (The Basics)

First, go to the mountaintop lookout point of Schilthorn to get an impression of the mountain world we live in. Then take a stroll through the village or down to Gimmelwald to get a sense of village life. And finally, if you have enough time, enjoy one of our many wonderful nature hikes.

In winter, there are skiing and snowboarding for the sporty among us and peaceful snowshoe hikes for those who want something calmer but still connected to the outdoors.

BERN & THE BERNESE OBERLAND

Hidden Gems for Seasoned Travelers
In summer, cross to the far side of the Lauterbrunnen Valley for spectacular waterfalls or hike to Kilchbalm for impressive alpine scenery or to one of the mountain huts for good local food and a panoramic view of the Eiger, Mönch, and Jungfrau.

Where to Stay
Stay in a local-owned chalet for a taste of Swiss daily life.

Day Trips
The mountaintop lookout points of Schilthorn, Jungfraujoch, and Männlichen are must-sees. Further away, I'd recommend Lake Thun and the city of Thun, with its creative small shops and boutiques.

What to Eat & Drink
Try our fresh fruitcakes, which you can find in most mountain huts. You can also pick up some alpkäse (Alp cheese) in the local stores or directly at the cheese factory at Winteregg.

In autumn, some local restaurants—like Hotel Bellevue in Mürren and Hotel Stechelberg or Berghaus Trachsellauenen in Stechelberg—not only serve the traditional wild game but also have owners that hunt and bring in the game themselves.

Where to Eat & Drink (Favorite Restaurants & Bars)
Hotel Eiger (across from the train station) has excellent food. Hotel Bellevue (on upper Dorfstrasse) has good food and atmosphere. Stägerstübli (on lower Dorfstrasse) is perfect if you're looking for local food and local people.

Budget Tips
The cafeteria at the Sports Centre (just up the hill from the train station) has excellent soups and snacks at reasonable prices. The Eiger Guesthouse has excellent and affordable Italian pizzas in different sizes. And some restaurants (like Stägerstübli) have a daily special (tagesteller) with soup, salad, and a main course for around 18 francs.

How to Fit In

Hiking with flip-flops is considered uncultivated and dangerous, as is walking around in shorts when it is cold. Other behaviors to avoid include using private benches in front of the houses for your lunch break, leaving garbage in public spaces, spitting on the floor in public, talking about money all the time (and how expensive everything is), being loud and drunk and badly dressed, and not greeting people when you are hiking.

How to Meet Locals & Make Friends

Stay in a local home and ask about people's daily lives.

Best Places to Take a Photo

I recommend Allmendhubel with its beautiful panoramic view.

Final Notes & Other Tips

All cities are pretty much the same, but in a mountain village you will find life at its most basic. Forget about your iPhone and iPad...just come and enjoy pure nature.

WENGEN
Ski slopes, scenery, & sports.

FIND WI-FI HERE: The Rocks Bar.

LANGUAGE: German   **CANTON:** Bern

Jennifer Zolla McDougall
Hotel & Restaurant Owner. BASE Jumper.

About Jenny
I grew up between Wengen and Italy and after finishing university in Milan, I moved back to Wengen to run the family business with my mother. We have a lovely historical hotel called Hotel Falken and a delicious Italian restaurant and bar called Ristorante da Sina and Sina's Mountain Pub where we serve Italian food as well as local specialties and steak.

What to Do In Wengen (The Basics)
First, take the cable car up to Männlichen and hike to Kleine Scheidegg. The view is absolutely breathtaking and the hike is very easy. When you arrive in Kleine Scheidegg, have lunch at the Bahnhof Buffet (definitely try one of their delicious roestizza (rösti with sausage, apples, and mozzarella). Make sure to arrive hungry, as the plates are very rich.

After that, you can either walk back down or take the train. If you arrive in Wengen early enough, head to the outdoor public pool and enjoy a refreshing swim. Otherwise choose a terrace and have what we call an *apero* (drink before dinner).

Where to Stay
If you're looking for something budget-friendly, I suggest staying in Lauterbrunnen. The Chalet im Rohr is very Swiss; you'll

get a simple room with shared bathroom and there are cooking facilities in the building.

If you are traveling with a group of friends or family, then renting an apartment is always a good idea. There are some lovely apartments for rent in the region, from very basic to luxurious. This option is ideal for people who will be in the area for at least a week. A beautiful, luxurious apartment shared by six or more people ends up having a really convenient price.

If you like to be taken back in time, our historical Hotel Falken is a perfect choice. It opened in 1895 and has been in our family since its founding.

What to Eat & Drink
When it comes to fondue, here's a little secret: book your fondue the previous day and ask for it to be cooked in Champagne and Cognac rather than wine and kirsch. I also prefer to have boiled potatoes with the cheese fondue rather than bread.

If it's rösti you're after, the best places to eat it here are the Bahnhof Buffet in Kleine Scheidegg or the Hotel Oberland in Lauterbrunnen (where you should try the Trucker Rösti).

Where to Eat & Drink (Favorite Restaurants & Bars)
In addition to my family's restaurant (Sina's), I like Hotel Bären. If you want to treat yourself to a truly amazing meal, the surprise menu at the Hotel Caprice (at Postfach 244) is divine. For bars, I like the Tanne Bar and the Rocks Bar.

How to Meet Locals & Make Friends
Go to local bars and don't be afraid to chat with the bartenders; they'll point you in the right direction.

Best Places to Take a Photo
Everywhere in the Jungfrau Region is simply stunning. On the Schynige Platte, there is a frame that you can stand in and

take an amazing picture. I also suggest going to Jungfraujoch (the highest train station in Europe) for incredible photos.

Find Jenny at wengenselect.com and dasina.ch.

Beverley Wood
Hiking Enthusiast.

About Beverley
I'm an English woman who lived in Germany for 20 years before moving to the Lauterbrunnen Valley and Wengen in 1998. I lived in Wengen for 11 years, then moved myself down the mountain to Interlaken. I've worked at the reception of the Hotel Oberland since 2009. And I've been a keen hiker for many years (even before living here, I'd come down from Germany all the time to hike the area).

Where to Hike
Some easy and popular hikes include the walk from Männlichen to Kleine Scheidegg, Grütschalp to Mürren, and the Lauterbrunnen Valley floor.

A few more hidden gems include the jeep trail that starts near Wengernalp. Follow the trail left just below the second farm to the Wixi moraine and down to Mettlenalp. You can sit below the glaciers in gorgeous pastures full of grazing cows and (if you're lucky) see some summer avalanches as the glaciers break. From there, you can continue along to Biglenalp and back onto the farmers' jeep trail down to Wengen (with a stop at Allmend for their lovely homemade herb ice tea).

Another favorite is the walk from Mürren to the Blumental (flower valley). If you don't feel like hiking far, take the funicular up to Allmendhubel and take the trail that weaves around to the right (when standing with the restaurant to your back). The Blumental will appear below you after a couple hundred meters. After descending into the Blumental, pass the Sonnenberg Restaurant and take the small trail behind the Suppenalp

Restaurant and up and around the mountain. You'll pass the cable car as it heads toward Birg and Schilthorn. From there the trail levels out and opens up with beautiful views of the mountains and you can continue onto Schiltalp, where you'll find a wonderful little farm that sells amazing homemade cheeses and farmers ice cream made in Meiringen. From here, you can take a walk down the valley back to Mürren or down to Gimmelwald.

My final hidden-gem pick is walking down from Gimmelwald to the Sefinen Valley. Take a picnic for this trip, as there are no places to get food or drinks on the way. As you leave Gimmelwald, take a trail down into this lovely valley (where there are steep cliffs on either side of the trail), following signs for Chilchbalm and Sefinental. Keep walking for an hour or so and you will come to a stream and a wooden bridge. Continue on, climbing up the trail and you'll end up in an amazing natural bowl with a stream running through it and hanging glaciers above you. In summer, there are cows grazing here, too. Kick back and enjoy your picnic. Take the same route back to Gimmelwald or hike down to the valley floor and Stechelberg.

For more experienced hikers, the trail to Obersteinberg is wonderful.

Finally, for more great views, take the bus to Isenfluh followed by a cable car to Sulwald and then hike up to the Lobhorn hut.

Day Trips
Take the cable car to Grütschalp and walk across to Mürren. Go up to the Schilthorn and back down through Gimmelwald, Stechelberg, and back to Lauterbrunnen. For something further afield, visit the towns of Gruyère and Broc and go to the Cailler chocolate factory.

How to Fit In
Wherever you travel, always learn the local greeting and use it. It will get you everywhere.

Final Notes & Other Tips

When you're heading into the mountains, get an early start to get the most out of your day. When passing farms in the summertime, buy the local cheese directly from the farmers.

GRINDELWALD
Hiking trails, mountain trains, & a special mountain energy.

FIND WI-FI HERE: Grindelwald Lounge, Avocado Bar, the sports center, & the tourist office.

LANGUAGE: German   **CANTON:** Bern

Elizabeth & Ueli Oehrli
Trekkers. Travelers. Artists. Outdoor Enthusiasts.

About Elizabeth & Ueli
Ueli grew up in Lauterbrunnen and Elizabeth in Iseltwald on the lake. We were both teachers and met at a school party. We have always both been big nature-lovers, so we bonded over skiing and hiking and the magnificent outdoors.

These days, we're retired. In our free time, we are painters (something we've done for a long time)—of mountains and plants and mountain guides. We have a nice studio in the house and you'll often find Ueli in the studio and Elizabeth painting in the sitting room. We're also avid travelers and have been trekking in places like the Peruvian Andes, the Nepalese Himalayas, Kyrgyzstan, and the High Atlas.

What to Do In Grindelwald (The Basics)
When the weather is nice, take the gondolas to Kleine Scheidegg and Gross Scheidegg. Then enjoy a simple walk from Gross Scheidegg to First. This walk has a panoramic view and is open and light and easy. It's also nice to go to Schwarz-waldalp. There's a beautiful, dramatic gorge there. In June, when the snow melts, it's so powerful.

We'd also recommend the Trümmelbach Falls (waterfalls inside the mountain) in the Lauterbrunnen Valley, the Glacier Gorge in Grindelwald, and the marble cave below Marmorbruch Restaurant.

Another beautiful walk is from First to Faulhorn. This is one of our favorites—amazing and beautiful. On one side, you can see to Germany and from the other you get the panorama of Eiger, Mönch, and Jungfrau.

If you take the popular trek from First to Bachalpsee, turn toward Busalp instead of going over the pass. That way is more interesting, taking you diagonally down narrow, stony paths.

If you aren't a hiker, try the Grindelwald Museum. It's not very big but is great for a rainy day. Another good rainy-day option is the sports center, which has a climbing gym, a swimming pool, and tubes for the kids to ride around in. And finally, visit the 1,100-year-old protestant church with its wooden posts and beautiful organ. Stay a while and check out the guestbook.

Hidden Gems for Seasoned Travelers

The Flower Path (from Waldspitz to Bort) is lovely and full of rare flowers. From there, you can walk to Bäregg and the Schreckhorn hut on a beautiful, wild path with an always-changing view. This path will take you over some ropes, across some iron stakes hammered into the rocks, and over gorges and wild rivers. You'll have to cross at least one broad river, so only go if the weather is good and you're experienced. If the snow is melting and the river is strong, save this for another day.

On the other side of the valley, by the upper glacier, Gleckstein hut is another nice choice.

From First, there is a steep, narrow, stony path to Waldspitz that's worth taking if you're used to tough hikes; it's tougher and longer than the Flower Path, but it's worth it. If you're not up for that, you can take an easier path from Bachalpsee to Waldspitz. And from Waldspitz, there's a beautiful path that runs flat for about 20 minutes and then heads up the mountain to a nice little pond called Kohlenweiher. It's stunning when the weather is clear. You can see the Eiger reflected in the pond, which is surrounded by pine trees.

In the summer, the hike from Gletscherschlucht to Alpiglen, along the foot of the Eiger, is something special. You'll find plants that you wouldn't see elsewhere (because of the shade here). And from Alpiglen you can go up to the Eigergletscher.

Finally, there's the Lauberhorn (home of the famous world cup race in the winter). In the summer, you can climb the peak and it's really simple and wonderful. Most people go to the upper station for skiing, but it's only 10 minutes past that to the peak and no one goes!

Where to Stay
If you like a little city bustle, stay in Grindelwald. If you prefer silence, go toward the Wetterhorn and Gross Scheidegg. We'd also recommend spending a night in Männlichen, which has a spectacular view down the Lauterbrunnen Valley. Kleine Scheidegg is also very quiet and has an ancient, elegant hotel.

Day Trips
If you're sporty, we suggest going from First to Schwarzhorn. It's a remarkable mountain and you'll only need to climb a little.

Beyond Gross Scheidegg, there's the Engelhorn or Wetterhorn. You'll need a guide for those and you'll have to do some real climbing, but if you want peaks, they're where you can go. You can also go to the Engelhorn hut, and you won't need a guide for that hike.

If you're staying for a while and want a city break, go to Bern. It's the capitol and they have nice shops and a great medieval town center surrounded by the Aare River. Thun is also nice. Zürich isn't that far. And Brienz, where you'll find the Ballenburg (an arrangement of old Swiss houses from every canton, where you can find exhibitions on silk-making, beekeeping, weaving, sausages, Swiss bread, etc.), is worth a visit as well. From Brienz, you can take the old steam train (Rothorn) for a pretty ride.

If you head toward Interlaken, the Harder Kulm viewpoint is another good choice, as are Iseltwald (along Lake Brienz) and the Geissbach waterfalls (which are best when the snows are melting in the early summer). If you hike to the Geissbach, wear long sleeves and pants. The woods are full of brambles and ticks.

Finally, a couple more sporty options include the hike to the Mutthornhütte (a mountain hut for which you'll need a guide), which will take you past a glacier, and from Stechelberg to Obersteinberg (which you can do without a guide). Plus, the area behind Stechelberg is a UNESCO World Heritage Site.

Where to Eat & Drink (Favorite Restaurants & Bars)

For coffee and tea, try C&M (at Almisgässli 1). It's a good tea-room and also has small meals. For restaurants, we like the well-cared-for, family-run Kirchbühl, located at Kirchbühlstrasse 23. It's famous, quiet, and beautiful and in summertime you can sit outside. The Wetterhorn in Grindelwald is reasonable. The restaurant in Hotel Kreuz (at Dorfstrasse 85) is good. Alpina (above the station) is recommended. And the two pizzerias in town are also good. The restaurant at the top of the Faulhorn has really good rösti and the view is wonderful.

Best Places to Take a Photo

The most photographed subject in town is the church with the Wetterhorn in the background. But we Swiss feel that this is a little kitschy. Instead, maybe go back on the trails toward Kleine Scheidegg or Baregg. You could take a great photograph there (or paint it). There are also gorgeous wildflowers along the way. The most important thing, really, is keeping your eyes open and taking everything in. You can find so many gorgeous places.

SPIEZ

A lovely lakefront & castle with a central location in the Alps.

FIND WI-FI HERE: Watch for signs around town.

LANGUAGE: German   **CANTON:** Bern

Margo Cummings
Translator. Tour Guide. Ski Instructor. English Teacher.

About Margo

I am a global nomad but have lived longest in Switzerland (15 years). I was born in Massachusetts and have lived in Saudi Arabia, Connecticut, DC, Germany, Colorado, and Alaska. Then my childhood dream (to live in Switzerland) came true and I got a job as a teacher and then became a ski instructor.

These days, I live in Aeschi bei Spiez and run my business—Margo Cummings Enterprises—as an English teacher, translator, tour guide, year-round ski instructor, and certified massage therapist. In my free time, I love to ski.

What to Do In Spiez (The Basics)

Spiez is a small town with a lovely lakefront and castle. It's tiny but centrally located, so there isn't a whole lot to do in the town itself, but it's a great base for exploring the region. Plus, it's outside the tourist areas, so it's more authentic.

That said, while you are in town, you should visit the castle (open Easter through October), walk along the lake, go swimming (in the summer), and take hikes. Also, I am in love with the Eisinsel (ice cream island), located at Seestrasse 28. This place has deliciously sinful homemade ice cream by the cup, cone, or to take away.

Nearby, you'll find the pyramid-shaped mountain of Niesen, which is a great outing. It has an amazing funicular and wonderful views in all directions.

Hidden Gems for Seasoned Travelers

A real secret gem is Swiss Indoor Skiing in the Jungfrau Park in Interlaken (*swissindoorskiing.ch*). This is a great rainy day activity for families. Beginners can learn to ski or pros can improve their technique while skiing on a moving carpet with a large mirror in front. Private lessons are available year-round with a reservation. Everything you need is included in the price.

Where to Stay

Airbnb.com has some nice places in town—and staying in a local apartment is a cozy way of getting a taste of the real Switzerland without the price of a hotel. Tourist information offices also have listings of alpine huts, which are available for a rustic, Heidi-like experience of living on the land.

Day Trips

Go to the Swiss Open Air Museum in Ballenberg. Original Swiss houses have been transported from the various cantons throughout Switzerland, so you can see all of Switzerland's architectural riches in one place. Exhibitions, hands-on activities, and theater performance enrich the experience. It's fun for all ages.

While you're there, check out the town of Meiringen and make a visit to the Reichenbach Falls, the setting for Sir Arthur Conan Doyle's "The Final Problem," where world-famous detective Sherlock Holmes fell to his death while fighting his nemesis, Moriarty. Also, the impressive Aareschlucht Gorge is nearby.

Where to Hike

The Suldtal nature reserve is a lovely family-friendly place for picnics along the steam. It offers some easy walks, as well as

101

more challenging hikes up along a waterfall. There is a char-ming chalet-style restaurant at the end of the valley called Pochtenfalls Restaurant with wonderful wild game specialties in the fall. (Open May – Oct.)

Where to Eat & Drink (Favorite Restaurants & Bars)

If you (like me) are tired of cheese and potatoes, head over to Appaloosa (at Thunstrasse 45)—a good Tex-Mex place with frozen drinks and delicious guacamole made right at your table. They've got a nice outdoor seating area and the Swiss military boys hang out here, so it's a fun atmosphere.

For burgers, wings, and live music, try ROX at Bahnhofstrasse 2. Then there's Bahnhofbuffet Spiez, which has daily menus of traditional fare for less than 20 francs. It also has a separate smoking lounge filled with colorful locals.

Outside Spiez itself, Cafe Mokka at Allmendstrasse 14 in Thun is a funky nighttime location for live music and an alternative scene. They have a lovely beer garden as well. Restaurant Chemihütte at Ebenenfeld 4 in Aeschireid has stunning views of the surrounding mountains and lakes. And Pier 17 at Schloss-gasse 10 in Oberhofen is a lakeside bistro with a great feel to it in nice summer weather.

Budget Tips

Switzerland has great second-hand shops (called *bröckis* or *brockenhauser*). There is a four-story one in the former Park Hotel at Haupstrasse 61 in Goldswil near Interlaken.

How to Meet Locals & Make Friends

Learn the language and join a club (skiing, dancing, etc.).

Best Places to Take a Photo

Living in Switzerland is like living in a postcard; just step outside.

Find Margo at linkd.in/1y0Yxg7.

KANDERSTEG
Authenticity, charm, beautiful hikes, & less tourists.

FIND WI-FI HERE: Most hotels & holiday rentals.

LANGUAGE: German   **CANTON:** Bern

Nicolas Seiler
Chef. Hospitality Expert. Family Man.

About Nicolas
I am 35 years old and married with three little ones. I was born and raised in Kandersteg, though I did my studies (at hotel management school) and apprenticeships (as a chef and waiter) elsewhere. I've been back for 10 years and now run the three-star Alfa Soleil Hotel and Nico's Restaurant, which I took over from my parents.

I am a big fan of the outdoors and I love the beautiful area around our village. In my free time, I hike, climb, mountain bike, snowboard, and ski. Kandersteg is a real cross-country paradise! My other passion is cooking. I love good food. My specialties are all made with local products. In spring, summer, and autumn, I collect lots of wild herbs, vegetables, roots, berries, and mushrooms in our woods. The goal is to bring the experience of the Alps to our table, to have the food reflect the place.

What to Do In Kandersteg (The Basics)
Start by visiting the Öschinensee, a UNESCO World Heritage Site in the mountains above Kandersteg. They call it the jewel of mountain lakes.

103

I also recommend the Blausee (blue lake) next to Kandersteg, the Sunnbüel hiking/ski area, and the Gasterntal (a pretty nearby valley).

Hidden Gems for Seasoned Travelers
Visit the wild, romantic Gasterntal (a nearby valley only inhabited in the summertime), the pure Uschinental (a very pretty valley where the famous Alp cheese is made in the summer), and the great Gemmi region (the rocky peaks between Kandersteg and Leukerbad).

The *via ferrata* (protected climbing route) from Kandersteg to Allmenalp is also something special.

Where to Stay
Frutigen, Adelboden, Thun, Spiez, Bern, and the Lötschental Valley are all excellent choices.

Day Trips
You should definitely visit the historic city of Bern, with its UNESCO World Heritage-designated old town surrounded by the Aarenschlaufe (the bend in the Aare River). It's charming and has stunning views of the alpine scenery.

Since Kandersteg is near the border of the Valais Canton, it is also very easy to visit the glacier villages of Zermatt and Saas-Fee.

And, of course, Locarno (in the Italian-speaking canton of Ticino) is just 2.5 hours away if you're craving some Mediterranean charm.

Where to Hike
In total, the hiking paradise of Kandersteg offers about 400 miles of excellent hiking paths, eight mountain huts (where you can stay overnight in the high Alps), and eight alpine passes that lead to other valleys. One hiking highlight is the walk from

Hirschegg to Heuberg, which offers great views down to the Öschinensee.

Where to Eat & Drink (Favorite Restaurants & Bars)
In addition to my own restaurant, I enjoy the historical dining room at Landgasthof Ruedihus (on Fielfalle), built in 1753.

For other great restaurants, I recommend browsing the members of the guild at *gilde.ch*, which maintains a high standard of quality, creativity, and hospitality.

How to Fit In, Meet Locals, & Make Friends
Learn a few German words and talk to people. Sometimes it takes time to get to know the mountain folk, but it's a worthwhile endeavor.

Best Places to Take a Photo
All of our hikes and natural areas offer fantastic photo ops.

Find Nicolas at alfasoleil.ch.

GSTAAD
Where cosmopolitanism meets authentic Swissness.

FIND WI-FI HERE: Most hotels.

LANGUAGE: German   **CANTON:** Bern

Anita Roth
Ski Instructor. Guide. Sports Enthusiast.

About Anita Roth
I was born in Gstaad and grew up in the famous Charly's Tea-Room next to the ice rink. After exploring the world as a Flight Attendant, my husband and I decided to live in Gstaad. In the winter, I am a private ski instructor; in summer, I work as a guide and guide manager in Gstaad-Saanen and I love to spend my free time in nature, doing sports, or traveling.

What to Do In Gstaad (The Basics)
First, visit the charming villages of Gstaad and Saanen and then hike on and explore our mountains. You should also attend one of our many events (ranging from the Beach Volley World Tour to Swiss Open Tennis to golf tournaments to classic local festivals like the Menuhin Festival or our Country Festival).

Visitors in summer should hike in the surrounding mountains. The alpine flora and fauna are astonishing.

Hidden Gems for Seasoned Travelers
Ski some of our quieter slopes and enjoy some powder skiing. It is also a great challenge to go snowshoeing.

Day Trips

Visiting a nearby farming village like Lauenen is always an experience. Take a horse-drawn carriage up to its beautifully embedded mountain lake surrounded by higher peaks and glaciers.

Where to Hike

Take the cable car up to Wispile, hike along the mountain rim, and visit some of the cheese-producing farms along the way (and buy some Alp cheese)—all while surrounded by a spectacular panoramic view. Another worthwhile experience is hiking across the Glacier des Diablerets and finding yourself on the unique terrace of Le Refuge, where you can try some local specialties.

Where to Eat & Drink (Favorite Restaurants & Bars)

One of my favorite places is Restaurant Sonnenhof above Saanen, with its beautiful terrace overlooking the Saanenland. A typical place where tourists and locals meet is the Hotel Kernen (at Dorfstrasse 58 in Schönried), which is run by former ski champion, Bruno Kernen. And for a nice drink in the center of Gstaad, I love the Rialto, where you can watch people walk up and down the promenade.

Budget Tips

If you're staying at one of the area hotels, you can purchase a Gstaad EasyAccess Card, which offers great savings on cable cars, local transportation, entrance fees, guided tours, etc.

Many restaurants, such as at Hotel Gstaaderhof or on top of Eggli Mountain, offer budget-friendly daily lunch menus.

How to Fit In

It is part of our culture to greet one another by saying *grüessech* (pronounced "groo-sah") or *grüess gott* (pronounced "groos got"). This is appreciated.

Best Places to Take a Photo

In the center of Gstaad, you'll find a perfect photograph of the Palace Hotel. And taking the cable car up to Rellerli Mountain offers a fantastic view of all of the Saanenland.

Final Notes & Other Tips

Our busy seasons include Christmas to New Year, February, and July through September. Mid-season is quieter. Winter can get cold (below zero) and summer gets hot (80s and up). The alpine spring with flowers blooming all over the mountains is most beautiful in June and we have an Indian summer in September.

Find Anita at guides-gstaad.ch.

SAANEN
Quaintness, tradition, & a seemingly endless array of activities.

FIND WI-FI HERE: Any hotel or pub.

LANGUAGE: German   **CANTON:** Bern

Jenny Waddle
Teacher. Traveler.

About Jenny
I'm from Bath in the UK, but after university I began to travel and live abroad. I'm a primary school teacher, so I've been working in international schools as a way to travel. I spent five years living in Saanen but have now moved to Trondheim, Norway to teach for a year.

What to Do In Saanen (The Basics)
Of course, the mountains are enjoyable year-round, as are the crazily indulgent Swiss food, the local shops and shopkeepers, the friendly villagers, and a great nightlife.

The old Spitzhorn Pizzeria (at Spitzhornweg 30) is awesome. There is an amazing cabin restaurant with excellent service, views, and fondue on the sled run from Wispile (Gstaad's local mountain) to Gsteig. Cafe du Cerf (at Rue des Allamans 8 in Rougemont), with one of the best fondues in the region, is a must-visit. And, by far the best place for food and wine in Saanan is Art Bar 16 (at Mittelgässli 16).

If you like walking, take a hike up our home mountain, Kohlisgrind. There's a great viewpoint on top, along with fire-wood and a BBQ pit. On the way up, there's a stone that they

109

used to behead people on and legend says they used to push criminals off the top. It's a sordid history but a pretty hike—steep, quiet, and full of wildlife.

There are also lots of markets here for Christmas, Easter, and throughout the summer. It's the region's original market town and draws cheese-sellers, confectioners, and even farm equipment sellers from all around. And at the end of each season, you'll find a special market where local businesses offload their seasonal items at heavily discounted prices. This is a great time to buy ski clothes.

Finally, if you can time your visit to see the farmers taking their cows up into the mountains in early summer or parading them back down in the fall, that's quite a spectacle. The farm families dress in traditional garb, the cows are decorated, and the noise from the cowbells is unbelievable.

Day Trips
The Lauenen municipality and Arnensee lake area are lovely. Grubenberg (a nearby mountain hut) is excellent for an overnight hike. And Glacier 3000—a mountaintop area perfect for skiing in winter and hiking in summer—is worth a visit. In Saanenmoser (another ski area nearby), there's a festival called Ride on Music, which is a great event.

Where to Hike
I love the hike from the Rinderberg back to Saanen via Schönreid. I enjoy hiking on Mounts Egli and Vildemanette and the Col du Pillon mountain pass. And the trails to Wildhornhütte and Mount Gummfluh are more challenging but also very beautiful.

Where to Eat & Drink (Favorite Restaurants & Bars)
My favorites are 16 Art Bar (mentioned above), Pub Saanen (at Dorfstrasse 121), and Mojo ski bar on Mount Egli. And wherever I eat, I like my fondue with Aigle white wine.

How to Fit In

Say hello in Swiss German, French, or English. Everyone says hello, especially on the walking paths. Look people in the eyes when toasting drinks. Wish people a good meal before eating. Use people's first names when saying hello. And if you are staying a while, learn the typical greetings, which involve a handshake on first meeting, three kisses on alternating cheeks once you've met them a few times, and a hug once you're good friends.

ZÜRICH & SURROUNDS

ZÜRICH
A hub of culture, shopping, quirk, & nightlife.

FIND WI-FI HERE: Starbucks, Casablanca Café, Café Lang, NENI Restaurant, the train station, or the Impact Hub co-working space.

LANGUAGE: German   **CANTON:** Zürich

Manu & Nina
Communicators & Explorers.

About Manu & Nina
We both grew up in the countryside not far from Zürich, moved into town to study, and stayed for work. These days, one of us works as a journalist, the other in corporate communications. We love to stroll around the city keeping our eyes peeled for new, exciting things. We also love cotton candy, flea markets, and jumping into lake Zürich.

What to Do In Zürich (The Basics)
First, stroll through the city center. Don't look at your map; just choose a direction and follow it. There is no dangerous spot in Zürich and it's small enough that you can't really get lost. While you're wandering, make sure to walk along the lake, by the Limmat River, and through the old town. Take tram 11 or 15 or bus 32 up to Bucheggplatz and walk up to the forest from there to enjoy the most terrific view over the town. Then spend as much time as possible in the most relaxed and trendy neighborhoods: Kreis 3, 4, and 5.

If it's rainy when you arrive, we suggest cozying up with a good book in one of Zürich's coffee shops (we like Casablanca, Kafi

112

Dihei, and Dini Mueter) or visiting one of the museums in town (we like Rietberg, Bellerive, and the Museum of Design).

Hidden Gems for Seasoned Travelers

If you want to feel local, eat chocolate (grab a bar at any grocery store or, for something special, head to the Sprüngli chocolate shop) and go shopping at the Freitag Tower (where you'll find bags, wallets, laptop cases, and more—all made out of used truck canvas; almost every Zürich local owns something from this shop). Then jump into Lake Zürich or bargain at a flea market (the two largest are held every Saturday at 7 a.m. at Kanzlei and Bürkliplatz and in summer there is another starting at 9 a.m. at Frau Gerolds Garten).

In wintertime, we recommend a visit to one of our top three saunas: Seebad Enge, City Hallenbad, or Stadtbad Zürich.

For the nature-lovers, the old botanical garden, the garden at Villa Tobler, and the park at Museum Rietberg are lovely.

Finally, for something quirky, have dinner at Blindekuh Zürich (at Mühlebachstrasse 148), the world's first dining-in-the-dark restaurant, take a ghost walk tour (*ghostwalk.ch*), or visit James Joyce's grave at Fluntern Cemetery.

Where to Stay

For a real taste of Zürich, we highly recommend Kreis 3, 4, and 5 (where we live). They are the most vibrant, young, artsy, relaxed, interesting, and colorful areas. Most of our favorite shops, restaurants, streets, and clubs are there.

Day Trips

Take a boat trip to Rapperswil. The trip itself offers nice views over Zürich and Lake Zürich and Rapperswil is a contemplative little city. Have lunch or dinner there and then take the train back to Zürich.

Other good options include the ski towns of Hoch-Ybrig, Davos, Engelberg-Titlis, or Flims Laax Falera. They all open in November/December and close in March/April (depending on the snow).

Where to Hike
Start with Üetliberg. From Triemli, it takes about an hour to reach the summit. From the summit, the two-hour walk to Felsenegg is very nice. If you still feel like hiking after that, continue to Sihlbrugg Dorf via the Albisgrat (Albis Ridge). From there, walk down through the Sihlwald and take the train back to Zürich. The whole trek should take about six hours.

Be sure though to stay on the marked trails and have a map and compass with you for orientation; rumor has it that a Dutch hiking group got lost in the Üetliberg woods and had to be rescued recently.

If you have more time, the areas around Walensee or Glarus County are beautiful and you can do day hikes in the real mountains there. (Compared to those, our mountain is a hill.)

What & Where to Eat & Drink
An absolute must is the Zürich gschnetzeltes veal dish, which normally comes with rösti. For the best of traditional Swiss fare, head to Helvetia (at Stauffacherquai 1; phone: +41 44 297 9999), Volkshaus (at Stauffacherstrasse 60; phone: +41 44 242 1155), and Bauernschänke (at Rindermarkt 24; phone: +41 44 262 4130).

The most popular drinks in Zürich are Aperol spritz, lillet (a French aperitif wine from the Bordeaux region), hugo (a German cocktail with elderflower and mint), or the classic gin and tonic. You can also try one of the local beers. We recommend Turbinenbräu, Amboss, or Bier Paul.

For cocktails, Dante (at Zwinglistrasse 22) can't be topped. Restaurant Volkshaus (mentioned above) is our pick for a great dinner and nice atmosphere. Chez Nhan (at Kehlhofstrasse 4; phone: +41 044 450 3262) offers reasonably priced Vietnamese food (and the best rice-noodle salad in town!). And Kronen-halle (at Rämistrasse 4; phone: +41 44 262 9900) is a classic (though very expensive).

Finally, for excellent coffee, we like Kafi Dihei (at Zurlinden-strasse 231), Babu's (at Löwenstrasse 1), Sprüngli (at Parade-platz), Dini Mueter (at Langstrasse 10), Markthalle im Viaduct (at Limmatstrasse 231), or Kafi Schoffel (at Schoffelgasse 7).

Budget Tips

You can save on public transportation by buying a day pass (for 8.40 francs you can use buses, trams, trains, and even the ship), taking the train (instead of a cab) from the airport, or, if you want to explore the whole canton of Zürich, buying a "9 o'clock pass," which gives you unlimited canton access for the day for 25 francs.

As far as activities go, dancing at the Cool Monday party at Mascotte only costs you what you drink. Tuesday is concert night at La Catrina and there's no entrance fee (just make a small donation to the local band). On Wednesday afternoons, admission at the Kunsthaus art museum is free. And you can borrow one of the free bikes at the züri rollt stands and discover Zürich on two wheels.

If you understand German, check the city's department of cultural heritage preservation; they offer free tours.

How to Fit In

If you are polite and sensible, you will be fine in Switzerland and if you say *grüezi* (hello), you'll be really popular.

How to Meet Locals & Make Friends

The Swiss are known for being a little shy. But if you're patient with us, we'll open up. Don't worry if you don't speak German. In the cities and amongst the young people, everybody speaks English pretty well.

Best Places to Take a Photo
Get off the beaten track and stroll the not-so-touristy neighbor-hoods of Kreis 3, 4, or 5. Not only will you meet the real Zürich, but you'll also find good photo opportunities. And don't miss the view from the sunny rooftop platform at Freitag Tower.

Find Manu & Nina at myfriendfromzürich.com.

Urs Michel

Hospitality Professional. Fitness Enthusiast.

About Urs
My name is Urs and I'm a Zürich native working as the Sales and Marketing Manager at the 25hours Hotel Zürich West. In my free time, I like to meet friends and explore Zürich. I'm also a tennis, soccer, and spinning enthusiast.

What to Do In Zürich (The Basics)
First, head to the beautiful old part of Zürich, called Niederdorf, and make sure to stop at Lindenhof Park's terrace and take the Polybahn up to the Polyterrasse. In both spots, you'll have a beautiful view over the old town.

Then, go to Zürich West. In the past, this was the industrial part of Zürich, but now it's famous for its small urban boutiques, fancy restaurants, and other interesting spots. Take a walk through the Viaduktbögen (an old viaduct whose base has been converted into shops and eateries) [editor's note: love this place!], stop by Gerolds Garten at Geroldstrasse 23 (for a nice cocktail in summer or a delicious fondue in winter), and visit the Prime Tower (the largest building in Zürich, which has a nice bar on top).

Hidden Gems for Seasoned Travelers
Visit Hürlimann Spa, located in Zürich Enge, where you'll find a

ZÜRICH & SURROUNDS

rooftop swimming pool with a sweeping view over Zürich. This is especially cool to do in winter, as the water is warm.

Day Trips
Basel is the heart of art in Switzerland and the people there are very friendly and Lausanne (in the French part of Switzerland) is beautiful, with its perfect perch on the lovely Lake Geneva.

Where to Hike
Üetliberg (our home mountain) is worth a visit. Plus, you'll find a good restaurant on top.

Where to Eat & Drink (Favorite Restaurants & Bars)
My favorite restaurants are JOSEF (at Gasometerstrasse 24; phone: +41 44 271 65 95), which serves small plates and is a great value, and Didis Frieden (at Stampfenbachstrasse 32; phone: +41 44 253 18 10). Try both if you can.

For a great bar, I recommend Old Crow (Schwanengasse 4), which has a large (possibly the largest) selection of whiskey.

How to Meet Locals & Make Friends
There are always friendly people on the Langstrasse in the evening, especially at the Olé Olé bar (at Langstrasse 138).

Best Places to Take a Photo
Check out the Quaibrücke. From there, you'll have views of the most famous churches and the Zürich skyline.

Find Urs at 25hours-hotels.com/en/Zürich-west [editor's note: this is one of my favorite hotels in the world].

The Real Picky Gourmet
Foodie.

About the Gourmet
I'm an anonymous food blogger from Zürich. I grew up in the

area, lived in various English-speaking countries for a while, and came back. I enjoy eating and am a big fan of the ladies.

What to Do In Zürich (The Basics)

Start by having a gemischter salat (mixed salad) and a cordon bleu or zürcher geschnetzeltes (mushrooms and thinly sliced veal with cream) with rösti (Swiss hash browns). And if you only do one thing (aside from eating), walk over the Quaibrücke and look back at the city.

Hidden Gems for Seasoned Travelers

For cordon bleu, try the Gertrudhof (at Gertrudstrasse 26 in Wiedikon). For geschnetzeltes, try Obere Flühgasse (at Flühgasse 69). Keep in mind that these are Swiss German- or French-speaking places and there are no gluten- or lactose-free or vegan options.

Where to Eat & Drink (Favorite Restaurants & Bars)

My personal favorites are Stef's Freieck (at Wildbachstrasse 42) for modern Swiss with a classic French touch, Riviera (at Dufourstrasse 161) for classic and avant-garde Italian dishes from Sicily, and Der Schwiizer (at Zwinglistrasse 3) for urban Swiss with extremely high-class products.

Budget Tips

If you want to save money, you can try the burgers at Holy Cow (at Zähringerstrasse 28). There's a decent selection of sausages with potato salad at the Zeughauskeller (at Bahnhofstrasse 28). And you can check out the very Swiss Gambrinus (at Langstrasse 103, in the red light district).

How to Fit In

Don't be fussy or loud. This isn't New York, where restaurateurs will sell their soul just to have you in their establishment.

Find the Real Picky Gourmet at therealpickygourmet.com.

ZÜRICH & SURROUNDS

Dimitri Burkhard
Marketer. Photographer. Magazine Founder.

About Dimitri

I grew up in the countryside near Zürich but lived in America for much of my adulthood. About six years ago, my wife and I (along with our cat from Texas) moved back to Switzerland to a town on Lake Greifensee.

From there, I commute to my day job in Zürich as a marketing project manager for a Swiss online directory. I spend most of my free time curating content for the Newly Swissed online magazine. As the founder, it gives me tremendous pleasure to coach writers, meet up with the community, interview business leaders or start-ups, and roam through Zürich with my camera.

What to Do In Zürich (The Basics)

Visit Lindenhof for a bird's eye view of the Limmat River. Walk the old town on both sides of the river. And stop by iconic places like Cabaret Voltaire, the birthplace of Dadaism (an avant-garde art movement). Augusto Giacometti used to mingle with the Dadaists and his colorful windowpanes can be seen inside Zürich's police headquarters across the river.

Hidden Gems for Seasoned Travelers

The Museum Rietberg has a beautiful collection of Asian, African, American, and Oceanic art. Look out for their traditional Japanese tea ceremony on Sundays. And Ankerstrasse between Zweierstrasse and Stauffacherstrasse has lots of little boutiques that are worth exploring.

For a time-traveling experience, visit vintage/retro boutique Swallow-d (at Josefstrasse 12). The owner, Tamara Rist, has a fascinating knowledge of the histories of vintage clocks, radios, and record players. She is always repairing something when I stop by.

ZÜRICH & SURROUNDS

Then there's Toni Areal, which used to be a dairy processing facility. Today, it is one of Europe's biggest art and design universities. It is worth visiting the campus for its fascinating architecture. Finally, the collection of historic industrial artifacts at the Schaudepot Design Museum offers yet another look into the past.

Day Trips
Rapperswil is a charming medieval town at the other end of Lake Zürich. Hop on a boat for two hours or on a train for 30 minutes. The reconstructed wooden bridge there is part of the pilgrimage route to Santiago de Compostela.

If you have less time, hop on a commuter train to Greifensee. Located just 15 minutes from Zürich, this lakeside village has a historic center with a castle. During the high season, the flower garden in front of the church is bursting with color.

Where to Eat & Drink (Favorite Restaurants & Bars)
There is a reason Switzerland is known for cheese and chocolate. Visit Truffe (at Schlüsselgasse 12) for a nice selection of artisan chocolates (not to mention one of Zürich's best hot chocolate) and the Jelmoli Food Market (at Seidengasse 1) for a peek at Switzerland's first cheese humidor. Make sure to ask for samples.

Coffee culture is big in Zürich and my personal favorite coffee bar is Café Henrici (at Niederdorfstrasse 1).

In the winter, warm your hands with some roasted chestnuts from any of the street vendors. The best can be had at Albisrie-derplatz, where they are roasted with red cabbage for extra flavor.

If you're here in the summer, start with Frau Gerolds Garten (at Geroldstrasse 23). It is the place where everyone meets for happy hour under the sun and it has become a staple in Zürich's hipster scene.

Another favorite is the distinctly Bohemian Les Halles (at Pfingst-weidstrasse 6. Go early for the famed moules et frites (mussels and fries) before they sell out.

Hiltl (at Sihlstrasse 28) is the world's oldest continuously open vegetarian restaurant (at least according to Guinness World Records). Try their buffet and don't forget to grab a bun (which comes with each plate).

Finally, The International Beer Bar (at Luisenstrasse 7) offers the widest selection of Swiss craft beers.

Budget Tips

All 1,200 public fountains provide crystal clear drinking water. Skip the expensive Evian at the convenience store and keep refilling a bottle like the locals.

Eat at the Migros Cafeteria at Limmatplatz (not to be confused with the Migros Restaurant). Located on the 4th floor, this restaurant offers delicious and budget-friendly dishes for emp-loyees and those in the know.

Climb the Grossmünster tower in the middle of the old town. A couple francs and 187 steps later, you will enjoy the most amazing view over Zürich.

If you already have a public transportation pass, don't miss a ride on the Limmat River Boats. The fare is included in the city ticket.

If you are into architecture, grab your camera and take a free walking tour (freewalkzurich.ch) through Zürich's formerly indus-trial neighborhood. Although it's un-Swiss to do so, show your appreciation by tipping your tour guide. The tour will conven-iently end near the Freitag tower (which is constructed from stacked shipping containers). It's free to climb them.

ZÜRICH & SURROUNDS

Best Places to Take a Photo
Lindenhof used to house Zürich's first settlement (from Roman times). This is no coincidence, as the bird's eye view of the old town is magnificent.

On a clear day, take the S10 train to Üetliberg. From atop the TV tower, you will have a perfect view of the entire lake—and possibly the Alps in the distance.

Find Dimitri at newlyswissed.com.

Tamir Wirz
Sporting Gear Sales Manager. Family Man. Traveler.

About Tamir
I'm Swiss and I have lived in Wetzikon just outside Zürich since I was born. I'm a sales manager for sporting goods distributor. In my free time, I love to travel, including around Switzerland.

What to Do In & Around Zürich (The Basics)
Well, I wouldn't recommend my own hometown. Wetzikon has nice surroundings and is in an excellent location, but the town is ugly. The nearest nice town other than Zürich is Rapperswil. It has a pretty old town, an impressive castle, and great views from the lake to the mountains. So I'd start with a visit there.

Another very popular place in the region is Jucker Farm in Seegräben (*en.juckerfarm.ch*). It's a farm where you can taste all the local fruits and vegetables. Kids will love it because they can cuddle the animals. The farm also offers a wonderful view of Lake Pfäffikon and the mountainous area of Glarus. Keep in mind, though, that on a sunny day it can be really crowded.

Probably the most popular lookout point in the region is the top of the Bachtel Tower (a radio tower on a mountaintop). The little (3,000-foot) mountain is located above the town of Hinwil.

The restaurant (Bachel Ranch) below the summit is easily reachable by car. To climb the tower on top is a 30-minute hike from there. There is another restaurant and some BBQ facilities on top. A little courage is necessary to climb the tower, but a great view is your reward—and it's free of charge.

In winter, when there is enough snow, they close the road for sledding, so it's fun to walk up and slide down. But don't forget to bring your own sled; there aren't any rentals up there.

Day Trips

One of my favorite day trips is to one of the nearby lakes— Klöntalersee or Obersee—in the Glarus region. Both lakes are located between mountains and are perfect for relaxing, swimming, and having a BBQ in high mountain surroundings.

The Klöntalersee is reachable by public transportation, but for the Obersee, you'll need your own car. Note: there are two Obersees. One is part of Lake Zürich and one is in the Glarus region. The one I'm recommending is the Glarus one.

For a real mountain feeling, I like Mount Säntis. The summit is reachable via gondola. From the top, you'll have a great view of Austria and Germany. And for more outdoor activities, go to the Atzmännig (atzmaennig.ch). It's a nice place to go skiing, climbing, sledding, and more. I'd also recommend the Rheinfall—Europe's biggest waterfall.

Then there's the Alpamare water park (alpamare.ch), the Science Center (technorama.ch) in Winterthur, and the Zürich Zoo (zoo.ch), which has a giant indoor rainforest and a brand new elephant park.

Where to Hike

Start with Taminaschlucht—a gorge where you can taste pure and healthy mountain spring water. Shuttle buses will take you there from Bad Ragaz. Around the gorge you'll find lots of hiking trails. And, even better, after a long hike you can go straight into the thermal spa in Bad Ragaz (*taminatherme.ch*) to relax. It's not cheap, but it is nice.

Another hike that my friends love (though I haven't been on it myself yet) is the 5-Seen-Wanderung (five lakes hike), which starts at Pizolhütte and includes a view of the glacier. This hike is near the above-mentioned gorge.

For something easy, cheaper, and family-friendly, I like the Sattel (*sattel-hochstuckli.ch*); a gondola takes you to the top and from there you can hike, ski, or sled down (depending on the season). The new hanging bridge adds an additional thrill.

Where to Eat & Drink (Favorite Restaurants & Bars)
For good Swiss food, try Restaurant Frauenfelder in Wetzikon (at Bahnhofstrasse 39). The dressings and ice cream are home-made and dreamy. And the most famous bar in the region is The Pirates Bar in Hinwil (at Ueberlandstrasse 14). It has good mix of people and on the weekends they have live music (rock and pop). The bar looks like a pirate ship and entrance is free.

I love the Jinshi China Restaurant in Wetzikon (at Bahnhof-strasse 285). For me, this is the best Chinese restaurant in the world...Very small but very good and cheap. I also like Restaurant Schlüssel in Tuggen (at Zürcherstrasse 19; phone: +41 055 445 1444). This place is famous for its chicken in a basket. Reservations are highly recommended. Then there's the Snack Bar at the Train station in Kempten. It's just fast food, but it's exceptional for its burgers.

Best Places to Take a Photo
One favorite spot is the top of the Grossmünster in Zürich. Climb all the way up the tower (I love the view here). Good views can also be found anywhere around Rapperswil, where you have a nice lake and impressive mountain views.

Final Notes & Other Tips
There are places with higher mountains, nicer cities, and better

ZÜRICH & SURROUNDS

views, but it's wonderful to live here. It's a lovely hilly landscape with lots of lakes and only minutes from Zürich and Rapperswil and many ski areas. So I would recommend my region for travelers who have a little bit more time than the usual three days. Most of the attractions and restaurants above are not that touristic, so this is your good chance to connect with local people.

WINTERTHUR
Peace & prettiness outside the city.

FIND WI-FI HERE: The train station & many restaurants.

LANGUAGE: German   **CANTON:** Zürich

Martin Mathis
Traveler. Car Enthusiast.

About Martin
I am 27 and Swiss and moved from the Thurgau countryside to Winterthur about a year ago. I work as a mechanic for Kyburz—the company that produces electric motorbikes for the post. My biggest hobby is traveling backpacker-style. I've been to 53 countries so far and I still love it. I also have an old-style car and fly remote-controlled helicopters.

What to Do In Winterthur (The Basics)
Winterthur is an old industrial town. The Sulzer and Swiss locomotive companies were huge here in the old days. Now, the old industrial buildings have been restored as bars, cinemas, and lofts to keep the flavor of the past while updating the city itself. It's quite cool. Also worth a visit is the technopark—a business park in the old industrial buildings. Finally, I like Goldenburg (a mountain viewpoint) and the Eschenberg Tower for a nice view over the city.

Hidden Gems for Seasoned Travelers
I enjoy the Bruderhaus—a small zoo here in Winterthur.

ZÜRICH & SURROUNDS

Day Trips
I recommend Rheinfall (the famous waterfall) in Schaffhausen. Winterthur is also good for exploring the Zürich area, which is just 25 minutes away by train.

Where to Hike
Appenzell and Glarus are nice hiking areas just an hour away.

Where to Drink (Favorite Restaurants & Bars)
Schmare Handtuch (at Turmhaldenstrasse 1) is a nice bar. Bolero (at Untere Vogelsangstrasse 8) is a good club. And Paddy O'Brien's Old Irish Pub (at Merkurstrasse 25) is my favorite pub.

Budget Tips
There's a hostel in town called Depot 195, where dorm spaces are just 35 francs per night.

How to Meet Locals & Make Friends
There is a meet-up (via *couchsurfing.org*) every second Friday at 9 p.m. in front of Restaurant National. This is a great way to meet people.

Best Places to Take a Photo
Goldenberg is my top pick.

SCHAFFHAUSEN
A small, peaceful city close to nature.

FIND WI-FI HERE: The train station & McDonald's.

LANGUAGE: German   **CANTON:** Schaffhausen

Denise Hirt
Artist. Swimmer. Reader. Cook.

About Denise
I grew up in a small town called Oberhallau, which is close to the German border but still part of Canton Schaffhausen. It's a farming town (sheep and cows mostly) and a lot of people have vineyards. When I was 19, I moved to Schaffhausen itself and, except for traveling, I have never lived in another city.

For work, I was an apprentice for a transport company, then trained apprentices (which I loved), and now work at the Swiss Post. In my free time, I like to cook, read books, do some artsy stuff (like crafting my own Christmas cards or painting furniture), spend time with family and friends, and, since I live next to the Rhine, take a swim or a boat up the river.

What to Do In Schaffhausen (The Basics)
The two must-sees in Schaffhausen are the Munot Fortress (which is famous and offers a nice view from the top) and the Rhine Falls. You can walk to the falls from downtown (you can also take a bus, but the walk is short and nice, so I recommend skipping the bus).

Old town Schaffhausen is also pretty nice for some shopping (not big brands but nice little shops) and just walking around taking photos of the bay windows and façades.

128

ZÜRICH & SURROUNDS

Hidden Gems for Seasoned Travelers

There is a cute flea market on Saturdays from 8 a.m. to 4 p.m. at Mosergarten on the edges of the city. Every Tuesday and Saturday morning, there is a farmer's market next to the St. Johann church. And just this summer a crepe food truck opened right beside the Rhine. Their crepes are delicious but only available in the summer on good-weather days.

Keeping things on a sweet note, the best homemade ice cream in town is at El-Bertin (at Unterstadt 13), which is open from March to September and always has a long line of locals.

Finally, I recommend a visit to Schaaren—a meadow between the wood directly at the Rhine where we locals arrive by boat (the flat-bottomed one called weidling) for a swim and a BBQ.

Day Trips

I like Stein am Rhein, which is a city on the Rhine. There is a ship that goes there in the summer and their old town is worth visiting. Another gem is the Bodensee region. And it's always fun to take a train to Zürich (45 minutes away) or Winterthur (30 minutes). I personally like Winterthur better than Zürich, as it's a bit more alternative and has a lot of nice bars and restaurants.

Where to Hike

There is a TV tower in Feuerthalen with a nice view of Schaffhausen, Germany, and the Rhine. It takes about 1.5 hours to get there from the city center.

Another good option is Randen, which is a nice hill with lots of hiking and biking trails. And there are two Randen towers, which are pretty cool to visit.

Finally, I love the walks around my hometown—Klettgau—which are best in autumn (though summer is a close second) when the vineyards are full of people harvesting grapes to make good wine.

ZÜRICH & SURROUNDS

What to Eat & Drink

In addition to our beloved Swiss classics, you should try the spätzle (local egg noodles). They're best at Restaurant Schäfli (on Unterstadt). For sweets, try schaffhauser zungen (a special type of sandwich cookie) and schaffhauser rickli (a pretzel-like cookie). And, of course, you have to try some local wine.

For good local drinks, head to Schäferei Bar (at Schäferei Webergasse 16) and order a mexikaner (shot). Then head to Cuba Club (at Safrangasse 2) for a Moscow Mule (vodka, Ginger Ale, cucumber, and a few other things served in a copper cup). Finally, make your way to TapTab (at Baumgartenstrasse 19) for a Dr. GO with vodka.

Where to Eat & Drink (Favorite Restaurants & Bars)

My favorite club is TapTab (mentioned above), which has concerts of all sorts. As for bars, I like Dolder 2 (at Zürcherstrasse 26 in Feuerthalen) and Cardinal (at Bahnhofstrasse 102 in Schaffhausen), which has the best veggie burgers in town.

For restaurants, I'd pick Kammgarn Beiz (at Baumgartenstrasse 19), with its always-changing menu, local veggies, good food, outdoor seating, and good concerts, Devi (at Repfergasse 26) for vegan and vegetarian options, and Cafe Vordergasse (at Vordergasse 79) for lovely atmosphere and good breakfasts, sandwiches, hot cheese tartlets, salads, hot chocolate, etc.

Budget Tips

There is a take-away soup bar called Suppenglück (at Webergasse 46), which offers tasty soups and an always-changing daily menu. Then there's an Italian restaurant called Romana (at Unterstadt 18) where you can get take-away pizzas for 10 francs. Beer usually costs about six francs and hard drinks run up to 14 francs.

You can also save money on transportation. The town is small and all the obvious attractions are easily reached on foot.

How to Meet Locals & Make Friends

Meet up with a local via *couchsurfing.org* for a drink, dancing, or a walk on the Rhine.

Best Places to Take a Photo

The Rhine Falls at night or the riverside on a sunny day.

ZÜRICH & SURROUNDS

ZUG
International community & small town charm surrounded by nature.

FIND WI-FI HERE: The Metalli Shopping Center, the library, & the central train station.

LANGUAGE: German   **CANTON:** Zug

Mary Fahsbender Gottschalk
English Teacher. Cook. Skier. Traveler.

About Mary

I'm originally from Pennsylvania but moved permanently to Switzerland almost 26 years ago (when I got married). My husband is also American but has lived here since he was three. We live in the small village of Hagendorn in the canton of Zug.

I work as an "Aunt Annie" in a program that brings native English speakers into the Swiss elementary schools. Children begin learning English in the 3rd grade and we visit them to talk, play games, and write for an authentic experience with the English language. It is a fun job. I also give a few English conversation lessons to adults and do volunteer work at the children's hospital in Lucerne.

In my free time, I love to cook. I have been in a cooking club for about 14 years with a group of women who have become my best friends. Every year we go on trip together.

Other hobbies include cross-country skiing, going to movies and concerts, reading, and playing a little-known sport called Indiaca (it's basically volleyball with a feathered bean bag disc instead of a ball).

What to Do In Zug (The Basics)

Zug is famous for its sunsets. The city is on the east side of the lake, so you see the sun sinking behind the lake and lighting up the mountains. It's magical.

Zug also has a very nice old town. It's small but well maintained. The highest point is the clock tower, which is open to everyone. Just go get the key from Wunderbox at Fischmarkt 10. Outside visiting hours, you can pick it up from the Restaurant Intermezzo (at Grabenstrasse 6).

The central plaza of old town is the Landesgemeindeplatz. It opens onto the lake and is used for all sorts of events and markets (including an annual open-air jazz festival, a cherry market, flea markets, and a weekly Saturday farmer's market). It's also a great place to hang out, with lots of bars and restaurants. From there, explore the pedestrian walking area with its little shops and beautifully restored buildings. At the casino (which is a performing arts center and not an actual casino), cross the street to the upper old town. From there, you can find parts of the original walls of the city and watchtowers. And keep an eye out for the fountains. The most famous is Greth Schell; it shows a weary woman carrying her drunken husband home after Fasnacht (the pre-Lent celebration).

You can also rent a pedal-boat, rowboat, or motorboat and spend a few hours on the lake for a great view of the fancy lakeside villas that are not visible from the street. If you are not feeling active, take one of the boats that ferry people around the lake and get off at any of the stops to explore the villages. It is easy to take a bus, train, or trail back to Zug.

Hidden Gems for Seasoned Travelers

Check zug-tourismus.ch for any events going on in the canton and then go! Words to look for are fest, which will be some kind of festival (for anything from jazz to cherries), chilbi, which is a yearly carnival in the late fall, and markt or märcht, which will be some kind of market.

The caves in Baar (the Höllgrotten) are very interesting to explore, especially during bad weather. And the very scenic towns of Unteraegeri and Oberaegeri, situated on a lake, are where author Richard Morais lived when he was young (they were the inspiration for the French village in his book, The 100 Foot Journey, recently made into a movie).

Finally, the Villette Park in Cham is worth a visit, as is the lake-side itself. Take bread to feed the ducks and swans.

Where to Stay
Zug is quite small and hotels are at a premium. But public transportation is excellent, so you won't to feel isolated, even if your hotel isn't centrally located.

Day Trips
Zug is located between Zürich and Lucerne, so either of those is easy to get to (with trains running hourly). Bern and Basel are also an easy train ride.

I really like the open-air museum, Ballenberg, in Brienz. There are all sorts of traditional houses from different parts of Switzerland and you can see different crafts and lifestyles.

Where to Hike
Take the Zugerbergbahn, a funicular railway, to the Zugerberg. There's lots of good hiking and a fantastic view up there. The Raten, above Oberaegeri is also very nice. There is an easy walk to the Gottschalkenberg (and more challenging hikes as well). Both places also have small ski lifts, cross country ski trails, and good restaurants. They also have the advantage that when it's foggy down below, they are in the sun. But there are also nice, well-marked hiking and biking trails all over Zug. Look for small yellow and red signs.

What to Eat & Drink
Cherries are a big crop in Zug and we are famous for our kirsch (a strong cherry schnapps). To sample and buy some, visit the

ZÜRICH & SURROUNDS

Etter factory in Cham.

Zugerkirschtorte, a cake made with kirsch, is a local specialty. It is often translated as "cherry cake," but it is really a very boozy dessert, no cherries! It was created at the Treichler Bakery, where you can still buy it and see it being made.

We also have our own fish, the zuger rötel, which lives in the lake and is a type of Arctic char. It is on the menu of many local restaurants.

You can also buy some bread and go to a local cheese shop. Try käse dubach in the Neustadt Passage in Zug or Wicki's Chäsland in the Neudorfcenter in Cham.

Finally, other things to look for include birchermüsli (oats, nuts, and fruit mixed with yogurt), mistkratzeli (a small, tender chicken...though the literal translation is "manure scratchers"), and the amazing variety of delicious bread.

Where to Eat & Drink (Favorite Restaurants & Bars)
The Wart (at Wart 1 in Hünenberg) is so beautiful. It is the old town hall, built in 1703 on the foundation of the original building from 1684, and has now become an upscale restaurant with very good food.

For fondue, the Zoll-Huus (at Zollweid 2 in Hünenberg) is a fun experience. It is decorated in a crazy Swiss motif...a mix of folkloric, kitsch, and military.

The premiere restaurant in Zug is the Rathauskeller (at Ober Alstadt 1), which has 16 Gault Millau points. It is fantastic and the old building is stunning. Their bar is also very nice.

My favorite bar is probably the Felsenkeller (at Kolinplatz 8), a wine bar located in the old town. The other place I really like is the Cafe Capra (at Sinserstrasse 8 in Cham)—a bar, restaurant, and coffee shop combo with good food and atmosphere.

Remember that the tip is included in the meal price (although I think it is still nice to give a bit for good service).

Budget Tips
The self-service Migros restaurant in the Metalli in Zug and Big Babas Döner Kebab at the Zug station are cheap options.

Museums are cheap. Also, use the tourist office and the travel services located at the main train station in Zug. They can tell you about events in the area and give you ideas for day trips and the most cost-effective way to travel.

How to Fit In
The Swiss have a reputation for being unfriendly, but I think it's more a matter of them being very formal. Never use some-one's first name unless you have been asked to do so. Shake hands upon meeting someone and remember their name. When drinking, always clink glasses and look your fellow drinker in the eye. Most people do speak English, but it's always nice to ask if they do.

Restaurants usually only book one seating per night and do not plan on turning the table. As a result, dinners out tend to be leisurely events and the service may be slower than you are used to. Try not to be impatient. If you have an appointment, let your server know to bring the bill with the last course.

How to Meet Locals & Make Friends
Talk to people when you are out hiking or skiing. Ask their advice about something rather than trying to make random chitchat. Or find a party. Look for a bratwurst stand and tables with benches and people drinking wine and beer and smoking crooked cigars. This is the time and place people tend to let their hair down a bit. And remember that, while the Swiss may have the reputation of being unapproachable, people are pretty much the same underneath and, if you approach them respectfully, they will generally respond in kind.

Best Places to Take a Photo

One of the best views in Zug is from the *hafen* (harbor) area of the lake. The tough part is getting the right weather for a good view of the Alps. The old town has a lot of good photo ops, as well...charming alleyways and ancient, restored buildings.

Final Notes & Other Tips

Zug is incredibly old. Roman artifacts have been found less than a mile from my house, including a waterwheel that has been reconstructed in Hagendorn. Some of the festivals go back centuries.

Zug is also incredibly modern. It transformed itself from a poor farming area to one of the richest cantons in Switzerland with its low taxes and commitment to foreign companies. Its infrastructure is incredible. The downside is that the cost of living is higher here than other places in Switzerland, especially in regard to housing.

Marina Fürst
Psychology Student. Snowboarder. Yogi.

About Marina

I grew up in Hünenberg (a village near Zug) and now live in Zug. I'm a student of psychology and I work on the side as a salesperson and interviewer for the university. At the moment, I have a lot to do for my master's thesis, but when I do have free time, I like to meet my friends and my boyfriend to go out or cook dinner together.

In winter, we're all really into snowboarding and skiing, so we're in the mountains a lot. In summer, I'm often at the lakeside swimming, playing beach volleyball, or just relaxing in the sun. Year-round, I do yoga and go inline skating. I'm also a movie and book lover.

What to Do In Zug (The Basics)

The nicest thing about Zug is the lake. As soon as the weather allows it, everyone is out for a stroll, a swim, or a BBQ at the lakeside. There are also lots of playgrounds there for kids.

One particularly nice place by the lake (outside Zug itself) is Brüggli—a huge grassland with spaces for BBQs, beach volleyball, a campsite, a small restaurant, and a swimming beach. It's about 10 minutes away by bus or train. Or if you're up for some walking, there's a nice walking path that leads there. It starts at Bahnhofsteg Zug train station at the crossroad of Chamerstrasse and Alpenstrasse and is well signposted.

The old part of the city is also quite nice to explore. There you'll find our one and only traditional sightseeing attraction: the Zytturm Clocktower. The old town also houses an art museum with ever-changing exhibitions and a prehistory museum.

Outside town, a really cool thing we have is the Zugerberg—our local mountain. You can go up there by cable car and have a good view over Zug and the lake. There are plenty of hikes up there and in winter you can sled down the hill or go cross-country skiing.

Another nice mountain option is Ägeri. It's not really a mountain, per se, but it's pretty far above sea level and has its own lake, which is really clean, very cold, and smaller than Lake Zug. You can get there by bus or car.

Hidden Gems for Seasoned Travelers
There are some wonderful festivals during summer here. The best one of all is the Jazz Night Zug, which is overflowing with jazz, blues, and world music. It's usually in August.

Then there's the Rock the Docks Festival—a free event with a lot of local, national, and international artists. In the afternoon, there are a variety of workshops you can take. It's normally on the last weekend of August.

In June or July, we have a Lakeside Festival, which features a fireworks show. Finally, there's the Boardstock Festival at the end of July. It's a sports festival with a lot of showcases and you can play different sports and games for free.

Day Trips
Zug is centrally located, so it's easy to get almost anywhere, including great ski areas like Engelberg, Stoos, Hoch-Ybrig, Melchsee-Frutt, and Sattel Hochstuckli, which is quite small and good for beginners and also has a sled run. You can also go hiking in Sattel Hochstuckli when the snow melts.

Then there's Mount Rigi, which is nice for sledding in winter and hiking in summer and has a thermal spa.

It's also easy to get to Lucerne and Zürich from here by train (in just half an hour). And Bern is just 1.5 hours away.

Where to Hike
In Zug, I like the routes between Zugerberg and Ägeri. Then there's the Sihltal (Sihl Valley) and Rigi, which are also quite famous for their hiking trails.

What to Eat & Drink
Our most famous dessert in Zug is the zuger kirschtorte—a special cake with cherry schnapps in it. (The cherry schnapps itself is quite typical for Zug.) We also have a locally brewed beer, the Baarer Bier. And there is a restaurant at the brewery, where you can eat typical Swiss food and really big cordon bleus.

Where to Eat & Drink (Favorite Restaurants & Bars)
For bars, I'd pick Chicago Bar (at Baarerstrasse 63) for meeting people, Blues Brothers Bar (a smoking bar at Unter Altstadt 12) for having drinks, and Skylounge Zug (at General-Guisan-Strasse 6) for drinks with a view of the lake.

For restaurants, my top three are Restaurant Brandenberg (at Allmendstrasse 3) for rustic décor and large plates, Café Capra (at Sinserstrasse 8 in Cham), and Da Pino (at Metallstrasse 9) for the best Italian food in town.

Budget Tips

There is one surprisingly affordable and good Italian restaurant called Colonia Italiana (at Zugerbergstrasse 14). And as for transport, you can borrow bikes for free just behind the train station in the warmer months. Riding around the lake or along the Lorze River are nice summertime pastimes.

How to Fit In

Don't take photos of people without asking them.

How to Meet Locals & Make Friends

A bar like the Chicago Bar is particularly good for meeting people, but you'll have to start the conversation. People here tend to be shy.

Best Places to Take a Photo

At the lake at sunset, from the Zugerberg, or in the old town.

Final Notes & Other Tips

The best time to visit Zug is in the summer during all the festivals. It's very lively.

LUCERNE

A famously pretty city, often voted most beautiful in Switzerland.

FIND WI-FI HERE: Starbucks, the library at Bourbaki, & all over town.

LANGUAGE: German   **CANTON:** Lucerne

[Editor's note: Lucerne is the French name of the town and Luzern is the German. Lucerne is what you'll often find it listed under online, but when speaking with a local, call it Luzern.]

Audrey Padilla
Outdoor Enthusiast.

About Audrey

My name is Audrey and I'm in my early 30s. I moved to Lucerne seven years ago and work in Zug in a trading company. I have a pretty stressful job, so I really enjoy being outdoors on the weekends.

What to Do In Lucerne (The Basics)

There are four must-sees in Luzern for me: First, the Lion Monument, which is such a beautiful sculpture. Second, the romantic Chapel Bridge (Kapellbrücke in German) and old town (where you can admire the fine, artistic work on the building walls). Third, the city walls, where you can climb a tower for a view of the KKL (an art and cultural center), the lake, and the old town. And fourth, Mount Pilatus, which can be a lovely place, parti-cularly in fall and winter, with views of the clouds below and blue sky and sun above.

Speaking of Mount Pilatus, in summer, it is a great adventure to combine a mountaintop walk with a boat ride. In spring or summer, hike ⅔ of the way up from Kriens (reachable via bus 1 from the main station) and take a gondola from there to the top. Then hike halfway down and jump on the steepest train in the world to Alpnachstadt where you can catch a boat back to Lucerne (if you are lucky, a steam one!).

Hidden Gems for Seasoned Travelers
If you are into culture and history, go on a scavenger hunt called Fox Trail, which takes you through the town and will teach you about Lucerne's history. You can book your hunt at *foxtrail.ch*.

In the summertime, after a long day of exploring, a great place to relax is the Sunset Bar (at Seeburgstrasse 53-61 by the lake). And when skies are clear, I love to walk or run the five-mile circuit around Rotsee pond. If you like nature, it's a nice place—and you won't find any other tourists there.

Where to Stay
The old town is cute, but hotels there can be very expensive and rooms can be small. Würzenbach is a nice, green area close to the lake. And I would avoid Baselstrasse, which is usually in the shade and doesn't look so welcoming.

Day Trips
I recommend Zürich, where there is a nice trail through town to the lake. One special place that I love there is the Cakefriends coffee shop at Torgasse 3. I also like Bern—our capitol city—which is only an hour away. It has an interesting town center and a bear park. Finally, I recommend a train journey to Schaffhausen to see the Rhine Falls.

Where to Hike
Mount Pilatus is a challenging but rewarding hike. Start from Kriens and head down to Alpnachstadt. Mount Rigi is also great...and you can even combine a hike on Rigi with a dip in the pool at the thermal baths. And Melchsee Frutt is another great area to hike around.

ZÜRICH & SURROUNDS

What to Eat & Drink
In the summer, have a schoggibrötli (chocolate chip bread roll) from Bachmann. [Editor's note: I love these!]

Where to Eat & Drink (Favorite Restaurants & Bars)
Taube (at Burgerstrasse 3) is the place to go for delicious local Lucerne dishes. Shamrock (at Wagenbachgasse 3) is a nice Irish pub. Gourmindia (at Baselstrasse 31) is a fabulous Indian restaurant. The affordable Dean and David (at Morgartenstrasse 4) is great for fresh salads, smoothies, juices, and curries.

Luz (at Landungsbrücke 1) is a tiny coffee place overlooking the lake with fabulous, delicious snacks. And Filou & Bengel (at Morgartenstrasse 7) has lovely cupcakes and a delicious vanilla latte macchiato.

Budget Tips
Go to the tourism office for a booklet of discounts for different activities. And for accommodation, check out the youth hostel in town; it is affordable and located near the Rotsee pond.

How to Fit In
Respect the rules. Don't jaywalk. Don't spit on the streets or throw trash on the floor. Don't put your luggage on the seats on trains or buses.

How to Meet Locals & Make Friends
This can be tricky in Switzerland, as Swiss people need time to let you in. So, unless you have years to spend here, your best bet is to go to the Irish pub and meet some expats. Ask for Mike (the owner).

Best Places to Take a Photo
My top picks are: 1) on the promenade along the lake with the mountains in the background; 2) from the city walls overlooking the town; 3) from the Suite Bar (at Pilatusstrasse 1) at night when the town is all lit up and dynamic looking.

Charlie Lucarotti
Theater Director. Traveler. Entrepreneur.

About Charlie

I was born in London, but when I was eight months old, my parents bought a catamaran and we spent the next eight years living on it in the Mediterranean. When it was time for school, we settled in Ajaccio, Corsica.

My grandmother left Switzerland to live in England with her English husband, so it was ironic when I met and fell in love with a Swiss man whilst studying in London. We moved back here 15 years ago.

I am a theater director and also run Living in Luzern, a not-for-profit organization aimed at helping expats ease into life here. When I'm not working or looking after our daughter, I ski, play golf, and cook for my family and friends.

What to Do In Lucerne (The Basics)

First, tour the city and climb the medieval towers, enjoy a cruise on the lake, and, of course, visit one of the mountain peaks surrounding Lucerne: Pilatus, Rigi, or Titlis. The Swiss Museum of Transport is also a worthwhile visit.

Hidden Gems for Seasoned Travelers

Go to one of the castles in the area. Schloss Heidegg is an excellent one with its own vineyard, wonderful gardens, and a fantastic play area on the top floors.

Where to Stay

Lucerne is small enough that anywhere downtown will give you an authentic experience. Though, of course, the hotels on the lake offer more romantic views.

ZÜRICH & SURROUNDS

Day Trips
One of my favorite trips is via ship to Weggis and from there (via train) up to the Rigi, where you can enjoy the view, have a fantastic meal at the Bergsonne, and finish the day at the spa at Rigi-Kaltbad.

Where to Hike
In the summer, there is a cabrio cable car (with an open-air top deck) that goes up to the Stanserhorn, where you can hike and enjoy the amazing views.

What & Where to Eat & Drink
Lucerne is known for its chugelipastete (a puff pastry casing filled with veal and sweetbread in a cream sauce) and it's simply delicious.

The view from the Hotel Gütsch bar (on Kanonenstrasse) is amazing. The Stern Restaurant (at Burgerstrasse 35) has great food made with local produce. Grottino 1313 (at Industriestrasse 7) serves good Italian. And, perhaps surprisingly, Gourmindia (at Baselstrasse 31) is a wonderful Indian restaurant.

How to Meet Locals & Make Friends
I recommend *meeup.com*. Find some events you want to attend and meet expats willing to show you the ropes.

Best Places to Take a Photo
The answer here is anywhere. Lucerne is so very beautiful with its lake and the mountains, you'll be taking pictures nonstop.

Final Notes & Other Tips
Fasnacht is our local carnival and it is unlike any other. The locals go crazy for the duration of event, dressed up in scary outfits, playing music through the night, dancing, and drinking. It's where the locals let their hair down and it's great fun—a once-in-a-lifetime experience.

Find Charlie at livinginluzern.info.

BADEN
Natural beauty & historic charm near the mountains.

FIND WI-FI HERE: Starbucks, McDonald's, & Manor.

LANGUAGE: German   **CANTON:** Aargau

Patty Jehle
Business Coach. Gardener. Writer.

About Patty

I am a U.S. citizen married to a Swiss man (and thus a Swiss citizen, as well). I lived in Canton Vaud for almost a year before getting married, in Zürich city for 10 years, and in the Argovian countryside near Baden since 2003. We have three kids, two cats, a dog, and five rabbits.

I work part-time at a university of applied arts and sciences as a business communications lecturer. It's a great job. After my recent training as a business coach, I also started my own consulting agency. This new adventure is a great balance to my classroom teaching.

In my spare time, I help with some church activities both in Zürich and in the Baden area with the International Protestant Church of Zürich. I also belong to our village women's group, which does fun and socially oriented things like walking to a local restaurant for dinner and serving a Christmas dinner for the seniors in town. I garden and really love to travel. I also belong to the Geneva Writers' Group, a wonderful organization that supports budding writers and has some really serious authors on its list of members. So, as you might have guessed, reading and writing are also passions of mine.

What to Do In Baden (The Basics)

Take a stroll down the Weitegasse (wide alley) toward the Catholic church and look up at the ruins of the old Baden castle on the hill. You can climb up to them and there is a nice restaurant next door where I recommend stopping for coffee.

Next, walk back down and along the river to the spa area. In medieval times, the German princes would come to Baden to discuss politics (these assemblies were called diets) and then enjoy the spa. In this area, a fun place to have a meal or coffee is the Hotel Blume (at Kurplatz 4). When you are finished with this, take a stroll through old town and visit some shops.

Hidden Gems for Seasoned Travelers

Check out the old wooden bridge across the Limmat River, which used to be a toll bridge. And, if you can get in, the old city meeting hall in the Rathaus is still set up for medieval diet meetings. My husband and I were married there.

Where to Stay

I recommend downtown (Weitegasse or the Blue City Hotel).

Day Trips

Of course, you have to start with Zürich, where you can visit the Fraumünster church (with its Chagall windows), Lake Zürich (for a boat ride in good weather), pretty Bellevue Square (where you'll find the historic and fun Cafe Odeon), the Niederdorf walking/shopping/eating area, the Sprüngli chocolate shop along Bahnhofstrasse (for the light mini-macarons called luxemburgerli), and the world-class art museum (even if you don't go in, Rodin's Gates of Hell are outside and fascinating). I also recommend a visit to the Grossmünster church (walk up the tower for an amazing view of the city), the beautiful Opernhaus (opera house), and the Federal Institute of Technology, where Einstein studied. For dinner, head to the Üetliberg (Zürich's mountain) for a fondue.

Aside from Zürich, some good day trips include Lucerne (a popular tourist city only an hour away), Lake Lucerne (for a

ZÜRICH & SURROUNDS

boat ride on a nice day), Thun and Lake Thun, Bern (the capitol), Gruyères (for the castle, cheese factory, and lots of cows and rolling hills), St. Gallen (whose lovely monastery library is a UNESCO World Heritage Site), Lake Constance (also very pretty), Geneva (which is a bit far but worth visiting, particularly for the UN—for which you'll need your passport), Basel (for its museums), Lugano (though that really needs more than a day to explore), Mount Rigi, and Einsiedeln (a very famous monastery with a black Madonna).

You can also easily head across the border to Colmar in France, Bregenz in Austria, and Milano in Italy (though the latter is a four-hour one-way journey).

Where to Hike
I am not much of a hiker, but the walk along Lake Lucerne is very nice and it would be easy to find other trails if you like.

What to Eat & Drink
In the fall, there's fresh-pressed apple juice called most and slightly sour grape juice called sauser. Local wines can be good, but it really depends on the year (and the weather that year). I also really like a hard cider made by the Rahmsier apple juice company. Beer is good here, too.

Where to Eat & Drink (Favorite Restaurants & Bars)
Near Baden, the Hertinstein (at Hertensteinstrasse 80 in Ennetbaden) is wonderful. In Zürich, the Blindekuh (for dining in the dark) wins the most interesting award. And my personal favorites in town are King's Kurry (at Freyastrasse 3), Gasthaus Rheinkeller (at Kirchstraße 13), and Hiltl (at Sihlstrasse 28).

Budget Tips
In Baden, there are a few inexpensive (Thai) take-away places.

How to Fit In
Don't talk loudly, especially while on public transportation. Be thoughtful: let everyone off public transport before attempting

148

ZÜRICH & SURROUNDS

to get on and give your seat to the elderly, the handicapped, and children. Don't ask for tap water (and don't argue when charged for it) in a restaurant. Instead, go a grocery store and buy a bottle of water and re-use it. All of the fountains in the city have drinking water. It's really okay to drink the water! Finally, don't sniff; it's better to blow your nose.

Best Places to Take a Photo
By the wooden bridge looking up and at the castle ruins looking down.

Find Patty at jehle-coaching.com.

BASEL & SURROUNDS

BASEL
Art, architecture, culture, seasonal markets, & family friendliness.

FIND WI-FI HERE: Unternehmen Mitte (the coffee shop), La Graziella, Starbucks, & Paddy's Pub.

LANGUAGE: German   **CANTON:** Basel

Dina Bonefacic-Mihaljek
Architect. Tour Guide.

About Dina
Originally from Croatia, I lived in the U.S. for 16 years before moving to the Basel area in 1999. I am an architect by training but worked in education for a long time. Since moving to Basel, I have been doing guided architecture tours and seminars on architecture-related topics.

What to Do In Basel (The Basics)
Go first to the heart of old Basel, to the Münsterhügel (Münster Hill). Here, you'll see an open-air archaeological display of one of the first Celtic settlements and defense walls (Murus Gallicus), Basel's most important historic building (the Münster—a cathedral from the Reformation in 1529), and the beautiful, well-preserved Münsterplatz (a square in front of the Münster), which is lined with stately houses. To get an amazing view of Basel and its tri-national surroundings, take the narrow steps spiraling up the Münster's Martinsturm (St. Martin's Tower).

Another place every visitor should go is the Rathaus (city hall)—a building complex whose architecture tells the story of Basel's historical development from the time it joined the Swiss Confederation (in 1501) to the very beginning of the 20th century, when its distinctive tower and the structures in the back of the courtyard were added.

Yet another historical landmark is the Spalentor—one of only three preserved towers/gates to the city, constructed in the late 14th century as part of Basel's outer defense walls.

Visitors interested in more contemporary architecture should go to the Messeplatz and have a look at the City Lounge—a round outdoor space that is part of an immense exhibition building designed by Basel's star architects Herzog & de Meuron. The interwoven metal skin of this most recent addition to Basel's Messe (fair grounds) shimmers beautifully and is visible from afar, as is the nearby Messeturm (the second tallest high rise in Basel, only topped by the new Roche Tower), which is the perfect place to go to during the impressive Art Basel or BaselWorld fairs.

Hidden Gems for Seasoned Travelers

Hidden behind one of the medieval gates on Münsterplatz is the renovated and extended Museum der Kulturen (Museum of Ethnology). It is well worth a visit, not only because of its progressive way of exhibiting the collection but also because of its architecture. The world-renowned architects Herzog & de Meuron designed an impressive, crown-like roof that encloses the new exhibition space.

Also very enjoyable is the area around the Spalenberg, Nadelberg, and Heuberg streets, where one can stroll through narrow medieval streets and enjoy some of the small shops and restaurants. The nearby Lohnhof complex is also worth a visit, with its mystical atmosphere and interesting history (it started as a monastery, became the city administration building, then turned into a jail complex before becoming multi-use today, with a hotel, restaurant, music museum, etc.)

A short stroll away is the Teufelhof—a medieval complex that houses an art hotel, two restaurants, and a small theater, as

151

well as an underground archaeological cellar that showcases segments of Basel's medieval defense walls.

Where to Stay
St. Alban-Tal still possesses the charm of the times past. It is quiet, yet full of culture-related places, including the Basel Papiermühle (paper museum) and the Museum für Gegenwartskunst (museum of contemporary art). A short, pleasant walk connects this area with the center of Basel.

For those interested in experiencing Swiss contemporary architecture integrated into a historical setting, the best place to stay is the St. Alban Jugendherberge (youth hostel).

Another special place is the Hotel Au Violin, located within the historical building of the former Lohnhof complex (rooms are in former prison cells that have been connected and remodeled) overlooking the busy Barfüsserplatz.

Day Trips
I enjoy Riehen, with its well-known Fondation Beyeler Museum and Wenken Park, Arlesheim (a wonderful small town known for its Baroque cathedral and beautiful English-style Eremitage park), and Dornach, which was the center of the anthroposophical movement, with a number of houses clustered around the Goetheanum and typical of Rudolf Steiner's approach.

I also like Weil am Rhein in Germany, especially the Vitra campus, which comprises many buildings by world's best-known architects (F. Gehry, Z. Hadid, T. Ando, etc.) and Ronchamp in France, where you can see Le Corbusier's Chapelle-Notre-Dame-du-Haut and Renzo Piano's convent.

Where to Hike
Walk from Arlesheim (starting at the Dom bus stop) through Eremitage to Ruine Dorneck, to Goetheanum, and back to the Arlesheim train station. Of interest along the way, you'll find Arlesheim's Baroque dam, views of two medieval castles, and

the Goetheanum (the center of the anthroposophical movement). The hike takes two to three hours and is fairly easy.

In Riehen, I like the trail from Hörnli to St. Chrischona to Wenkenhof. This is a three-hour moderate hike with some longer uphill sections. Of interest along the way are Basel's highest point (St. Chrischona church, terrace, and TV tower) and Wenkenpark (a beautiful French garden with a Baroque-style villa and nearby English-style park).

A bit farther away, I like the trail from Bubendorf to Schlosspark Wildenstein. The easy three-hour hike starts at the Steingasse bus stop in Bubendorf (take bus #70 or #71 from Liestal) and ends in Hölstein, where you can get a train back to Basel. Of interest along the way are the ancient oak trees and the Wildenstein Castle.

What to Eat & Drink
Around Fasnacht (Carnival), try mehlsuppe (flour soup), zwiebelwähe (onion pie), and fasnachtskiechli (deep-fried, sugar-dusted sweets). And for drinks, try the local beer (Ueli Bier), Baselland kirsch (cherry brandy), and Rivella (a soft drink made from milk whey).

Where to Eat & Drink (Favorite Restaurants & Bars)
My top three are Zum Isaak (at Münsterplatz 16), Volkshaus Brasserie (Rebgasse 12 - 14), and Bonvivant (Zwingerstrasse 10).

Budget Tips
Staying at the St. Alban Youth Hostel is more affordable than at a hotel, yet it offers an authentic Swiss experience. The Roman town of Augusta Raurica, whose large area includes many ancient remnants, can be visited for free. Only the museum requires a ticket. Some city museums offer free admission on the first Sunday of the month. And the Basel-Card—available at the tourist office—offers many discounts.

How to Fit In
The Swiss culture is a quiet one, so make sure you aren't too

BASEL & SURROUNDS

loud. In Basel in particular, people do not like to show off; neither extravagant clothing nor boasting is appreciated.

How to Meet Locals & Make Friends
Follow your interests and join a local Verein—a group that pursues a particular activity (sports, singing, visual arts, etc.).

Best Places to Take a Photo
Head to the Münster towers, the top of Margarethenhügel (the hill with the church of St. Margaret on top), or the Wasserturm (water tower) in Bruderholz for panoramic views. Beautiful views of Basel's historic skyline can be had from the promenade along the Rhine, on the Kleinbasel side.

Final Notes & Other Tips
Basel is famous for its collection of some of the best works of the Northern Renaissance artists. It boasts one of the first art collections ever opened to the public (the 16th-century Amerbach collection, parts of which are included today in Basel's Kunstmuseum), as well as the first European museum dedicated exclusively to contemporary art (Museum für Gegenwartskunst). In mid-2016, the new extension on the Kunstmuseum will open its doors and even more impressive artworks will be on display.

In addition to the almost 40 museums of various kinds all over Basel, annual fairs like Art Basel feature art brought into the city from 100s of leading galleries around the world.

Architecture fans can find buildings designed by numerous well-known architects, including Jacques Herzog and Pierre de Meuron, who were both born and raised in Basel and have maintained their main offices here, employing some 300 architects from all over the world. Another Basel-based office well established internationally is that of Diener & Diener. A number of smaller offices, such as Miller & Maranta, Christ & Gantenbein, Buchner & Bründler, and HHF, have also contributed to the local architectural landscape, thus strengthening the perception of Basel as the architecture center of Switzerland. Also, the one and only Swiss Architecture Museum (SAM) is in Basel.

Find Dina at architecture-walks-and-talks.net and facebook.com/archiwalkstalks.

Daniela
Designer. Culturist. Foodie. Hiker.

About Daniela
I'm from Mannheim, Germany and moved to Switzerland in 2008, first to Rickenbach, then Binningen, and now Basel. For work, I'm a web designer, working part-time at the MCH Group, Messe Basel, and studying sociology, pedagogy, and cultural studies at the University of Basel. In my free time, I like to meet my friends for a concert, a beer, a modern dance class, or hiking. I also like art and digital photography and love vintage markets and good food.

What to Do In Basel (The Basics)
Go for a walk (the Erasmus walk is a great one) using the little signposts on the houses as a guide and have a look at the old city. (You can find a brochure with five self-guided walking tours at *basel-virtuell.ch*.) Then, take one of the ferries across the Rhine to Kleinbasel, walk along the Rhine to the Wettstein Quarter, and climb up the green stairs at the old Warteck Brewery to the Kulturbeiz for coffee with a bird's eye view.

In the evening, have a vegan burger at Cafe Salon (at Sperrstrasse 94) and then go to a concert in the Kaserne or the Goldenes Fässli (at Hammerstrasse 108).

Hidden Gems for Seasoned Travelers
Landestelle is a seasonal, open-air restaurant and bar at Uferstrasse 35 close to the Rhine. It's a great place to have a cold beer near the river in the summertime.

Also in summer, the cinema in the harbor area (on top of one of the silos) is an interesting place. And there's a great vintage market at Petersplatz on Saturdays.

Where to Stay
If you like multicultural quarters, then hang around Kleinbasel, Klybeckstrasse, and Matthäusquarter. If you are looking for glamour, go to Grossbasel or Spalentor.

Day Trips
Wasserfallen in Reigoldswil is a great region. You can hike or go up by gondola and go down on a scooter. You can search for trails in the region at *wanderland.ch*.

There are lots of little hikes in the Jura area (St. Ursanne or Porrentury are great for hiking along the Doubs River). I also recommend a visit to the Vitra Design Museum in Weil am Rhine or to Freiburg im Breisgau just across the German border.

Where to Hike
St. Chrischona is very close and nice. The Klimaweg (climate trail) there explains a bit about Basel's sustainable energy.

What to Eat & Drink
Basler leckerli (honey cakes) are a famous local sweet. Beggeschmutz (chocolate shells filled with sweet foam) are also very local, but they are only sold at the Herbstmesse (an amusement fair) or the Christmas Fair.

Where to Eat & Drink (Favorite Restaurants & Bars)
Hirscheneck (at Lindenberg 23) is an alternative bar and restaurant, as is Zum Goldenen Fass (at Hammerstrasse 108). Da Francesca is a good bar and restaurant in Kleinbasel. La Fourchette is a super nice café. And Kulturbeiz (at Burgweg 15) is a good bar on top of the former Warteck Brewery. There are also very good Thai restaurants in the area (Thai Family at Drahtzugstrasse 32 or Lily's at Rebgasse 1). Jêle Café (Mülhauserstrasse 129) is nice for Turkish food.

Budget Tips

Restaurants in Kleinbasel are a bit cheaper than in Grossbasel. Cinemas are cheaper on Mondays. Vintage markets are cheaper than buying clothes in the shops. The botanical garden is free. And in Klybeckstrasse there's good Turkish food.

How to Meet Locals & Make Friends

Use Airbnb and *couchsurfing.org*. Take a class at Klubschule Migros. Go to a Quartiertreffpunkt (neighborhood meeting places with scheduled activities) and have a look at the local programs there. Go to a concert. Use *meetup.com*. And once you've met a couple people, organize a party.

Best Places to Take a Photo

Dreirosenbrücke (the big bridge) and the top of the former Warteck Brewery are both excellent choices.

Final Notes & Other Tips

Visit in the summer for a walk along the Rhine, in autumn or winter for the Herbstmesse or Weihnachtsmarkt fairs, or in spring for the famous carnival or the amazing art fair in June.

Andrew Gigax
Traveler. Wine-Lover. Hiker. Biker.

About Andy

I was born in the US and have been in Basel for nearly four years working in finance for a pharmaceutical research company. I have a wife and an 18-month-old daughter. Together, we enjoy traveling around Europe and our holidays typically involve a wine region or two, maybe some biking/hiking, and the occasional beach.

What to Do In Basel (The Basics)

Our typical itinerary for guests always includes stops at the Basel Münster (the main church) to climb the tower, the Spalenberg/Marktplatz old town for shopping, Basel's old city walls, and some time along the river at a café or bar.

Hidden Gems for Seasoned Travelers

The best gem is Fromagerie Antony just across the border in France. It's well hidden (at 5 Rue de la Montagne) in a small French village called Vieux Ferrette and can really only be accessed with a car.

Antony is widely considered to be one of the greatest cheese shops in the world. The owner provides cheeses to more Michelin-starred restaurants across the planet than anyone else. It's a very small shop and you can call ahead to reserve a spot for a tasting (phone: +33 3 89 40 42 22). I highly recommend it for anyone who wants a culinary experience. And the best part is that it's very reasonably priced.

Where to Stay

Any area with access to Basel's tram system is ideal. My particular favorites are the Schutzenmatt Park area (which has some great restaurants/bars and a park that's perfect for family picnics); Gundeli (which is located behind the train station and has a TON of nightlife and some cool bars/restaurants); and the city center (which is the best area for hotels and daily activities, of course, but can be a little hectic for families or those who prefer peace and quiet).

Day Trips

For mountain lovers, Basel is just an hour or two from the heart of the Alps. A good starting point is Lucerne, with its old town on the lake at the base of Mount Pilatus. From the center you can access the mountain via gondola and even stay at the top in a beautiful hotel. Lucerne has a good balance of city and alpine views.

For a true alpine experience, head to Mürren and Grindelwald. From there, you can get to Jungfraujoch (Europe's highest train station) and there is an incredible amount of recreational activities year-round. The whole area is absolutely breathtaking and is a must for someone who wants to experience the Alps.

[Editor's note: For those traveling by train, Mürren and Grindelwald are a bit far for a day trip from Basel, so consider adding them as an overnight or multi-day portion of your itinerary.]

Finally, outside the Alps, another excellent day trip is Alsace—the French wine region west of Basel. The region starts in Mulhouse and extends north nearly two hours (by car) to Strasbourg. Particularly interesting is the Route de Vin—a marked road that snakes its way through the vineyards from one storybook village to the next. My favorite villages are Kaysersberg, Eguisheim, and Turkheim. In each village, you'll find dozens of wineries that host free tastings and bottles can be purchased for as little as a few euros. Each village also has a fantastic selection of local restaurants that serve specialties like tarte flambe, foie gras, and escargot.

Where to Hike
The entire country is connected with a network of trails marked with yellow signs. Each sign details the distance and estimated time to hike to any number cities/landmarks/vistas/etc.

Personally, I enjoy the area just east of Basel, starting in Liestal and wandering toward the towns of Sissach, Frick, and Olten. This area has some nice, not-too-difficult hills and beautiful scenery. One stop that is an absolute must is the Sissacherfluh. It's just outside the town of Sissach and is well marked. The hike begins in the city and heads up a large hill to a cliff high above the town where there's a restaurant that serves great local food with picturesque views.

What to Eat & Drink
In Basel, particularly common dishes are bratwurst in an onion sauce and frikadelle (meatloaf). Switzerland isn't really known for its beer, but the largest brewery in Switzerland (Feldschlossen) is just outside Basel. Its beer can be found everywhere. For a more local (and better tasting) brew try Ueli Bier.

BASEL & SURROUNDS

Where to Eat & Drink (Favorite Restaurants & Bars)

First, I like the Schlusselzunft (on Freiestrasse near Marktplatz) for its incredible, elegant interior and food to match. Second, I recommend Biersekerhof (at Binningerstrasse 15). It's an Italian restaurant with a fantastic wine list and even better food. Prices are a bit on the high side and service can be slow, but it's well worth it!

Finally, I like Klingental (on Kasernenstrasse in the red light district). This place is a Basel institution. It goes without saying that any restaurant located in a red light district attracts some colorful clientele. That being said, the food is very traditional, the experience is very local, and prices are reasonable.

As for bars, I like Irrsinn (at Rebgasse 43), which is cool underground cellar with a great selection of cocktails, a younger crowd, and good prices. It's a nice change of pace from the normal bars in town. Another good bar option is Campari Bar (at Steinenberg 7). In the summer, it has an amazing patio. The inside is very nice as well but is on the small side. Then there's Schluggstube (at Gerbergässlein 28)—a really cool little pub that fills up quickly where you can spend hours looking at all the interesting stuff hanging from the ceiling. Staff here is always fun and friendly.

Budget Tips

Basel sits on the border of France and Germany. When in need of groceries, many Baselers will travel to the towns of St. Louis in France or Weil am Rein in Germany to do their shopping. It can save you more than 50%! Do be careful coming back across the border, as there are limits on the amount of food one can buy (these limits are posted online and usually in the cross-border grocery stores of Geant, Casino, or Heibers). Another big tip is to avoid buying anything at the Kiosks. The prices are nearly double for the same items purchased in a grocery store. If you have to buy groceries in Basel, go to Migros or Denner; their prices are usually the lowest around.

Some great restaurants to try on a budget are Braunen Mutz (at Barfusserplatz), Restaurant Linde or Fischerstube (in Klein Basel), or Lily's (also in Klein Basel).

How to Meet Locals & Make Friends
Be friendly and take interest in local things like FC Basel (local soccer) or Fasnacht (our carnival celebration). When you find similarities with someone, the ice always breaks much faster.

Best Places to Take a Photo
The best view in the city is from the top of the Basel Munster. It's not very well marked, but when you enter the church you can ask the desk about touring the tower. It costs about five francs and the climb is quite long and not recommended for someone with a fear of heights. But keep going all the way to the very top and you won't regret it. Marktplatz and the Rathaus are always good for photos as well.

Billy Meyer
Linguist. Traveler. Coach.

About Billy
I was born in Basel in 1958 and, except for one year in New Zealand, I have always lived here. After a career in journalism, in 1986, I opened my own firm, where I currently work as a coach, supervisor, mediator, personal counselor, and family counseling facilitator. I also invented a course called Authentic Writing. In my free time, I love to learn, travel, practice my Chinese, chat with strangers and friends, and sit in coffee shops.

What to Do In Basel (The Basics)
For a dose of Basel atmosphere, stroll along the Rhine early in the morning (and I mean *early*). Cross the Mittlere Brücke from Gross Basel to Klein Basel. Exit the bridge and turn right. Take the stairs toward the Rhine And then stroll along the river until you hit the Tinguely Museum. In the summer, take your bathing suit along, change in the bathroom of the Tinguely Museum

coffee shop, put your valuables and clothes into a waterproof plastic bag (which you can buy at the Bider & Tanner book-store), and float back down the Rhine to the Mittlere Brücke.

For the less-outdoorsy: visit the Beyeler Foundation Museum in Riehen (tram #6), take a ferry or water taxi ride across the Rhine, visit the Pfalz viewpoint behind the Münster, have a look at the houses in the old part of town, and take a tram ride on tram #6 from Riehen, changing to tram #8 at Claraplatz, to Weil (Germany). If you happen to be there (in Riehen) on a Saturday, enjoy the beautiful market in Lörrach (about a 20 minute walk from the border).

Hidden Gems for Seasoned Travelers
One interesting hidden gem is the small park (called Leonhard-skirchplatz) next to the former prison Lohnhof.

If you like architecture, try to get an invitation from a Novartis employee to visit the Novartis campus. There are a lot of interesting examples from world-renowned architects. While you're there, have a coffee at the Italian restaurant.

Another place you should visit (I have never been there, but all my friends and visitors like it) is the Bar Rouge in the Messeturm (at Messeplatz 10). It's almost 350 feet above the city and the bathroom is something special (trust me).

Finally, a place that is becoming more and more popular with the younger generation is Klybeckstrasse—a street full of new coffee shops and restaurants.

Where to Stay
Try to stay near the Rhine. There is a B&B—La Vie En Rose—(run by a friend of mine) just three minutes from the river at Oetlin-gerstrasse 25.

Day Trips
First, wander to Alsace in France. Take a train from Basel via

Mulhouse to Dannemarie Gare. Cross the road and have a tasty lunch at Restaurant Ritter on the Rue de la Gare. On the way back to Basel, stop in Mulhouse and pay the beautiful fabric print museum (Musée de l'impression sur Etoffes) a visit.

Next, take the train to Freiburg, with its old town full of small shops. If you rent a car, you can make a detour across the Schwarzwald (Black Forest). It's very picturesque.

Around Basel, I highly recommend the 500-year-old oak forest (Eichenwald) near Bubendorf. Take the train to Liestal and then catch a bus to Bubendorf from the train station.

Where to Hike
For something easy and wonderful, walk around the Eichenwald oak forest (mentioned above). For something longer, head to the Black Forest (the area around Titisee is very picturesque) or the nearby Jura Mountains (particularly the Saignelegier area).

What to Eat & Drink
For sweets, try Jakob Läckerli—a little shop in the St. Johanns-Vorstadt neighborhood. If you are here during the Fasnacht (Carnival) in late winter, try the onion and cheese tarts. They are typical for both the city and the event. And don't forget the fasnachtsküechli (a thin pastry dusted with powdered sugar) also available around Carnival.

Where to Eat & Drink (Favorite Restaurants & Bars)
To drink coffee, meet locals, and enjoy a good atmosphere, try La Graziella (at Feldbergstrasse 74), La Diva (at Ahornstrasse 21), Amici Miei (at Allschwilerstrasse 99), and El Mundo (at Güterstrasse 158). Also nice are the so-called buvettes (summertime cafes run out of old shipping containers) along the Klein Basel riverside.

For food, start with my favorite Turkish place, Marmaris (at Spalenring 118) and So'up (a soup bar at Fischmarkt 10). For a very beautiful location, try Restaurant Veronica (at Sankt

Alban-Rheinweg 195) on the Rhine. Sitting there on a warm night with a glass of wine is wonderful and very Baselish.

Budget Tips
One fairly priced restaurant is Ristorante Borromeo (at Byfang-weg 6). It is run by a foundation called OVERALL, which helps connect employers with job seekers. They are only open for lunch and only Monday to Friday from 11:30 a.m. to 2 p.m.

Another inexpensive and very cosmopolitan place is the food stall area in the Markthalle near the train station. They are also only open for lunch.

How to Fit In
If you participate in the Fasnacht (Carnival), get a costume and a mask (larve). Do not paint your face.

How to Meet Locals & Make Friends
A good place to meet locals is the Markthalle (mentioned above). You can also enter a restaurant, choose a table where somebody is already sitting, and ask if you can join. Then just start with small talk. Good luck!

Best Places to Take a Photo
On a sunny day, go to the car-free Münsterplatz, where the cathedral makes a great background. Of course, there are also many beautiful spots along the river walkway. Stroll along the river, cross the bridges, and come back to the walkway. Or take your camera on a ferry crossing. Finally, in nice weather, the terrace at the Manor restaurant is great.

Find Billy at sprachraummeyer.ch.

AARAU
A small, typical Swiss town at the foot of the Jura Mountains.

FIND WI-FI HERE: Starbucks, the city library, & the Tuchlaube bar.

LANGUAGE: German

CANTON: Aargau

Silvia Dell'Aquila
Sociologist. DJ. Editor, We Love Aarau.

About Silvia

The daughter of Sicilian immigrants, I grew up in Lenzburg and now live in Aarau. I work as a sociologist and, in my spare time, I am a DJ and organizer, I run the site We Love Aarau, and I am active in municipal politics.

What to Do In Aarau (The Basics)

Although Aarau is a small town, it has a lot to offer. Start in the heart of old town and look up at the famous giebel—elaborately painted eaves that are unique to this city. The old town also has some great restaurants and shops, as you might imagine. And the most beautiful part of old town is the halde, which also has a mysterious side (rumor has it that it's haunted by the ghost of an executioner).

Another must-do here is a walk by the river, where we have some great summer cafes and views. And I always recommend a visit to the Kunsthaus art museum, not only because of its unique architecture but also its lovely exhibitions and good café.

Hidden Gems for Seasoned Travelers

The Meyerschen Stollen—a series of tunnels originally built for textile dying—near the train station are well worth seeing. And for art lovers, there are also galleries and spaces full of experimental art in the city.

Day Trips
Aarau is very central, just half an hour from Zürich, Basel, and Solothurn and slightly farther from Bern and Lucerne. Baden is the second largest city in Aargau and can also be interesting. And Lenzburg—with its castle and beautiful old town—is just seven minutes away by train. This is part of Aarau's appeal. We're so close to everything.

Where to Hike
Start with a walk by the river, where preservation efforts have kept ancient flora and fauna intact. For something a bit farther afield, the Jura Mountains are only a short train ride away. And you can walk over those hills forever, discovering new worlds and enjoying great views.

One nice hike is from the clinic at Barmelweid to the Naturfreundehaus (Friends of Nature House) in Schafmatt. It's an intense 90-minute trek and there's an observatory where every Friday you can head up and view the night sky.

Finally, the nearby Wasserfluh and Gislifluh mountains are not to be missed.

What to Eat & Drink
Aargau is known for its rüeblitorte (carrot cake) and its white Küttiger carrots. The first Wednesday in November, you can find our famous carrots at the Rüeblimärt market.

Where to Eat & Drink (Favorite Restaurants & Bars)
For cocktails and burgers, check out Waldmeier (at Im Graben 31). The best Thai in town is at Thai Time (at Pelzgasse 10). The best pizza is at La Caverna (at Graben 14). My favorite tearoom and lunch spot is Brändli (at Bahnhofstrasse 37). And Tuchlaube Café & Bar (at Metzgergasse 18) is great for everything.

BASEL & SURROUNDS

Budget Tips
Budget-friendly restaurants include Thai Time (mentioned above), Signor Rossi (for pasta) at Laurenzentorgasse 6, and Brotkorb (at Metzgergasse 22).

Entertainment-wise, the deals are Barracuda, Butcher Street Pub, and Bar Tuchlaube, which all offer free concerts and DJed music (and all three are located on Metzgergasse).

How to Fit In
As with anywhere in Switzerland, we appreciate our peace and quiet.

How to Meet Locals & Make Friends
The Tuchlaube, the Butcher Street Pub, and Barracuda are all good places to meet people.

Best Places to Take a Photo
The best shot is along the Aare River with the old town and the town church as a backdrop.

Find Silvia at weloveaarau.ch.

BASEL & SURROUNDS

OLTEN

Small, beautiful, & full of Roman-era gems.

FIND WI-FI HERE: Hotel Arte, Hotel Olten, & Astoria Hotel.

LANGUAGE: German   **CANTON:** Solothurn

Max Frey
Retired Teacher. Sailor. Skier.

About Max

I was born in Olten and grew up at the Römerstrasse (the place where the Romans used to live in the center of town) and the Amthausquai (at the Aare River near the administrative buildings). I used to work as a teacher at the high school, but I'm retired now. In my free time, I do all kinds of sports—from sailing and rowing on Lake Biel to skiing the Alps.

What to Do In Olten (The Basics)

Have a look at the lovely Altstadt, which is the oldest part of the town. When you walk across the wooden bridge, you are already in the center and those buildings are mostly between 300 and 800 years old. Then, relax a little and walk along the Aare River. There is a nice walk along the banks on the right side of the river. And if the weather is good, just sit in a garden restaurant in the old part of the town and enjoy watching the everyday life of the Olten citizens.

Hidden Gems for Seasoned Travelers

Start with the beautiful classicist church (the so-called town church). If it's not open, ask for the priest, who lives in the neighborhood.

Next, head to the old monastery with its 17th-century church. There is a wonderful garden open several days a week. If it's closed, knock and ask the priest if he'll open it for you.

Finally, walk up the Säli Schlössli; it's an old castle with a restaurant on the top of a hill close to Olten. The view is great and you can watch the most beautiful sunset in the region. If you're walking, take good shoes. If you don't want to walk, you'll need to take a taxi.

Where to Stay
The most typical place to stay in the city is Hotel Kreuz (next to the Rathskeller garden restaurant), where you can find hotel rooms in a very old typical house. And if you want to visit a nice hotel or restaurant with a beautiful view of the area, go to the hotel Mövenpick (about five miles from Olten, reachable by bus or car).

Day Trips
Aarau and Solothurn are both very nice. You can also take the train to Zürich, Basel, Bern, Lucerne, or Biel (on the lake). It takes only about half an hour by train, because Olten is in the middle of all these nice places. Even a day trip to the Alps is possible. I recommend heading to the Bernese Oberland or the Titlis (or Rigi) near Lucerne.

Where to Hike
Hiking in the Jura Mountains is a must! This mountain chain is north of Olten and there are many buses that can bring you up to nice villages where you can start your hike.

Nearby, there's Frohburg (where Olten's founders' old castle used to be). From there, you'll have a beautiful view of the Alps. For something higher, head to the Belchenfluh, which is about 4,000 feet above sea level.

If you prefer to walk in the flat area, stroll along the Aare River down to Aarau (7.5 miles) or up Solothurn (18.5 miles).

BASEL & SURROUNDS

Where to Eat & Drink (Favorite Restaurants & Bars)

There are not many bars in Olten, but the one on top of the Hotel Astoria (Le Sisième) has really gorgeous views. Address: Hübelistrasse 15. The bars in Kreuz (at Hauptgasse 18) and Vaudois (at Marktgasse 23 next to the bell tower) are nice, too.

For restaurants, check out Aarhof (at Froburgstrasse 2) near the Aare River, Salmen (at Ringstrasse 39), where you'll find the walls covered with old photos of Olten, Felsenburg (at Aarauerstrasse 157) for excellent Italian fare and steaks, or Schlosserei (at Schützenmattweg 14), which is in an old black-smith's shop at the junction of two rivers.

Budget Tips

In Schönenwerd, there is the Fashion Fish outlet store and you can find cheap food and supply prices at Otto's.

How to Meet Locals & Make Friends

Go to the Rathskeller restaurant. That's where people from Olten go to have a beer and meet friends. You can sit at the round table and start talking to someone.

Best Places to Take a Photo

Go to the banks of the Aare River. From the eastern bank, you can take pictures of the town with the old wooden bridge. If you have enough time, go to the Säli Schlössli—the old castle on the top of the hill. You can see everything there.

Final Notes & Other Tips

Olten is in the heart of Switzerland, with major railway and motorway junctions. So not only can you enjoy staying in a lovely place, but you can easily take day trips to many other nice places. The airports of Zürich, Bern, and Basel are all less than an hour by train and Geneva is only 30 minutes farther.

GENEVA & SURROUNDS

GENEVA
Culture, architecture, food, wine, international politics, & Lake Geneva.

FIND WI-FI HERE: Starbucks, the Lady Godiva Pub, Boreal Coffee, Café du Lys, Cottage Café by the lake, & city parks.

LANGUAGE: French   **CANTON:** Geneva

Lynn Sorrentino
Hiker/Walker. Media Professional.

About Lynn
I consider Seattle my hometown, even though I was born and raised in California. Now, I live in Geneva and work as a project manager in media and communications. In my free time, I love to hike, walk, and snowshoe (depending on the season) in Geneva, its surrounding cantons, and France.

What to Do In Geneva (The Basics)
If you are flying in, the first thing to do is pick up a free public transport ticket at the airport (in baggage claim) to get to your local destination with no hassle.

Once you are settled in and can get to the old town in the city center, I recommend a walking tour—starting from Parc des Bastions, where you'll see Reformation Wall. From there, head across Place de Neuve to the sign on the large wall about Isaac Mercier, the man who alerted the Genevois guards on the night of L'Escalade (December 11, 1602) about the attack on Geneva by the French Savoyards.

Next, walk up the hill (called Promenade de la Treille) to Old Town proper. Once inside the walls, enjoy a nice lunch of fondue or raclette at one of the many cafes or a Calvinus beer

GENEVA & SURROUNDS

in Place du Bourg-de-Four before you climb the steps to the best view of Geneva: the Cathedral of St Pierre.

There is a small charge (about $4), but the 157-step climb on a clear day is well worth the effort. John Calvin, the Protestant Reformation leader, preached in the cathedral and there is a lot to see inside, as well as outside on the viewing platform at the top. If the city is cloudy, there is a Roman ruin museum under the cathedral that is also well worth a visit; it explains the founding of the city and has some amazing archeology. For another small charge, you can get a guided tour (with headphones) that explains a lot about Geneva and the Allobroges who were first to settle here.

After that, wander through old town to see the architecture and maybe take a tour of the Maison Tavel, Geneva's oldest private residence ("a unique testimony to medieval civil architecture" per the Geneva tourism website).

Once you are done touring old town, its shops, restaurants, and the little places to sit and people watch, I recommend heading to the other side of town where the United Nations is located. The UN is served by several buses (5, 8, 11, F, V, and others) and tram 15. Place des Nations has water fountains and several pieces of art dedicated to banning land mines (the large chair) and promoting peace. From the large chair, one can walk directly across the street to see the UN flags and the front of the Palais (the headquarters building), then go left up the street for 10 minutes (near the statue of Gandhi) to the free Ariana Museum of Textiles and Pottery, which is always open and has a cafe and no charge.

After that, keep walking up that street to the Pregny Gate of the UN for one of two daily guided tours (at 10 a.m. and 2 p.m., I believe). The art and history inside the UN is amazing and this two-hour tour (at about 12 francs) is done is several languages with a guide. My favorite room is the Spanish Room...the ceiling art piece is stunning.

Finally, I recommend a walk to the lakeside and to the Jardin Botanique. The garden is also free and in spring and summer is full of floral displays and blooms and pleasant places to picnic. The lake walk on a clear day has gorgeous views of the French Alps—Mont Blanc, Les Dents du Midi, and more.

Walking around the lake, across the pedestrian footbridge near the Four Seasons, will take you to the Ile de Rousseau and the area where a lot of water birds congregate and there are sometimes art displays. Continuing across the bridge into the edge of old town takes you back to the shopping area, more restaurants, and open-air markets.

Hidden Gems for Seasoned Travelers

It's not quite hidden, but the Bains des Pâquis sauna, massage, and restaurant is a great place to relax and enjoy the longer summer evenings. You can swim in the lake here, as well, and the sunset alpenglow on the mountains on clear summer nights is quite memorable. You can get here via buses 1 and 25.

In my neighborhood, Champel, the Parc Bertrand is very large and a great place to picnic or read a book on the lawn. There is a kids' pool in summer and a nice playground. The park is away from traffic noise and is large enough to have a quiet spot to yourself if you'd like. Buses 1, 3, and 8 serve this area.

A walk along the Arve River is also a favorite pastime of mine for quiet time and bird watching. Getting to the river by tram 12 or bus 11 or 21 is easy.

Finally, the little Sardinian neighborhood of Carouge is quite the joy to discover. It has low buildings that are very old, amazing Sardinian restaurants, great little bars, cafes, and ice cream shops, and nice ambiance.

Where to Stay

Stay in old town or in the Paquis. Avoid staying by the airport (it's too far from town). [Editor's note: This is excellent advice, even if you have an early flight. If you stay out here, you'll actually often need to take a bus *back into town* to catch one to the airport—nonsensical but true.]

Day Trips

Take a boat around the lake to see several places along the lake in France and Switzerland. Boats and ticket offices are near the Pont du Mont Blanc at the lower part of the Paquis area on the lakefront. Go to the medieval town of Yvoire, France, or up to Montreux, Switzerland, and enjoy a day on the water and wandering through historical cities.

For another very easy day trip, take the train from Gare Cornavin (Geneva's main train station) to Nyon to see the castle and the waterfront there. The ride is just 15 minutes.

Where to Hike

Head up to La Dôle by car through the small towns of Cheserex and Gingins and hike near La Barilette or all the way to the top of La Dôle. That area has great views of the French Alps and on a cloudy day in Geneva there can be a lot more sun above the clouds on these hills.

As for hiking near the lake, there are trails along Lake Geneva easily accessible in Nyon, Geneva, Morges, and Gland.

By far, my favorite hiking is a little bit out of town, along the wine trail of La Vaux. The trail—from St. Saphorin to Lutry—is a UNESCO World Heritage Site and has terrific views of wineries and the lake. St Saphorin is a cute medieval town with great photo opportunities (I recommend starting here and exploring the town before your hike). The hike is about 3.5 hours long, well marked, fun, and has some medium difficulty sections. The wineries are not usually open along the route (as they are working wineries), so stopping to picnic means bringing a lunch and wine of your own to enjoy in one of the tiny towns or near the edge of the vines at a small picnic area.

GENEVA & SURROUNDS

What to Eat & Drink

My favorite fondue and raclette are served in the old town in a restaurant called Les Armures (at Rue du Puits-Saint-Pierre 1 by the old armory). The food, wine, and staff are really great.

Wines of Dardigny, Satigny, and Russin near Geneva are terrific (particularly the whites). The red Gamaret is very local and very good. My favorite Gamaret is by La Clemence, a local winery. Local wines can be purchased at most grocery stores here.

And, of course...chocolate. Try the type of cure truffles called pave. They are sold in several chocolatiers and grocery stores. These are a Geneva specialty.

Where to Eat & Drink (Favorite Restaurants & Bars)

Les Armures (at Rue du Puits-Saint-Pierre 1) is excellent for food and wine. Chez Ma Cousine (at Place du Bourg-de-Four 6) is good for chicken, fries, and small budgets. And Parfums de Beyrouth (on Rue de Berne in Pâquis) has the best Lebanese food—falafel, hummus, etc.—you'll find in Geneva. It's also inexpensive.

Budget Tips

For 39 francs you can buy a one-week pass that will work on all buses, trams, and mouettes (tiny boats that go across Lac Léman) in the city. The office of TPG behind Gare Cornavin sells these passes, which also cover the airport train. And taking the mouette boats across the lake to places like Eaux Vives then back to Pâquis and over to old town (Molard) is a fun thing to do that is covered by a bus pass.

As noted above, try Parfums de Beyrouth and Chez Ma Cousine for inexpensive food.

Several of the sights in Geneva are free or cheap—like the view from the cathedral. At the tourist office (in the main post office on Route de Mont Blanc, directly across from the train station down into the Pâquis) you can also get some passes for Geneva sights and tours.

Water fountains are operational most of the year except freezing winter…if they say eau potable on them, fill up your water bottle; the water is clean and completely safe to drink and will save you tons on buying water in the stores. Same goes for hotel water, it's all ok to use and drink.

How to Fit In
Be quiet on your phone or when talking in groups on public transport. Don't play your music without headphones. Let people get off the bus, train, etc. before you get on and help little old ladies, pregnant women, or women with babies in a stroller get on or offer them your seat as a courtesy. Say *bonjour* (hello) to people when you see them on the street (unless there are crowds) and say it again when you walk into a shop. When you leave, say *merci, au revoir* (thank you, goodbye).

How to Meet Locals & Make Friends
Being polite to people in your apartment building is key, as is finding groups to network with based on interests. *Glocals.com* is a great resource.

Best Places to Take a Photo
The best shots are from the St. Pierre Cathedral, the Place des Nations, and the lakefront on a clear day.

Final Notes & Other Tips
Check out the myswitzerland.com for fun things to do and *cff.ch* (the train website) for deals and itineraries in the region. For accurate bus and train schedules, visit *tpg.ch*.

Marisa Ribordy
Health Coach. Yoga Teacher. Outdoor Enthusiast.

About Marisa
I'm Marisa—a Swiss/Dutch girl in her early 30s who grew up

in Geneva. I quit my job at the beginning of the year, completed my yoga teacher training in Bali, traveled for a few months, and then came back home to do what I love, which is coaching people to regain their health and energy while connecting with their body through yoga.

In my free time, I love to travel, hike, snowboard, and spend time outdoors. Nature and activity are essential for me.

What to Do In Geneva (The Basics)
In summer, start with breakfast at Bains des Paquis (address: Quai du Mont-Blanc 30) and then go for a swim. This part of Geneva is a beautiful place to watch the sunrise while listening to live music—and you can see the Jet d'Eau (the big fountain on the lake).

In the winter, check out the Turkish baths (hammams) and saunas and eat a cheese fondue.

Hidden Gems for Seasoned Travelers
Parc de la Grange is one of my favorite places to hang out, laying in the grass with a book. I love the trees and the view over the lake.

Any time of year, head to the old town for a stroll and a drink at Café Clémence (address: Place du Bourg-de-Four 20). In December, you'll find a great Christmas market in Carouge. On the first Saturday in December, check out the Escalade Run. During the race, the town is always packed with people cheering the runners on. It's a very popular event. There's also a costume run in the evening, which is fun to watch with a cup of mulled wine.

In summer, at Plage du Reposoir, you can hire paddleboards. There's also a restaurant/bar boat called Le Bateau, where you can eat in the evenings. And one of my favorite things to do is watch movies in a park by the lake (*cinetransat.ch*).

GENEVA & SURROUNDS

Where to Stay
Stay in Old Carouge or the old town. Around the train station or lake is also practical, as you are close to everything.

Day Trips
Montreux is lovely and has an amazing view (particularly at sunset) over the lake and mountains. Lavaux is perfect for a walk in the vineyards (which are a UNESCO World Heritage Site). And if you have more time, head to the Alps for a weekend. Zermatt, Saas-Fee, Verbier, and Crans-Montana are all great.

Where to Hike
I often go hiking in the Jura, which is 30 minutes away. Around St-Cergue and La Dole there are a few hiking trails. The countryside around Geneva is beautiful, full of farms and vineyards, so walking in the region can be really nice. And in winter, you can go snowshoeing in St-Cergue. They have a night snowshoe walk in the forest under the moonlight. It's a great experience.

Where to Eat & Drink (Favorite Restaurants & Bars)
Helveg Café (at Avenue de Miremont 31) is a good vegan restaurant (pretty much the only one in Geneva). Cottage Cafe (at Rue Adhémar-Fabri 7) is good for tapas or drinks. And Comme à la Maison (at Rue Ancienne 36) has a cozy brunch in Carouge.

Kraken (at Rue de l'Ecole-de-Médecine 8) and Café du Lys (right next door) are in the student area and are fun to stop in for a beer. Yvette de Marseille (at Rue Henri-Blanvalet 13) in the Eaux-Vives neighborhood is a good choice, too.

Café du Soleil (at Place du Petit-Saconnex 6) is an old and charming café where you'll find good salads in summer on the terrace or cheese fondue in winter.

Budget Tips

Mikado is a Japanese place (at Rue de l'Ancien-Port 9) with good price for sushi or warm dishes (take away or eat-in). And Bains des Paquis (mentioned above) is also very good option for good food and cheap prices.

How to Fit In

Start with a few words in French before launching into English.

Best Places to Take a Photo

From the top of the cathedral in old town. Take the stairs all the way up for a nice view of the city. The view from the mountain Salève is pretty amazing, too.

Final Notes & Other Tips

I recommend visiting in the spring or summer, as there's more to do and the city is beautiful in the sunshine. Winter is quiet and grey and the place to be is in the sunny, snowy mountains.

Find Marisa at wildhappyheart.com.

Aleks & Sophie
Bloggers. City Girls.

About Aleks & Sophie

Our names are Sophie and Aleks and we're originally from Singapore and Russia/America. We are currently full-time bloggers—a career that took off once we got to Geneva (where we are currently based). We both had a lot of visa issues when we arrived in Switzerland, but this turned out to be a blessing in disguise as now we are doing what we really love (writing and running our own blog).

What to Do In Geneva (The Basics)

Start off with a wander around the old town. As the name implies, it's the oldest (and nicest) part of the city. If you're feeling a bit cultural, pop your head into the cathedral and pay a visit to the Maison Tavel (the oldest private house in Geneva, located at Rue du Puits-Saint-Pierre 6). While you're there, have a coffee (or something stronger) and people-watch at Le Clémence, which is a great cafe right in the main square of the Old Town (at Place du Bourg-de-Four 20).

Next, make your way back toward the river—with a mandatory stop at the flower clock, the most random and surprising of tourist attractions—and enjoy a little walk and the views of Mont Blanc (one of the best views is from the Mont Blanc bridge). On the bridge you'll also see Geneva's most famous attraction, the Jet d'Eau (the huge water fountain).

Finish with a hearty dinner in Geneva's most famous steak restaurant, Le Relais d'Entrecôte (at Rue Pierre Fatio 6). Make sure you get there at exactly seven or you'll never get a table.

Hidden Gems for Seasoned Travelers

Geneva is something of an open book, as it's so small, but one place both new tourists and seasoned pros should visit is Carouge. Carouge is a village next to Geneva and we love it because it feels so much like a medieval town, with cobbled streets, charming façades, and little shops everywhere. There is also a small market on Saturdays and it's just one of those great places to walk through when you want to get away from the bustle of the city center.

Where to Stay

We'd choose somewhere central, close to the station (great for day trips) but not quite at the station (as it's not the nicest neighborhood). A great hotel is the L'Hôtel d'Allèves at Rue du Cendrier 16. It's reasonably priced, nice, and a five-minute walk from Mont Blanc Bridge, while also really well connected to the rest of the city.

The Paquis area is also a hidden gem of sorts. It may not look like the nicest neighborhood, but you can always find a tasty restaurant that's open on a Sunday (which any Geneva resident knows is a miracle!).

Day Trips
Annecy! It's a very quaint French village with great restaurants. And it's small enough to wander around and see in a day.

Another favorite is Gruyères, the birthplace of the famous cheese. It's a charming medieval village perched on top of a hill and feels unaffected by the passage of time.

Where to Hike
Every summer, we make various trips to the Jura Mountains. There you will find no end of hiking trails for all levels. Our favorite part is the celebratory drink when we make it down.

Where to Eat & Drink (Favorite Restaurants & Bars)
L'Apothicaire (at Boulevard Georges-Favon 16) has great cocktails. Key and Eagle (at Rue De-Grenus 7) is great for a bit of pub life and expat fun. And Soleil Rouge (at Boulevard Helvétique 32) is good for wine.

As for restaurants, we'd have to say Entrecôte (Rue Pierre Fatio 6), Le Trois Verre (on Rue Hornung) for great Italian, and Cafe du Centre (Place du Molard 5) for a great brunch.

As far as hidden bars and restaurants go, two places we definitely recommend are Sesflo (at Route de Florissant 16) and Bar du Nord (Rue Ancienne 66). Sesflo is really good Italian place tucked away in Champel—a residential area. Bar du Nord's main feature is tons of whiskey, pretty much any brand you can imagine, as well as good cocktails.

Budget Tips
Most things in Old Town (like the cathedral) are free. At night, have a look around Planpalais, which is the student area of Geneva. And walk down Rue de l'Ecole de Médecine and you can find some bars and restaurants with reasonable prices (The Kraken, Cafe du Lys, etc.).

GENEVA & SURROUNDS

How to Fit In
Be sure to say *bonjour* (hello); locals find it rude if you don't greet them on your way in to a shop, bar, etc. Even if your grasp of French is lackluster, try and make the effort.

How to Meet Locals & Make Friends
Learning French helps. It's hard to break into Swiss friendship circles if you don't have a strong grasp of the language. I know that a lot of our friends here met people off *glocals.com*, which is a site for expats to find activities, nights out, etc. Another similar site is *meetup.com*, where you can organize or join groups based on your interests.

Best Places to Take a Photo
Our top picks are the Mont Blanc Bridge, the views from Bain de Paquis, in front of the Jet D'eau, the cathedral in the old town, and the large chess sets in the Parc des Bastions.

Find Sophie and Aleks at sisterhoodofthetravelingwags.com.

MONTREUX
Home of the Montreux Jazz Festival.

FIND WI-FI HERE: Everywhere—the town is well-wired.

LANGUAGE: French   **CANTON:** Vaud

Mathieu Jaton
CEO of the Montreux Jazz Festival. Music Enthusiast.

About Mathieu
Born in Vevey, I now live in Attalens, not far from Montreux. I'm the CEO of the Montreux Jazz Festival. And in my free time, I like reading comic books (a passion of mine since childhood), playing golf, and, of course, listening to music!

What to Do In Montreux (The Basics)
Take the lovely little train from Montreux to Les Rochers-de-Naye and enjoy the magnificent view at the top while eating a delicious fondue at the restaurant.

Hidden Gems for Seasoned Travelers
In spring and summer, definitely visit the Gorges du Chauderon. It's a wild and refreshing canyon with a shaded trail just a few steps away from Montreux train station.

The Montreux Jazz Café at Montreux Palace is a place full of history, passion, and, of course, music. The stamp of festival founder and local son Claude Nobs is on every square inch of the place. And emblematic photos and memorabilia from a half-century of musical history make this a new town must-see showcasing artistic and culinary treasures.

Where to Stay
The old part of Montreux city: Les Planches.

Day Trips
Head to the summit of the Rochers-de-Naye, enjoy a picnic, and spend the night in a Mongolian yurt at an altitude of 6,500 feet—year-round. Book ahead at *goldenpass.ch*.

There are some beautiful spas/thermal cure centers in the mountains of the Canton of Valais that are really wonderful.

Another nice option is to take the regional (slower) train from Montreux to Lausanne. Along the way, there are lovely places for sunbathing, including the tiny harbors at Saint-Saphorin, Cully, Rivaz, and Epesses. These villages are also all surrounded by vineyards (the Lavaux region is a UNESCO World Heritage Site known for its white wines), so a day spent exploring the vineyards and tasting the wine is also a day well spent. At the end of your explorations along the lake, slip into Lausanne's nightlife. It's the biggest city in the area and has a lot to offer.

Finally, another really nice thing to do is take a boat from Lausanne to Thonon-les-Bains or Evian. The Compagnie Générale de Navigation (CGN) runs the world's most important and most elegant fleet of side-wheel paddleboats there. Traveling on a steamer on the lake is an out-of-time, unforgettable experience.

Where to Hike
I recommend Les Avants—a nice location up in the mountains with a sledding slope in winter—and the hamlet of Derborence, just under 5,000 feet above sea level in an isolated valley. Derborence is not permanently inhabited, is completely surrounded by mountains (with the Diablerets to the north), and has a really unusual landscape, due to two landslides in the 18th century.

GENEVA & SURROUNDS

What to Eat & Drink
Filets de perche is a delicious specialty, but make sure the restaurant serves fish from Lake Geneva. I also recommend white wine from Epesses.

Where to Eat & Drink (Favorite Restaurants & Bars)
Visit Funky Claude's Bar in the Montreux Jazz Café at Montreux Palace (at Avenue Claude Nobs 2) for its live concerts. (Reservations are recommended: +41 21 962 1400.)

Another favorite is the Yatus Winebar (at Rue des Deux-Marchés 24 in Vevey).

I also recommend Le Pont de Brent (at Route de Blonay 4 in Brent). Under the direction of chef Stéphane Décotterd and with 18 Gault Millau points, the restaurant is well known in Swiss gastronomy.

Best Places to Take a Photo
On market square, with an unforgettable view on the lake, the mountains, and the statue of Freddie Mercury.

Find Mathieu at montreuxjazzfestival.com.

GENEVA & SURROUNDS

NYON
Scenery, vineyards, & lake views tucked away outside Geneva.

FIND WI-FI HERE: The train station and many restaurants.

LANGUAGE: French   **CANTON:** Vaud

Evren Kiefer
Writer. Content Manager. Comedy Enthusiast.

About Evren
Despite being half Turkish, my roots are firmly planted on the shores of Lac Léman. I was born in Vevey, a town in the wine country of Lavaux. And I've been living in the center of Nyon for almost a year now. I'd never lived in town before. I love it.

My work is in web content management and publishing for the University of Geneva. Outside the office, I struggle to establish a writing habit and, for fun, I watch and listen to a lot of stand-up comedy.

What to Do In Nyon (The Basics)
Nyon's old town is adorable and small. From the chestnut tree square with its four Roman columns (which became a symbol of the town), pass by the St. Mary gate without going through. Then continue toward the stairway, which leads to the priory and the temple. Take the narrow streets for a look at the nice shops and houses. Since we have lots of expats, you may come upon the English bookshop with its colorful kids' books.

Or you may happen upon a statue of Caesar, which marks the square where you'll find the Roman Museum (*mrn.ch*). The museum is nested in the remains of the forum's basilica. I encourage everyone to visit at least one Roman museum in the region to see how the empire shaped Europe by reclaiming farmland, establishing towns, and planning the roads that our transportation systems are still indebted to.

If you walk through Nyon for a while, you're bound to come out on the Place du Château. The castle was renovated and reopened in 2005, as good as new. Some people think the renovation was heavy-handed but it's well done. It houses a history museum, which I've heard is interesting.

Whether you visit the museum or not, be sure to go through the castle to the terrace. The view of the lake is priceless. After having completed your tour of upper-Nyon, exit the terrace on the right and go down to the lakeside enjoying the flowery parks on the way.

Hidden Gems for Seasoned Travelers

You should definitely visit the European Centre for Nuclear Research (CERN) in Geneva, which houses the Large Hadron Collider. Parking is scarce there, so you may want to take public transit (Tram 18). They have impressive pedagogical exhibits and admission is free. With a little prior notice, you can book an above-ground guided visit or (if you're part of a group of eight or more and book months in advance) a group tour that could include a peek at underground installations. Book at *outreach.web.cern.ch*.

To continue with the science theme, even if it is less impressive, Geneva's Science History Museum exposes a lot of antique scientific precision instruments that were made by the areas' watchmakers for 18th- and 19th-century scientists. It's in an old house nestled in the beautiful Perle du Lac Park. And it's a good place to take an hour's respite from the city and the crowd if you ever need one.

Where to Stay

If you stay in Nyon, stay as close as possible to the center, the train station, and the harbor. This will grant you rapid access to

GENEVA & SURROUNDS

Geneva and Lausanne by train and France over the lake. If you rent a car, staying in Nyon might not be the best idea since the highway between Geneva and Lausanne is crowded with commuters and there are speed radars everywhere.

Day Trips

If you come in the summer, definitely sail the lake in an old steamboat. They use fuel instead of coal to make steam, yet the machinery you see is really propelling the boat. You can watch the red wheels on the side turn through a shield window. It's impressive.

A short boat ride away, there's the charming fortified medieval town of Yvoire. It's in France, so you'll need your passport and some euros. The village is full of nice little attractions. For example, I wouldn't miss Le Jardin des Senteurs, which is a garden full of plants selected specifically for their scents and a maze. There are also a few places that make good crepes.

If you want longer boat rides, there are cruises to go to Lausanne or Geneva.

Where to Hike

Take the train to La Givrine. It's 46 minutes away from Nyon in a cute red train and the ride itself is very scenic (though the convenience also means it can get crowded, as locals go hiking in the Jura quite regularly on weekends). From the Givrine station, you can hike to La Dôle. At the top, there is a passive radar station that receives signals from airplanes for traffic control. On a clear day, you can see the town of Nyon, of course, but also a large part of the canton and the border area with France. It's breathtaking.

Keep in mind that you don't need to go all the way up to experience the characteristic environment of the Jura.

Another good option is the Sentier des Toblerones (Toblerone Trail), which is way less steep. It's a hiking trail that follows a fortified line from World War II. The concrete structures designed to make it impossible for armored vehicles to pass resemble Toblerone pieces. On the way, you'll pass forts, two bunkers painted in trompe-l'oeil style to resemble houses, and a variety of streams flowing in between dense forest.

If you like the forest, there's an old oak forest natural reserve not too far away. It's called Bois de Chênes and is just north of Vich. In places, the forest is very old and has a mystical quality to it. It found its way into a new-age list of energetic places not too long ago. In other parts, the forest suffered severe damage from Roman over-exploitation and has been on the mend ever since. I've seen deer, boar, and a few hares there.

What to Eat & Drink

Saucisson Vaudois is our local sausage. It's served with mashed potatoes or rösti or lentils. If you want to try fish, filet de perche is a classic served in lakeside restaurants in Nyon and every other town in the area. And the region's cheese dish is without a doubt the malakoff Vaudois, which is made with a grated cheese and egg paste on bread that is then fried.

Where to Eat & Drink (Favorite Restaurants & Bars)

In Nyon, next to the castle, there is the Auberge du Château, which is quite a nice place. It was in the news when Hillary Clinton went to eat there unannounced on a state visit with President Clinton in 1994.

In Geneva, where most of my social life happens, the Rue de l'Ecole-de-Médecine between the Plaine de Plainpalais and the Arve River is a street full of bars where college students have gone since time immemorial. My favorite is the Café du Lys (at Rue de l'Ecole-de-Médecine 7). Have an Elmer Citro (fizzy elm water with lemon) or Gazosa Swiss soda there.

Also in Geneva, Inglewood Burger (at 44 Boulevard du Pont-d'Arve and 17 Rue de Montchoisy) won best burger in the French-speaking part of Switzerland in a consumer advocacy

TV show last year. Their Plainpalais location is small and popular with the locals.

Budget Tips
In old town Geneva, there are places few tourists ever visit, like Terrasse Agrippa d'Aubigné, the surrounding mosaics, and the narrow streets around the cathedral. You can also walk to the Promenade St-Antoine on the edge of the old town. Below is a car park. In the process of digging it, they have uncovered a large section of Geneva's fortifications, which are now on display there with explanations. Archeological digs continue around this part of town and soon there will be more to see.

The first Sunday of every month, a lot of museums have free admission. Otherwise, if you plan on doing lots of touristy things in a short period of time, you might want to consider the Geneva Pass, which you can get at the tourism office.

As for food, Asian cantinas are quite common in Geneva and they're usually on the less expansive end of the spectrum without being too mediocre. In the summer, you can spend time in the Parc des Bastions and picnic, which is something groups of students do to save money.

How to Fit In
Use your common sense and everything will be fine. The beauty and tidiness of the place sometimes leads a tiny minority of visitors to forget that people live and work here. I mean, does anybody really need to take pictures of the sandwich stands where commuters buy their lunch?

Our transportation infrastructure is on the brink of overflow in the region between Lausanne and Geneva. If you take that fact into account, we'll all have a much better experience. For example, avoid regional trains when travelling with your large suitcase, because the new carriages are not designed for luggage at all and that's just annoying to everybody. In the InterRegio or the ICN trains, use the space below and in-between the backs of the seats to put your luggage. I know the looping messages about pickpockets at the airport and the train station sound scary. But you don't need to have your giant suitcase in between your knees with your hands on the handles at all times. Watching them intently is enough. Besides, if you let me sit in front of you on the train we might have a nice chat. Who knows?

How to Meet Locals & Make Friends

Swiss people are quite difficult to approach, even for other Swiss people! The geek connection works great, however. There are monthly meet-ups, blogger dinners, and Twitter aperitifs that you could try. I have attended the #taloz (the Twitter Apéro Lausanne) and #HTAGG (the one for Geneva).

If you don't mind getting up early and registering online, you can also come to the local chapter of Creative Mornings (*creativemornings.com/cities/ge*), where you can listen to a local speaker (in English), get breakfast, and meet people from the design/communication scene. You can also come to the WordPress Geneva meet-up, which you can find on *meetup.com* (events are in English or French on a case-by-case basis, depending on the speaker).

If you're in the web industry, Lausanne has great community events. For back-end folks, there is #WebMardi (*techup.ch/tag/webmardi*), which means Web Tuesdays. For front-enders, UXRomandie is the local IxDA group (*uxromandie.ch*). Both events are vibrant and popular.

If it's summer and the local groups don't have meetings planned, all hope is not lost. If you know a local, they can introduce you to their friends with a picnic at CinéTransat's free movie nights or the municipality's free music in the park events.

Best Places to Take a Photo

In Nyon, check out the chestnut tree square (Place des Marronniers) with its Roman columns, the castle, or the pier. In

GENEVA & SURROUNDS

Geneva, it is the Jet d'Eau, the Reformation Wall, or the Reformed Cathedral.

You can skip the horloge fleurie, which is a clock made out of flowers. I don't get why people flock to it. Tour buses park right in front of it; it's next to a busy bridge and a busy street. Moreover, the park behind it is where drug dealers work.

Final Notes & Other Tips

Geneva airport has a separate train station. All InterRegio trains going through Geneva stop at the airport. Please, don't go off the train at Geneva Central with your luggage, exit the station, and ask how to get to the airport. It breaks my heart to tell people they have to haul their luggage back to the platform from which they came.

LAUSANNE
Natural beauty & lakefront access.

FIND WI-FI HERE: Starbucks, the Eclau or La-Muse co-working spaces (book ahead at *coworking-romand.ch*), & the city center.

LANGUAGE: French   **CANTON:** Vaud

Katherine Zachary
Public Relations Pro. Foodie. Traveler.

About Katherine
I'm from Detroit and moved to Lausanne in December 2012 for my job, which is in public relations. In my free time, I love to cook, travel, explore new cities, walk, read, and spend time with friends.

What to Do In Lausanne (The Basics)
Lausanne is seasonal. Winter means ski trips and summer means leisure time at the lake. I recommend exploring the winding, multi-leveled streets of the old town, strolling up to the cathedral, experiencing the farmers market on Wednesdays and Saturdays (in old town from 8 a.m. to 1 p.m.), going on hikes through the Lavaux vineyards, visiting the Olympic Museum, taking a boat ride across Lac Léman to France, having a glass of local wine at the lake, and, last but not least, eating fondue!

Hidden Gems for Seasoned Travelers
The Art Brut Museum is quite a find—a world-class collection unlike anything most people have ever seen.

Where to Stay
Stay in Ouchy for a view of the lake and mountains and easy access to all of Lausanne and the neighboring towns. And the city center offers some good options, too.

Day Trips
Must-sees include Montreux, Gruyère, and the Lavaux region.

Where to Hike
Hike through the beautiful vineyards (all terraced down to the lake) of the Lavaux region. The scenery is spectacular and there are little towns with their open wine cellars along the way in case you want to pause for a glass of local wine.

Where to Eat & Drink (Favorite Restaurants & Bars)
Le Chalet Suisse (at Route du Signal 40) offers a very authentic experience. Watergate (Avenue Emile-Henri-Jaques-Dalcroze 9) has a great lakeside vibe. Le Pinte Besson (at Rue de l'Ale 4) has a special old-world charm. And when it comes to bars, choose Le Comptoir (at Rue de la Barre 1) for cocktails, Yatus (at Rue du Petit-Chêne 11) for wine, and Café Bruxelles (at Place de la Riponne 1) for beer. Outside town, check out Le Deck (on Route de la Corniche in Chexbres) for the view.

How to Fit In
In Switzerland, it pays to follow the rules. Cross at the cross-walks. Don't litter. Always say hello and goodbye (in French) when you come into or out of a shop or restaurant. And, whatever you do, drive at the speed limit! There are traffic cameras everywhere.

How to Meet Locals & Make Friends
Like anywhere, if you go out and start chatting with strangers, they typically respond positively. It's difficult to define what exactly a local is in Lausanne, as the town's population is over 40% non-Swiss. With so many people from all over the world, it's easy to make friends and have a casual chat with strangers.

Best Places to Take a Photo

You can take some great photos from Ouchy, as well as in front of the Lausanne Cathedral and from the Lavaux Vineyards. It's hard to go wrong, especially if the sun is shining.

Final Notes & Other Tips

Lausanne is a city of steep hills, winding streets, secret stairways, and back passages. It's super charming but easy to get turned around in and wish you were wearing better shoes. An excellent public transportation system (bus and metro) makes it navigable for tourists and locals alike.

Stephanie Booth
Outdoor Sports Enthusiast. Blogger. Consultant.

About Stephanie

I'm half British, half Swiss, born in U.K. but raised in Lausanne. For work, I'm a Social Media Consultant. I started in 2006 as a blog consultant and now I help clients understand what online communities and social media are about and how to do intelligent things around that.

As for my free time, I love sailing, skiing, walking around in the mountains—all kinds of outdoor sports type stuff. I also play Ingress and I like taking care of my plants and cats, cooking, reading, watching movies, and talking with people over a cup of tea. And then there are my online activities. It's not always clear if it's work or free time, but I love blogging and online communities.

What to Do In Lausanne (The Basics)

The cathedral, the lakeside, and La Citée (old town) are definite must-sees. I also take people up the hill to the top of the town at Sauvabelin. There's a viewpoint there (Signal de Sauvabelin) where you can see the lake and in the forest there's a wooden tower that gives a 360-degree view of the area.

There are also lots of museums here, including Musée de l'Elysée (the world-renowned Olympic museum), the Natural History Museum in the city center, Palais de Rumine (a palace housing several museums), and Musée de l'Hermitage (for the art-lovers).

Hidden Gems for Seasoned Travelers

Walk. Lausanne isn't very big, so you can walk from the lake to Sauvabelin in just over an hour and you'll have been across the whole town. One of the nice things about Lausanne is it's a 3D city, built on three hills. The roads and houses are on various levels. You have staircases and lifts that take you from one level to another and that's fun to explore.

There's one particular lift that takes you up from Vigie to Chauderon. There are staircases between Le Flon and Bel-Air and at both ends of Font Bessieres. There's also a staircase quite hidden between Rue Centrale and Rue de la Mercerie that you can go searching for (it's the kind of thing you wouldn't find unless you knew it was there).

There are nice parks for exploring, too. They are tiny and, again, some of them are tucked away between buildings. There's one big one near where I live called Parc de Valency and it's nice because you have a view of the lake.

A truly tiny park is hidden in between Avenue de France and Avenue de Echallens near the Aubepines bus stop. Look for a little passageway through the row of buildings. This will take you to the park.

Another nearby park is Mont-Goulin. From the bus stop, you'll see a huge opening in the apartment block that towers above you. When you walk through the passage, the u-shaped gardens inside the apartment blocks have a bench or two and there's a really nice view of the lake.

Finally, make sure to visit the open-air market at Place de la Riponne on Wednesday and Saturday mornings in the city center. It's quite the experience.

Where to Stay

By bus, anywhere is just 20 minutes away, so where you stay doesn't make a big difference to your options when it comes to visiting the town. La Citée is really lovely and the central pedestrian area in the middle of the city is also nice, as are the streets below the train station, popularly called Sous-Gare.

Day Trips

One of my top must-sees is a village called Saint-Prex just past Morges, 15 – 20 minutes away by train. It's a medieval village by the lake with an old center. Another nice little town (on the other side of Lausanne) is Vevey.

If you want something further out, but fine for a day trip, choose Gruyères. You have the lake, the castle, the Giger Museum, and overpriced (but good) fondue. It's touristy but very typical and nice.

Another option is to head into the countryside around Lausanne. Take the LEB train to Echallen or one of the buses to the more rural areas. In just 15 - 20 minutes, you're really in the countryside.

You can also take the boat (a 40-minute ride) across to Evian or Thonon in France. Evian is the more touristy and Thonon is nicer, in my opinion. Walk around. Have a nice French lunch experience and then come back with the last boat in the evening.

And since Switzerland is so small, you could easily take a day trip to Geneva, as well.

Where to Hike

By Swiss standards, Lausanne is not near the mountains. But the countryside and the forests are great. So if you want to walk, go and hike in the woods north of Lausanne. Start from Le Mont (drive or take bus 22 to the end) and then walk toward Le Bois du Jorat. North of Le Mont, you'll reach a really nice forest full of walking paths. You can walk all the way to Chalet-à-Gobet.

A little closer to Lausanne, the Sauvabelin woods are also nice for a stroll. And there's also a lot of uphill walking in the city itself. Just walking in Lausanne feels like a lot of hiking. You can also walk all the way to Lutryie—an hour or two along the lake.

If you want a real mountain hike, you need to go at least as far as Montreux. From Montreux, take the train up to Caux and walk up to Dent de Jaman. Or, stay on the (quite expensive) train, which goes all the way up to Rochers-de-Naye. You can hike all the way up if you're courageous.

Another nice day hike is the Dent de Vaulion. And for other authentic mountain experiences, I recommend the trails above Bex (the area where I have a little chalet).

What to Eat & Drink
The Vaud specialty is the papet vaudois: a particular type of sausage with cabbage in it (saucisse aux choux) and leek and potatoes cooked together. There's also the malakoff (pieces of cheese battered and fried), boutefas sausage, and tomme cheese. For a savory snack, try the taillé aux greubons (puff pastries made with bacon and apples).

In the dessert department, there's raisinée (thick pear or apple syrup used to make tarts), les beignets des brandons (dough-nuts), and meringues topped with thick Gruyère cream (I promise, it's not cheesy).

Where to Eat & Drink (Favorite Restaurants & Bars)
Coccinelle Café (at Rue Pichard 18) is nice. They are only open for lunch and are great for afternoon tea and a piece of

cake or a nice lunch.

La Bossette (at Place du Nord 4) has really lovely local and fusion food, as well as a huge collection of beers.

Brasserie du Chateau (at Place du Tunnel 1) is another nice one...I like their pizzas a lot. They also brew their own beer (I don't drink beer, but they are famous for it). If you go early— 6:30 or 7 p.m.—it's not too noisy.

Baz'Art (at Avenue de France 38) is good for pizza, pasta, salads, and the plat du jour at lunch.

For something different, try L'Indochine (at Avenue d'Echallens 82) for good Vietnamese food. Also in the international department, I like L'Abyssinia (at Rue du Valentin 14) for Ethiopian food and Le Couscous (at Rue Enning 2) for North African. The secret with Le Couscous is that at the top of the stairs there's a carpet and it's traditional to lift up the carpet and take a voucher on your way in. Give the voucher to the waiter and you'll get two merguez (sausages) as a starter. When you leave, they'll give the voucher back and you replace it under the carpet. Even locals who are unfamiliar with the restaurant miss out on that one.

Finally, in the neighboring town of Morges, don't miss the Balzac Café (at Rue Louis de Savoie 37; phone: +41 21 811 02 32). They only serve at lunchtime and you should definitely book ahead. But the most important thing to know is that their specialty is hot chocolate. Not the powdered stuff but real hot chocolate from all over the world. There are dozens of options to buy and make at home.

Budget Tips

The cathedral is free. And even the climb to the top costs just a couple francs. So that's one really cheap thing to do. Oh, and you should buy a sandwich at a kiosk called Metropole at Place Chauderon. It's doesn't look very exciting, but they have the best sandwiches in town.

GENEVA & SURROUNDS

Another option for budget food is kebabs. These are our version of fast food, a North African equivalent of the burrito. If you're in a hurry for lunch, they are affordable and nice. It's not local food, but it's a local habit here to eat them at lunch. Finally, in the summer, there are three free swimming pools at Valency, Boisy, and Bellevaux. Swimming pools are normally horrendously expensive, so take advantage of the free ones.

How to Fit In
The Swiss take their peace and quiet very seriously. Normally, you aren't supposed to make noise that can be heard outside your apartment between 10 p.m. and 6 a.m. and on Sundays and holidays. If you rent an Airbnb apartment, you need to know that.

Another important thing is to look people in the eye when toasting. Not making eye contact during a toast is very rude. We also say hello, goodbye, thank you, and excuse me a lot. And people don't really like telling you that you're bothering them, so you have to be on the lookout to make sure you're not disturbing someone. If you're in the way, Americans will tell you. Swiss people won't tell you. They'll sit there and fume. And maybe glare at your back. So be conscientious.

Finally, let people get off before you get on trains/buses.

How to Meet Locals & Make Friends
Join some group activities. There are singing groups, dancing groups, sports groups...especially if you're studying here. The university has tons of extracurriculars.

Also, learn the language if you want to settle here. I'm amazed at the people who arrive and think they can get by in English. People here don't really speak English. Do a tandem language exchange to improve your French and meet people. There are also inexpensive classes (of various types) at Ecole Club Migros.

If you are a pub person, we have plenty. The Captain Cook Pub attracts a big expat crowd, as does The Great Escape.

Best Places to Take a Photo

The cathedral and the old market stairs that lead to the cathedral. I'm sure the marketplace on Wednesday and Saturday mornings is great. And by the lake you'll get a good mountain backdrop on a clear day.

If you want a view, go to the Signal de Sauvabelin viewpoint and the tower in the woods above town. You'll get a great 360-degree view from there.

For something quirky, there is a design school in the area that has put together a little group called COFOP (Centre d'Orientation et de Formation Professionnelles). They graffiti the electric boxes in town. Over 100 have been graffitied with people, gorillas, smiley faces—all sorts of weird stuff.

Find Stephanie at eclau.ch and climbtothestars.org.

MORGES
Lakefront promenades, vineyards, & a 13ᵗʰ-century castle.

FIND WI-FI HERE: Balzac coffee shop.

LANGUAGE: French   **CANTON:** Vaud

Yannick Rosset
Traveler. Sports Enthusiast.

About Yannick
Hi everyone...I'm Yannick, a 31-year-old born in Morges, raised in Lausanne, and now returned to Morges for the more affordable rents.

I work as an electrical engineering consultant for plastic industries, which allows me to travel frequently. After traveling so much for work, I fell in love with the idea of travel and quit my job to spend a year on the road in North and Central America. Now, I'm back in Morges but dreaming about a move to Germany to improve my German.

I am passionate about running and sports. I like to enjoy a beer in the bar with friends. And I like comedy and would like to someday perform.

What to Do In Morges (The Basics)
Go to the market (Wednesdays and Saturdays 8 a.m. – 12:30 p.m.) on the main pedestrian street (Grand Rue). Hike or bike along the lake. Attend La Fête des Tulipes tulip festival in Parc de l'Indépendance in the spring (where you'll be awed by a display of 120,000 flowers). In September, check out the free

Paillote music festival. See something at the Théâtre de Beausobre, which is famous in this area and offers a lot of comedy shows. And enjoy the town's view of Mont Blanc from a nice public bench.

Hidden Gems for Seasoned Travelers
Walk or run the Sentiers des Truites pedestrian walkway along a river. Nobody goes there, and it's very beautiful and calm.

In the summertime, go to Preverenges Plage—a nice beach area about 20 minutes to the east on foot. Visit on a weekday (weekends are busy) and rent a paddleboard.

Finally, visit La Foire du Livre (literally "books on the docks"), a literary festival held in September.

Day Trips
Take the train to Lausanne, get a day pass for the boat (CGN), and visit some of the other towns on the lake.

Where to Hike
There are a lot of hiking trails (indicated by the yellow signs) that split off from the Sentiers des Truites (mentioned above). My personal favorites are the trails on the west side of Morges.

For a great day hike, take the Bière–Apples–Morges Railway (BAM) from Morges to Montricher. From there, follow signs for Mont Tendre. It should take two to three hours to get to the top. And your end reward is an amazing view of Mont Blanc and a good fondue from local farm at the top.

Where to Eat & Drink (Favorite Restaurants & Bars)
For wine, go to Linpasse (at Rue des Fossés 55). For a lounge bar, try Alembic (at Rue Louis-de-Savoie 50 et 52). For a typical bar, visit Jameson (at Rue de la Gare 1). For a good restaurant with a little of everything, try the Tennis Club (at Promenade du Petit-Bois 15). For a great lunch, visit Le Mont Blanc (on Quai du Mont-Blanc). And in the summer, check out the outdoor bar La

Paillote (inside the sailing club at Place de la Navigation 1) for beers and burgers.

Budget Tips
At the train station office, you can ask for a special family discount for a day trip on the boat. It'll save you over 50%.

For a cheap, small meal, go to La Tartine (at Rue Centrale 9) and order two big pieces of bread with jam for 4 francs.

How to Fit In
When a car stops to let you cross the street, say thanks to the driver.

Best Places to Take a Photo
My favorites include sunset shots from Preverenges Plage, shots of the lake from the benches at the lakefront, and shots of Mont Blanc from Mont Tendre.

VEVEY

The flower-covered lakeside late-life home of Charlie Chaplin.

FIND WI-FI HERE: Starbucks & La Place du Marcher.

LANGUAGE: French   **CANTON:** Vaud

Rebecca Santos
Wine Lover. Walker.

About Rebecca

I was born in Montreux but now live in Vevey. I work in sales for a wine company called Obrist. In my free time, I like to walk in the mountains and spend time with friends and family. I'm a very active person; I can't stay still too long.

What to Do In Vevey (The Basics)

Everyone should see Lac Léman (Lake Geneva) from above. Les Avants, Caux, and Mont-Pélerin have the best views. You can take the train or hike up to any of those lookout points.

Walking by the lake is also very nice. Everyone should see the famous fork in the lake.

Vevey is where Charlie Chaplin lived, so you can also visit the two new towers in the District of Gillamont (just a 15-minute walk from the center), where his house has been converted into a museum.

Finally, the open-air market (Tuesdays and Saturdays from 8 a.m. to noon) is very nice.

Hidden Gems for Seasoned Travelers

The town is very small and doesn't have many hidden corners,

GENEVA & SURROUNDS

but whenever I want to do something special, I take a walk in the vineyards and find myself a bench to sit on and appreciate the view of the lake.

Where to Stay
For a nice view, stay up on le Mont-Pélerin (though the hotels there are expensive). In Vevey itself, the old town is the best place to stay. It's close to everything, including the lake.

Day Trips
Switzerland is small, so if you have the money, you can take the train and visit everywhere, including Lausanne, Montreux, Geneva, Lucerne, Zürich, and Bern. [Editor's note: Zürich and Lucerne are a bit far for a day trip, so plan to at least stay overnight if you really want to spend time there.]

I also tell people to visit Gruyères. It's a small and cute village just 30 minutes by car (1.5 hours by bus and train) from Vevey. While you're there, visit the cheese and chocolate factories and have a typical Swiss cheese fondue.

Finally, in the winter, you should go somewhere in the mountains to see the snow. And in summer, you should walk in the vineyards at Le Lavaux. (There is a small tourist train there if you don't fancy a walk.)

Where to Hike
When I feel like walking in the mountains, I go to Les Pleiades or Les Paccots, which are not too far away.

What to Eat & Drink
When people come to stay with me, I make them try Lavaux's Chasselas white wine. And for dessert we have a meringue et crème double (a Swiss dessert popular in Gruyères).

Where to Eat & Drink (Favorite Restaurants & Bars)
I enjoy Les Négocians at Rue du Conseil 27, La Bodeguita at

Rue du Lac 35 (for nice Spanish tapas), and Les Trois Sifflets at Rue du Simplon 1 (for typical Swiss food).

As far as bars go, my favorites are Kavo (at Rue Jean-Jacques Rousseau 5), which has an excellent wine selection, Le Ve (on Place de la Gare), which is always full of young people and loud music, The Latino (at Rue de Fribourg 2), which features Latin music and dancing, attracts a 30- to 50-something crowd, and doesn't close till 4 a.m, and Le Deck (on Route de la Corniche in Chexbres), which is a lovely bar with an incredible view of the lake (though it's only open in the summer and closes early).

How to Meet Locals & Make Friends
Couchsurfing.org seems to be the best way to meet people.

Best Places to Take a Photo
Anywhere along the lake, especially at its fork.

Final Notes & Other Tips
We speak French, but a lot of people can speak English (or other languages). I can speak Spanish, English, German, and French, myself. So don't be afraid to approach people and strike up a conversation.

Every 25 years, there is an enormous and famous wine festival called La Fête des Vignerons. If you can make it during that (the next one is in 2019), you're in for something special.

The Montreux Jazz Festival (during the first two weeks of July) is also extremely famous, as is the Christmas market in Montreux during the month of December.

LE CHENIT

Wilderness, watchmaking, & wild, beautiful people.

FIND WI-FI HERE: The tourist information office.

LANGUAGE: French   **CANTON:** Vaud

Jade Rochat
Sports Enthusiast. Nature Lover. Hiker. Traveler.

About Jade

My family name (Rochat) is a typical name in the Vallée de Joux, and our ancestry runs deep here. For 22 years, I lived in the village of Le Solliat, which is part of the municipality. Since then, I've lived in Cheyres (a small village on Lake Neuchâtel), then a small village called Le Lieu back in the valley.

I am an electrician, but in summer of 2014, I quit to pursue an obsession with travel, adventure, scenery, and change.

In my free time, I like to be outdoors—hiking, skiing, biking, running, or climbing. Everything that starts with "extreme" attracts me. I also started doing some photography recently. And when the weather is not favorable for being outdoors, I appreciate talking with friends about hikes or vacation plans over a good cup of tea.

What to Do In Le Chenit (The Basics)

For first-time travelers in La Vallée de Joux, I recommend a visit to a watchmaker and the clock museum, as well as a cheese tasting.

In summer, take advantage of the lake (swimming, water skiing, paddle boating, canoeing, etc.), ramble along on your bike, have a meal in an Alpine restaurant (and try some typical regional cuisine), climb to the top of La Dent de Vaulion, relax in the spa at l'Hotel des Horlogers in Brassus, have a steak at l'Hotel de Ville in Sentier, and visit Jura Parc—an interesting zoo with wolves, bears, bison, horses, and goats. In winter, go skiing in the mountains or ice skating on the lake.

Hidden Gems for Seasoned Travelers

The big tip for savvy travelers coming to La Vallée de Joux is to come in May, June, September, or February, which are the best months for outdoor activities. In May and June, the weather is often better than in July and August. Autumn begins in September, but the Indian summer is also present in February, when the lake is frozen and you can enjoy skiing on long, sunny days.

After a day outdoors in any season, go to the tearoom on the docks in the village of Le Pont. They have excellent tea and pancakes with a beautiful view of the lake.

In the evening, treat yourself to a meal in the restaurant Hotel des Horlogers (at Route de France 8 in the village of Le Brassus; phone: +41 021 845 0845). They have very good food and a charming atmosphere and the hotel has a spa area where guests can relax in a Jacuzzi. Book before you go.

For a beautiful view, go to La Dent de Vaulion by car or on foot (just a one-hour walk from the village of Le Pont).

In September, try the Vacherin Mont d'Or, a winter cheese available starting in mid-September when we celebrate the opening of the season in Les Charbonnières with *désalpe*, an event where you'll find cows coming down the mountains in headdresses, local products, music, and a variety of activities.

Where to Stay

When visiting the French part of Switzerland, I would actually advise you to stay in the vicinity of Lausanne. It's so central (on the lake and just an hour from the Alps and an hour from La Vallée de Joux) and such a beautiful city.

If you want to stay in La Vallée de Joux, try l'Hotel de Ville in Le Sentier, which is the center of the region and close to amenities and shops. And if you want to be in the center of Switzerland itself, stay in Fribourg.

Day Trips

Lausanne is a beautiful city with many museums and an active nightlife right on lovely Lake Geneva. Geneva is big city with a luxury image, a famous fountain on the lake, and a moderate nightlife. Fribourg has a very typical old town, good cheese tasting, chocolate, and a beautiful landscape. The Lavaux Region on the shores of Lake Geneva (between Lausanne and Martigny) is beautiful and covered in vineyards.

The Canton of Valais is nestled against the Alps with every out-door activity you can imagine, as well as many vineyards, ski resorts, thermal baths, and luxury options. In Valais, some of the towns worth visiting include Zermatt, Saas Fee, Gtaad, Crans-Montana, Zinal, Verbier, Leysin, Chateau d'Oex, and Les Diablerets.

If you're interested in a smaller village in the region, I recommend Chatel Saint Denis, which is a heaven for traditional Swiss food and good cheese. In nearby Broc, you'll find the Cailler chocolate factory, as well as some relaxing thermal baths and beautiful views of the Alps and the lake.

Where to Hike

The Dent de Vaulion hike I mentioned above is one not to be missed. And for the more energetic, another beautiful walk is along the Col du Marchairuz pass to Col du Mollendruz. It takes about four or five hours, is rather hilly, and has some great views. There are also restaurants at both the start and finish and a snack shop halfway up if you need some refreshments.

GENEVA & SURROUNDS

Both walks can also be done in winter on skis/snowshoes.

What to Eat & Drink

In addition to the classics, don't miss the chocolate, les meringues crème double (double-cream meringues), cenovis (a salty food paste used in soups), and our good coffee.

Also, we have a lot of vineyards here in Switzerland, so try some of our good wines (Côte, Lavaux, Chablais, etc.). In particular, don't miss the Gamaret Garanoir.

Where to Eat & Drink (Favorite Restaurants & Bars)

My favorite is Le Chalottet, located above the village of Les Charbonnières on the mountain and open only in summer. They do an excellent fondue and les pâtes du chalet (macaroni with Swiss cheese), as well as double cream meringue and gourmet coffee.

My second favorite place is Le Chalottet, the tearoom on the docks at Le Pont, where you'll find wonderful tea and good crepes and pancakes with a view.

My third favorite is the restaurant and wine bar La Maizon (at Chemin des Bruyères 1 in Le Sentier). They have an excellent *menu du jour* (menu of the day), decent prices, a great atmosphere on Thursday and Friday after work, and very good beer. Often, they offer special entertainment.

My fourth favorite is the restaurant at l'Hotel de Ville in Le Sentier. The meat and lake fish there are excellent and one of their specialties is pizza rösti, which I love. For dessert, don't miss the raspberry gratin.

How to Fit In

Switzerland is a very clean country. We recycle and sort our waste. There are bins everywhere, available to everyone. Please never ever leave your waste in nature. This is one of the most disrespectful things you could do here.

How to Meet Locals & Make Friends

The best places to meet people are the restaurants and tea-rooms I mentioned above, as well as the disco bar Nautilus, which is open on the weekends in Le Sentier. There is also a sports center where you can play a multitude of sports, watch hockey games, book massages, eat, and get whatever information you need from the tourist office.

Best Places to Take a Photo

The best photos are from the top of Dent de Vaulion.

Final Notes & Other Tips

La Vallée de Joux is located in the southwestern Jura Mountains in the Canton of Vaud. Situated at an altitude of about 3,000 feet, it includes three lakes (Lac de Joux, Lac Brenet, and Lac Ter).

LEYSIN

Postcard-quality views & quiet getaways.

FIND WI-FI HERE: La Farandole (for a fee) & many restaurants.

LANGUAGE: French　　　　　　　**CANTON:** Vaud

Gadiel Rachelson
Hiker. Skier. Climber. Outdoorsman.

About Gadiel

I'm originally from the San Francisco Bay area and I came to Switzerland for the beautiful surroundings and to work at an international boarding school. I spend my weekends outdoors—hiking, skiing, climbing, on *via ferratas* (self-attaching climbing paths), and pursuing anything else that's challenging and exciting.

What to Do In Leysin (The Basics)

If you find yourself in the mountains in Canton Vaud, consider yourself lucky. This is one of the most quiet, humbling places in the world and you can truly feel the power of the planet.

There are many amazing natural places to explore, but start with the two towers: Tour D'Aï and Tour de Mayen. They are both rock formations accessed by challenging five-hour (each way) day hikes that require perseverance but will change your life. The elevation change is about 3,000 feet.

In winter, the skiing here is a really enjoyable experience, too.

Hidden Gems for Seasoned Travelers

One of my favorite gems in Leysin is the Eagle's Nest hike, which leads to views of Lac Léman and the Prafandaz Chalet.

For a real challenge, we have a *via ferrata* (a self-led mountain climbing path) that takes you up the face of the Tour D'Aï mountain clipped into a long metal rope until you reach the top with an incredible 360-degree view. This is not only for climbers but for any intermediate outdoorspeople. You'll need the right gear, which is rentable in town for about 20 francs.

Day Trips
Skip touristy Montreux and head to Vevey instead. There is great shopping, a cool old town, nice walks on Lac Léman (Lake Geneva), and a killer Saturday farmers market, which becomes a wine festival in the summer. For a fee, you can get a glass and taste many local wines. It's a sweet scene.

Where to Hike
From easy to difficult, these are some of my favorites: 1) Eagle's Nest, 2) Les Fers, 3) Lac du Mayen, and 4) either the Tour D'Aï or the Tour de Mayen (all-day hikes).

Where to Eat & Drink (Favorite Restaurants & Bars)
In Leysin, you must eat at either La Fromagerie on Rue du Village (for the best fondue) or Café Leysin next door (for a more varied upscale dining experience). Up in the village is the Top Pub (on Avenue Secrétan), which has great weekend parties with special themes (Cuban, Norwegian, Gatsby, Mardi Gras) with a special dinner and drink menu.

How to Fit In
In Suisse Romande (the French-speaking part of Switzerland), people expect you to greet them on the streets or in shops with a *bonjour* (good day) or a *bonsoir* (good evening).

Best Places to Take a Photo
We have a lovely view (every day and from everywhere) of the Dents du Midi mountain peaks across the valley, so it is a very photogenic town with a marvelous Alpine backdrop. Anywhere up the mountain, away from the houses and cars, will provide a great photograph.

GRUYÈRES
Home of panoramas & cheese.

FIND WI-FI HERE: McDonald's or the public library.

LANGUAGE: French   **CANTON:** Fribourg

Franck Douard
Hiker. Musician. Skier. Wine & Food Aficionado.

About Franck
I come from the center of France, near Lyon, and now live in Epagny, a little village near Gruyères and Bulle. I work at an engine research center for crane and excavator programming software. In my free time, I like playing piano, skiing, and hiking. I'm also passionate about cars, gastronomy, and wines.

What to Do In Gruyères (The Basics)
First, visit the old town center, which is a medieval village with a big castle. Everything is well preserved and beautiful.

Second, visit the Cailler chocolate factory. It's one of the oldest chocolate factories in the world and is a blast to visit. Plus, the chocolate shop is awesome and not that expensive.

Hidden Gems for Seasoned Travelers
The Moléson, which is 6,500 feet high, is worth seeing. You can hike up (the hike is very beautiful), take the big *via ferrata* (self-attaching climbing route), or take the cable car.

Where to Stay
Le Pâquier is the typical Swiss village, very nice and quiet and with only one hotel.

Day Trips

For something really beautiful, go to the Montbarry Chalet in Le Paquier. It's a stunning chalet and the perfect day trip if you like old Swiss architecture.

In the summer, go for a swim in Lac de la Gruyère (the lake) at Morlon beach.

Where to Hike

In addition to the Moleson, I like the Le Vanil Noir mountain, which requires a higher fitness and experience level. And the paths around the Gorges de la Jogne are perfect for a summer day, with waterfalls everywhere.

What to Eat & Drink

Of course, the gruyère cheese is very famous and very good. Even more typical is the vacherin fribourgeois, which you can eat on its own or in cheese fondue (pro tip: that's the best type of cheese fondue, very creamy and easier to digest, as it isn't made with wine).

The cuchaule (shortbread with saffron) is also typical and you can eat it with the Bénichon mustard.

Where to Eat & Drink (Favorite Restaurants & Bars)

My favorite restaurant is the Fribourgeois (at Place des Alpes 12 in Bulle). They have the best vacherin fondue in the region—truly excellent. Moreover, they have a mechanical music box that plays every hour.

My favorite bar is the Buro (at Rue de la Sionge 29 in Bulle). This is the place to be if you want to meet the local young people. The ambiance is very good and the drinks are affordable.

Budget Tips

The chocolate factory ticket is only 8 francs and you can taste all the chocolate you want. If you want to go out, the Indus Bar (at Grand-Rue 64 in Bulle) is cheap, as is the Mellowcoton Club (at Grand-Rue 30 also in Bulle).

How to Fit In

People here are very polite and like a quiet way of life. Thus, they are not so patient with frenetic behavior. Be respectful, quiet, and, above all, clean.

How to Meet Locals & Make Friends

Go out, play sports, and attend events.

Best Places to Take a Photo

At the top of the Moleson on the panoramic terrace.

Final Notes & Other Tips

Do not visit the La Maison du Gruyère in Pringy. It's expensive, not interesting, and kitschy.

NEUCHÂTEL
A small, easygoing community with outdoor activities for all.

FIND WI-FI HERE: McDonald's & most pubs or restaurants.

LANGUAGE: French   **CANTON:** Neuchâtel

Florence Vehier
Speech Therapist. Hiker. Photographer.

About Florence
I'm French, 42 years old, and have lived in Switzerland since 1997. I taught in Vaud for four years, then moved to Neuchâtel to study and then work as a speech and language therapist. In my free time, I like to meet up with friends for dinner, go to the cinema, hike, snowshoe, swim, skate, and dabble in photography. I'm also an avid traveler and diver.

What to Do In Neuchâtel (The Basics)
Go to the Vue des Alpes (a nearby high mountain pass) for a perfect view over the Alps, weather permitting. I like snowshoeing up there, too, and eating a fondue.

After that, take a tour through town to admire the interesting and area-specific architecture.

And finally, if you're fond of theater, we have three or four of them in town. Check out the programs. There's always something interesting going on.

Hidden Gems for Seasoned Travelers
You can take a cruise on Lake Neuchâtel over lunch. You can cruise from Lake Neuchâtel to Lac de Morat (Murten Lake) or

NORTHWESTERN SWITZERLAND

Lac de Bienne (Biel Lake) on the connecting rivers. Or you can rent a bike for free at the port, bring it on the boat, cruise the lake, get off in Cudredin or Portalban, have a cycling tour, then come back with the next boat.

Day Trips
I always take visiting friends to Gruyère to visit the medieval village and the chocolate factory (Cailler) in Broc (choco-emotions.ch), to Montreux with its nice view of Lac Léman, and to Bern, which is the capital and is bursting with typical Swiss architecture.

What to Eat & Drink
There's a wide variety of traditional fondue served at the La Pinte de Pierre-à-Bot (at Route de Pierre-à-Bot 106). You can also try jambon à l'asphalte (yes, ham cooked—quite literally—in asphalt) from the Mine d'Asphalte in the Val de Travers. As for drinks, the region is famous for absinthe.

Where to Eat & Drink (Favorite Restaurants & Bars)
Café l'Aubier (at the bottom of Rue du Chateau in Neuchâtel or at Les Murailles 5 in Montézillon), Café du Concert (at Rue de l'Hôtel-de-Ville 4), and the Wodey Suchard choclaterie (at Rue du Seyon 5) are three favorites.

Budget Tips
Restaurant Max et Meuron and many other local restaurants have a special lunch menu under 20 francs. Some restaurants have student pricing if you're a younger traveler (including Le Bleu Café at Faubourg du Lac 27). And there are lots of kebab take-aways and crêperies, which are a bit cheaper.

How to Fit In
The Swiss always wait for the walk signal before crossing the road. Always. They never cross outside the crossing. And they definitely don't litter on the streets.

How to Meet Locals & Make Friends
You can make friends with other travelers and expats in Café

du Cerf, but to make friends with locals, you have to live here and do theater or belong to a music or sport association.

Best Places to Take a Photo
By the lake, for sure, and on the Vue des Alpes.

Alicja Wytrzymaly
Traveler. Expat.

About Alicja
I am Polish but have been living in Neuchâtel for about five years now. I'm an office assistant at a gaming company and I spend my free time traveling or hanging out with friends.

What to Do In Neuchâtel (The Basics)
When I'm showing someone around, I use Neuchâtel as a base and take people to the surrounding towns of Gruyère, Montreux, and Bern. Gruyère is, of course, well known for cheese and chocolate, Montreux for festivals, Charlie Chaplin, and Freddie Mercury, and Bern as the capitol and one of the most important cities in Switzerland.

In Neuchâtel itself, you must visit the castle and old prison tower (which has a sweeping view of the lake and town), the Latenium archeological museum (fancy and interesting!), and the art and history museum (entrance is free on Wednesdays).

Hidden Gems for Seasoned Travelers
If you love to hike, check out Creux du Van—a nearby natural rocky cirque—and Chasseral—a mountain overlooking Lake Biel. Both are amazing.

Where to Stay
Personally, I prefer the town of Auvernier, which is nearby and offers easy access to Neuchâtel itself.

NORTHWESTERN SWITZERLAND

Day Trips
Start with Bern, Gruyères, and Montreux. Bern has a lovely old town, mini bear zoo, and Albert Einstein's house and museum. In Gruyères—the chocolate and cheese capitol—you absolutely must take a chocolate tour at the Callier factory and a cheese tour at one of the cheese factories. Then have a fondue in one of the tiny restaurants in the center. And Montreux is home of the beautiful Chateau Chillon and Freddie Mercury's memorial.

I also always take visitors to Auvernier. It's so pretty there every season of the year.

Once you've hit those favorites, try Geneva (bursting with cultural activities, fine art, modern art, lovely gardens like Jardin Anglais, and, of course, the gorgeous lakefront with its big fountain), Lausanne (with its lovely lakeside, international environment, and lively clubs and concerts), and Chasseral (with its breathtaking views and excellent hiking and biking).

Finally, the town of Boudry has an awesome castle, which often offers cheese and wine tastings. And for these who want sweeping views without hiking or climbing, Chaumont hill is a great choice.

Where to Hike
Mount Chasseral has some excellent trails, Creux du Van (mentioned above) is fascinating, and Pierre-a-Bot forest is a wonderful place to stroll.

What to Eat & Drink
Well, you simply have to try our absinthe. There is an absinthe house in Motiers (*maison-absinthe.ch*) and it's a must-see.

Where to Eat & Drink (Favorite Restaurants & Bars)
For drinks and nice chat in English, try Cafe du Cerf (at Ancien Hôtel de Ville 4). For 27 types of fondue in a nice atmosphere, try Pinte de Pierre-a-Bot (at Pierre-à-Bot 106). And every visitor should go to Les Brasseurs (at Faubourg du Lac 1). Try their

221

famous flammenkuchen (thin bread with toppings), but don't drink their beer.

How to Fit In

The Swiss are very polite. Make sure to say good morning when you enter a shop and goodbye when you leave.

Best Places to Take a Photo

In Neuchâtel, the best shots are at Place des Halles (the heart of old town), at the port, and from Chaumont and Auvernier.

BIEL/BIENNE
Switzerland's largest bilingual city.

FIND WI-FI HERE: Starbucks, Migros, Coop, & McDonald's.

LANGUAGE: German & French   **CANTON:** Bern

[Editor's note: Biel is the German name for this bilingual town. Bienne is the French.]

Chrissie S.
Guide. Fitness Enthusiast. Reader. Traveler.

About Chrissie
I work part time as a guide, though my main occupation is in administration. I'm 49 years young. I was born in Biel/Bienne, grew up in a village of 600 inhabitants between Aarberg and Ins in the Seeland (lake-land), and have lived in Biel/Bienne for over 16 years. My hobbies include aerobics, zumba, fitness, reading, traveling, cinema/theatre, skiing, and shopping.

What to Do In Biel/Bienne (The Basics)
In any season, start with a guided tour of Biel's old town. In the summertime, take the funicular to Magglingen and hike from Magglingen through the Twannbach Gorge (via Twannberg). From there, take a stroll through the wonderful wine-growing villages of Twann and/or Ligerz and catch a boat back to Biel.

If you have more time, rent a bicycle and ride along the south shore of Lake Biel from Nidau to Erlach to St. Peter's Island (a nature reserve), where Jean-Jacques Rousseau spent some time here in 1765. You can load your bike on the boat and taste the local wine on your cruise back to Biel.

Hidden Gems for Seasoned Travelers
Visit Solothurn (a beautiful baroque town) and take a cruise on the Aare River from Solothurn to Biel. If you're in a small group, attend a glassblowing workshop at the Glasbläserei-Atelier-Restaurant Twannbachschlucht (*glas-atelier.ch*).

Explore the Jura Mountains, the Three Lakes region's small, historic towns, and Switzerland's largest vegetable garden (Das Grosse Moos), which you can bike through near Murten.

Day Trips
Erlach is a small, historic town with a nice view of the lake and St. Peter's Island from its Castle Hill. It's an ideal starting point for an excursion on the lake and/or to the island.

Büren an der Aare is also a small, historic town, situated on the Aare River. It's a great place for hiking and biking.

Murten is a historic town (where the Battle of Murten took place) on Lake Murten with nice ramparts and museums.

Solothurn is Switzerland's most beautiful baroque town—a gem, really. And the Jura Mountains and La Grande Cariçaie nature reserve (near Yverdon-les-Baines) are must-sees.

What to Eat & Drink
Taste the excellent wine and local fish from the Lake Biel area, Twann, Ligerz, and Murten, the nidlechueche (cream pie) in and around Murten, and, in the wintertime, the treberwurst sausage (a local specialty) in Twann or Ligerz.

Where to Eat & Drink (Favorite Restaurants & Bars)
Try Hotel Villa Lindenegg (at Lindenegg 5) and Opera Prima (at Jakob-Stämpfli-Strasse 2) in Biel/Bienne, La Péniche (at Schlossstrasse 25) in Nidau, and Kloster Hotel und Restaurant St. Petersinsel (at Heidenweg 26 on St. Peter's Island).

Budget Tips
Stay at the Lago Lodge hostel in Nidau.

Best Places to Take a Photo
The best shots are Biel's old town or the wine-growing villages.

Final Notes & Other Tips
Don't hesitate to contact the local tourist office for more information: *biel-seeland.ch*.

FRIBOURG
Gastronomy, culture, & beautiful bridges.

FIND WI-FI HERE: Café le Mondial & the old station.

LANGUAGE: French   **CANTON:** Fribourg

Pascal Jenny
Professor. Humanitarian. Outdoors Enthusiast.

About Pascal
Hello everyone! My name is Pascal Jenny and I have lived in Fribourg my whole life. I have two professions: I am a professor at the vocational trade school in Fribourg and I am responsible for administration of a social organization that cares for the homeless in Geneva. In my free time, I play a lot of sports, I often go to the mountains, and I love to travel.

What to Do In Fribourg
To appreciate the beauty of Fribourg, you have to take it all in from the top of the tower at St. Nicolas Cathedral or from the heights of Loreto Chapel (accessible by a small tourist train). This unforgettable look at a medieval architectural ensemble has survived modernity. Founded in 1157 by Duke Berthold IV of Zähringen, Fribourg is now a young university town and a popular place to meet.

Once you've seen Fribourg from above, I recommend a walking tour of the city. Here's my ideal itinerary: Start at Place de Notre Dame and walk to the cathedral, then walk through the old city following this route: Grand-Rue - Gold Street – Pont de Bern - Place Petit St-Jean – Pont du Milleu - Planche Inférieure –

Planche Supérieure – Pont St-Jean – Court-Chemin. Finally, return to Place de Notre Dame.

If you love nature, I propose a boat ride at Vallée du Gottéron (a tributary of the Sarine River).

Finally, consider a walk across the Pont de Bern toward the pretty Gottéron Gorges. The gorge area's bridges and sturdy wooden steps make access easy.

Where to Hike
Schwarzsee is an absolute must-see for nature-lovers, families, or sporty types. Located about 18 miles from Fribourg and about 3,500 feet above sea level, it's in the middle of impressive mountains and features an idyllic lake.

What to Eat & Drink
Our specialties include chocolates from Callier and Villars, le gateau de vully (cream cake), and cuchaule (sweet dessert bread).

Where to Eat & Drink (Favorite Restaurants & Bars)
Fribourg is well known for excellent cuisine at reasonable prices. It is impossible for me to limit myself to three, but here are my favorites: Hôtel de Ville (at Grande Rue 6; phone: +41 26 321 2367), which has good prices and is often full; Café Mondial (at Rue de l'Hôspital 39), which has a simple interior and good food; Restaurant Zum Brennenden Herz (at Im Dorf 24 in Rechthalten), which is just 10 minutes from Fribourg; Auberge Aux 4 Vents (at Route de Grandfey 124 in Granges-Paccot), which has beautiful gardens; the Chez Mon Cousin kebab shop; Crazy Horse (at Rue de l'Hôpital 39) for burgers; Le Gothard (at Rue du Pont-Muré 16), which is the most authentic local restaurant; and Le Trois Canards (at Chemin du Gottéron 102), which is located in an idyllic setting at the entrance of the Gotteron Valley.

As for bars and nice places to drink, Cafe Villars is a small cafe located in the factory where Villars Chocolate is produced.

Not only can you drink coffee for just 2.50 francs in a beautiful setting, but you can also buy chocolate produced on site. Auberge Aux 4 Vents (mentioned above) is also a nice place for a drink. Café du Belvédère (at Grand-Rue 36) has a beautiful terrace. And the café at L'Ancienne Gare (at Gare 3) is excellent as well.

Budget Tips
Food-wise, you won't find anything cheaper than Idées Crétoise (a Greek restaurant at Boulevard de Pérolles 30, where the average price is 12 francs), Café le Mondial (mentioned above), and Les Cantines des Universités (at Boulevard Pérolles 95),

Best Places to Take a Photo
Go to the Loretto Chapel. Once there, you will be overcome by the sight of the old town and the Pont de la Poya bridge.

MOUTIER
Home of deep ravines, rolling fields, & very little tourism.

FIND WI-FI HERE: Migros.

LANGUAGE: French   **CANTON:** Bern

Allison Zurfluh
Writer. Translator. Traveler. Runner. Reader.

About Allison
Born and bred in Hollywood, I spent my childhood in the Los Angeles basin before moving to Chicago, spending half a year in Seville, Spain, and then settling in Switzerland about 21 years ago. I've been a translator for the French-English language pair for the past 20 years, as well as a journalist and writer. In my free time, I enjoy early and classical music, running, reading, knitting, and time with my family. I like to travel and do so about twice monthly.

What to Do In Moutier (The Basics)
We live in a very rural part of the country, in the heart of Watch Valley, in a town of about 7,000 called Moutier. The natural, outdoor offerings are really what set the area apart. However, this is also where décolletage—the process of producing precision-machined parts for the watchmaking industry, as well as for the fields of medicine and aviation—was born.

Here, a tour of Omega S.A.'s museum in Bienne is a great start, followed by a visit to the International Museum of Horology in La Chaux-de-Fonds.

Hidden Gems for Seasoned Travelers

Start with a walk around the Etang de Gruère near Saigne-légier, a town that also hosts a prestigious international horse-racing competition in August, and a visit to the medieval town of Saint-Ursanne (possibly taking in a concert during the Piano Festival in August or the Festival du Jura in September).

Moutier has the highest concentration of dinosaur tracks in the world and a wonderful festival called Stand d'Eté, held in June and July, which takes place at an old shooting range and includes an opera performance, as well as jazz and classical concerts.

Hang-gliding is a popular sport and reservations can be made for tandem flights across the splendid Jura Mountain range.

Where to Stay

Moutier has one great B&B (Prévôtoit B&B) for nature lovers who like sterling accommodation (*prevotoit.ch*). Otherwise, this area is ideal for agritourism, staying on farms and enjoying locally-made organic food.

Where to Hike

The Etang de la Gruère I mentioned is fabulous for hiking, with a path that circles a pond and nature sanctuary. In summer, wild blueberry picking complements a swim across the pond and it's nice to stop to roast a sausage and have a bottle of wine. In winter, rolling hills with pine trees set the backdrop for sled dog races, cross country skiing, and snowshoeing and you can hire a horse-drawn sleigh for a dash across the fields.

Fairytale-looking gorges and ravines are typical in this rock-climbing paradise. Natural trails through the Pichoux, Perrefitte, Moutier, and Court gorges are idyllic.

What to Eat & Drink

The local schnapps is made of damson plum (called damassine) and many people press their apple juice locally. The St.

Martin's Feast is a typical Jura celebration for anyone with a taste for pork.

Where to Eat & Drink (Favorite Restaurants & Bars)

My top pick is Relais des Chasseurs in Les Ecorcheresses. I stumbled upon this farm-turned-restaurant on Valentine's Day, when, incidentally, it is always fully booked. Homegrown food is shaped into handcrafted gastronomy and served to classical music and candlelight that feels 200 years old. Organic and crusty, the chef appears as a rural Captain Jack Sparrow (he doesn't know I think that). This is a hidden gem for people looking for something local and tourist-free.

Budget Tips

Visit the Tête de Moine cheese-making establishments in the Jura Mountains, where monks at Bellelay Abbey started making their Monk's Head cheese eight centuries ago. The abbey is wonderful to see at no cost.

How to Meet Locals & Make Friends

Bars and pubs are a good gathering place in this area. Town fairs and expositions tend to bring people together and a vernissage (art exhibition) is always the talk of the town. Hikers are always friendly and you might meet a lifelong friend just by asking a few questions and walking a few steps together.

Most importantly, in this area it is important to listen, observe, and be interested in the way locals do things. Many foreigners will try to share interesting facts about their own countries and cultures, which really ends up undermining the relationship. When you're in someone else's country, be there with your head, too. Not back in your own world. If they want to know about your country, they will go there or ask you.

Best Places to Take a Photo

Saint-Ursanne on the river Doubs! It's a medieval paradise nestled between luscious mountains that keep it completely hidden and off the beaten track. The Christmas market is delightful, with hand-knit socks at about 15 francs a pair. In the summer months, bike there or rent a canoe.

Even more photo worthy is Weissenstein Mountain, which has a brand new ski lift. Visit the 1:1 billion-scale model of our solar system that spans the Jura Mountain range.

Also, hike up to Le Tour de Moron for a breathtaking panoramic view of Jura/Jura Bernois. You can see all the way to France!

Find Allison at allisonzurfluh.com.

PORRENTRUY
Authenticity, charm, & simplicity.

FIND WI-FI HERE: Many restaurants & public establishments.

LANGUAGE: French & German   **CANTON:** Jura

Jean-Carlo Zornio
Pub Owner. Mountain Biker. Skier. Gamer.

About Jean-Carlo
A native of Delémont (the canton's capitol), I now live in Porrentruy, where I own a pub called Brasserie-Pub Au Faucon. Hobbies include mountain biking, video games, card games, tennis, pétanque (a popular French game), skiing, and travel.

What to Do In Porrentruy (The Basics)
The city (and I use the word city loosely) of Porrentruy is very small but very charming. For first-time visitors, the best place to start is the Secret Circuit—a self-guided tour with a key card that gives you access to various secret spots that were previously not open to tourists. These include the castle, La Tour Réfous tower, and the ancient town dungeons.

Porrentruy is the capital of the Jura region called Ajoie, which is known for the discovery of traces of dinosaurs. As a result, it's a town full of museums and sites for dino-lovers (jurassica.ch).

Hidden Gems for Seasoned Travelers
The area is a paradise for mountain bikers, trail riders (on horseback), and hikers. The trails are well marked and well preserved. My personal favorite routes are Roche-d'Or (for views of the area and into neighboring France) and the walk from

233

Porrentruy to Saint-Ursanne, a medieval town on the Doubs River.

Another wonderful little natural place is l'Etang de la Gruère—a small, beautiful lake in a protected natural reserve.

As for events, the November Feast of St. Martin here in town is not to be missed.

Day Trips
The best places to explore nearby are medieval Saint-Ursanne, the Caves of Réclère, and the town of Saignelégier and its surrounding region.

What to Eat & Drink
Local specialties are traditional peasant dishes, including tête de veau (cow brains), les pieds de porcs (pigs' feet), and potatoes in many forms.

Where to Eat & Drink (Favorite Restaurants & Bars)
Les Deux-Clefs (at Rue des Malvoisins 7; phone: +41 32 466 1831), Le Château (at Le Chateau 18 in Pleujouse; phone: +41 32 462 1080), and Chez Wenger (at Rue de la Gare 2 in Noirmont; phone: +41 32 957 6633) are my favorites.

As for bars, in addition to my own, Chez Steph (at Grand-Rue 1) and Pépin (at Rue des Malvoisins 11) are also excellent.

Find Jean-Carlo at le-faucon.com.

SAINT-URSANNE

A local-loved hub of nature, serenity, & medieval architecture.

FIND WI-FI HERE: The town center & tourist office.

LANGUAGE: French   **CANTON:** Jura

Michel Marchand
Artist. Family Man.

About Michel

I am from Delémont but have lived in Saint-Ursanne since 1984. I am an artist (painter, sculptor) and that is, above all, my passion. Any time I'm not with my art is spent with my family. I love cooking and I often daydream by the Doubs River.

What to Do In Saint-Ursanne (The Basics)

First, soak up the place by strolling through the streets, visiting the church and its cloister, and, finally, walking over Le Pont Saint-Jean—the old stone bridge over the river.

Hidden Gems for Seasoned Travelers

One special gem is the crypt in the heart of the church in the forest above the Ermitage (chapel) where St. Ursanne once lived in a cave. Another is the platform (formerly a castle) overlooking the city, which you can reach by following a path up from the chapel. The view there will take your breath away.

And for a truly authentic experience of the area, go to the top of the hill via the Fin du Teck walking path (near Epauvillers) and follow it up into the mountains where you can see the looping River Doubs. In good weather, you can see the French

235

NORTHWESTERN SWITZERLAND

Vosges Mountains in the north and the Swiss Alps in the south.

Day Trips
Head to Soubey and visit its church, with its beautiful modern art-style stained glass by the artist, Coghuf. Then walk back along the banks of the Doubs to Saint-Ursanne, making a stop at Tariche for some trout (a local specialty) on the restaurant's terrace. It's simply divine.

Where to Hike
The Les 66 du Doubs trail (41 miles) along the Doubs and through the mountains is a great introduction to the region. The route is well marked and dotted with restaurants and hotels. It's also possible to sleep in a barn and eat with a peasant family for a change of scenery.

What to Eat & Drink
To eat like a local, try our trout with local herbs. Then taste the Tête de Moine AOP—a local semi-hard cheese that melts in your mouth. And you absolutely must try the incomparable cochonnaille (pork) from the feast of St. Martin. Finally, the tiny damassine plums are made into a brandy that is very typical and important to the region (and not made anywhere else).

Where to Eat & Drink (Favorite Restaurants & Bars)
My favorites are Restaurant Clairbief (at Clairbief 85 in Soubey; phone: +41 32 955 1220) for its trout, l'Auberge de la Fontaine (at Grand Rue 10 in Seleute; phone: +41 32 461 3030) for its wild game and morel sauce, and l'Hôtel-Restaurant de la Couronne (at Rue du Vingt-Trois Juin 3; phone: +41 32 461 3567) for fine dining.

Budget Tips
Chez le Baron in Epauvillers is a good family restaurant with hearty, affordable food made from local farm products.

How to Fit In

Always wish people good morning/good day/good night. This is so important to us.

How to Meet Locals & Make Friends

Stop in one of the city taverns or play pétanque (boules) under the lime trees in front of the church.

Best Places to Take a Photo

The best photo opportunities are from the old castle platform (above the city), the bridge, and the Fin du Teck (Epauvillers).

Find Michel at michelmarchand.com.

YVERDON-LES-BAINS

A haven of protected natural areas, water sports, & spas.

FIND WI-FI HERE: The tourist office & Pestalozzi Square.

LANGUAGE: French   **CANTON:** Vaud

Dominique Faesch
Tourism Director. Avid Traveler. Former Tour Guide.

About Dominique

I am currently the regional director (in charge of tourism and economic development) for seven tourist offices for the Yverdon-les-Bains region.

I was born in Orbe, a small city where my family ran a very successful brewery. So perhaps it was escaping from a predictable future that led me to develop ties and an attraction to foreign cultures. Whatever the reason, I was on the road at 18 as a tour director and guide for an international travel company. Extended stays in Sri Lanka, India, Thailand, Greece, Spain, the USSR, the USA, Brazil, and Canada gave me the opportunity to discover some of the beauties of this planet and to learn about foreign cultures, as well as my own fellow citizens and myself.

I have an MBA from the University of Sherbrooke in Canada, as well as a diploma from the Lausanne Hotel School. I have worked abroad and in Switzerland for companies such as the Lausanne Hotel School, Crowne Plaza, and Hyatt Hotels.

What to Do In Yverdon-les-Bains (The Basics)

Yverdon-les-Bains is famous for its thermal baths. The healing waters come out of the spring at over 86° (Fahrenheit) and are then cooled so you can swim in the indoor and outdoor swimming pools. In the winter, when it's snowing, it is a particularly unforgettable experience. A hydrotherapy session gives you an immediate feeling of well-being. In the summer, tourists can swim at the Thermal Centre, the municipal swimming pools (indoor and outdoor), and a magnificent beach on the shores of Lake Neuchâtel.

Yverdon's history dates back to the Neolithic age and the 45 dolmens (single-chamber megalithic tombs) at Clendy, not far from the lake, are an impressive testimony to the lake's history. At the Musée d'Yverdon et Région (Yverdon region museum) in the town center, you can explore the ages and the area's successive inhabitants—the Celts, Romans, Savoyards (who built Yverdon Castle), Bernese governors, etc.

The 18th century saw the construction of some wonderful buildings and they still stand today in the pedestrianized old town and Pestalozzi Square, which has a statue of the great pedagogue who lived in Yverdon for many decades.

Meanwhile, at the castle, you'll find not only the above-mentioned museum but also the Pestalozzi Research Center and the Swiss Fashion Museum. Another peculiarity of Yverdon-les-Bains is its Museum of Science Fiction, a unique institution in Europe, which holds a number of permanent and temporary exhibits on subjects related to the philosophical and cinematographic literary movement that is science fiction.

In between museums in the spring, soak up the atmosphere at the cafés and terraces on Pestalozzi Square surrounded by majestic historic buildings. Then stroll through old town and explore the boutiques, where you can buy unique crafts.

Hidden Gems for Seasoned Travelers

The Centre d'Art Contemporain (contemporary art center) is housed in the historic town hall building and has unusual temporary exhibitions that brim with ideas, forms, sounds, and color. The cultural program here also extends to three theatres:

Benno Besson, Echandole (located in the castle cellars), and the Petit Globe (on the banks of the lake in the summer months).

For visitors who want to try our farm produce and regional specialties, La Ferme (at Rue de la Plaine 15) is a unique shop concept, allowing you to stock up every day as if you were at the market, as well as offering a range of produce and regional wines. The weekly markets held in the old town from 8 a.m. to noon on Tuesdays and Saturdays also allow you to experience local and regional life through a wonderful selection of farm produce.

I also recommend a walk by the lake and along the banks of the Thiele, where sailing boats and small vessels are moored. Continue past the port to the Iris quarter where, with an unobstructed view of Lake Neuchâtel, lucky residents spend the summer in colorful wooden cabins.

Day Trips

On the French border, the city of Vallorbe is an important part of the region. It is known as the iron city because iron mineral has always been processed there, thanks to the River Orbe and the paddle mills on its banks (seven of those paddle mills are still in operation and its product can be seen at the Iron and Railway Museum where blacksmiths produce some beautiful handicraft pieces). The museum recounts not only the history of iron and the craft that made the region wealthy but also the history and structure of the railway, with a room dedicated to miniature train circuits (a big hit with children).

The famous Vallorbe Caves attract 60,000 visitors each year. The caves cover approximately 2.5 miles, with many galleries (formed over millions of years) and extraordinary concretions, which are illuminated to showcase their contours. The river is still active and in some places you can see the turbulent waters filling the caves. The path ends in a hall that is 260 feet high and more than 300 feet underground, rightly called "The Cathedral," where a sound and light show is held.

NORTHWESTERN SWITZERLAND

In Vallorbe, you can also visit a fortress (Fort Pré Giroud) that guarded the Swiss border in the last war. Under a chalet that acts as a decoy, a lift takes visitors more than 150 feet underground. The galleries, observation post, cannon casemates, dormitory, kitchen, and infirmary housed some 100 soldiers for long months and guides passionate about military history are available to show you around.

Not far from Vallorbe, Romainmôtier, a town of 500 inhabitants, nestles in a small valley that is wonderful for walks and is home to the oldest abbey in French-speaking Switzerland. This church dates back to the 6th century and formed part of the Cluny network, the first and most important of the European monastic networks (with approximately 1,400 sites in all of Europe), which had its center at Cluny Abbey in France. The Romainmôtier Abbey, the prior's house, and a number of other historic houses exude a unique atmosphere in a location steeped in history. It is definitely worth a visit. On Saturdays, you will often spot a happy wedding procession and on Sundays there are church services, as well as a magnificent concert program.

15 minutes from Romainmôtier, the small town of Orbe (where I grew up) is worth spending a few hours in. Following the footsteps drawn on the pavement and the itinerary and map provided by the tourist office, visitors will pass the castle esplanade (with a magnificent view from the round tower across the plain to the Alps) and walk along the ramparts. Orbe is also the departure point for an unforgettable hike through the Orbe Gorge. However, the most important jewel is, without doubt, the Boscéaz Mozaics on the way out of town. The protected mosaics, which offer insight into Roman Helvetia, belong to a vast Roman villa open to the public.

Grandson, 10 minutes from Yverdon-les-Bains, has one of the most beautiful castles in Switzerland. Built in the 13th century, it stands above Lake Neuchâtel and has a breathtaking view from its towers and esplanade. The castle houses numerous collections that describe the battles that led to the partitioning of today's Europe. It also houses the Museum of Vintage Cars, as well as an impressive collection of crossbows.

NORTHWESTERN SWITZERLAND

In Grandson, the Maison des Terroirs is a magnificent showcase for wines from the Bonvillars region, along with other regional products.

For magnificent panoramic views of the Alps and the Jura Mountains, take a 45-minute ride on the small mountain train from Yverdon-les-Bains up to Sainte-Croix/Les Rasses. Or, for another natural experience, take the train toward the Grande Cariçaie wetland. You'll pass a magnificent manor house (now turned into a natural history museum) at Champ-Pittet and arrive in Yvonand, a small village surrounded by pine forests and famous for its beaches. In the summer, the edge of the lake has a holiday atmosphere, with numerous chalets, camp-sites, and lake activities.

In Sainte-Croix, four museums trace the village's history of music boxes and automated machines. At the Baud, CIMA, and MAS museums you can admire an automated poet (a real character), an orchestrion (a machine that plays music like an orchestra), and a wonderful collection of valuable music boxes. Opposite CIMA, you can pre-book and visit Dr. Wyss's music box collection, housed in a reconstructed 19th-century workshop. If you consider that art mechanics were the starting point for clock mechanics, the guided visit of this old workshop is a real discovery, particularly since each one of these machines can be activated and is explained by an enthu-siastic guide.

From Sainte-Croix, there are a number of hikes in the Jura. You can walk back down to Yverdon through the Covatannaz Gorge or enjoy some specialties in one of the numerous moun-tain chalets, still often used for summer grazing pastures. In the winter, a few miles from Sainte-Croix is Les Rasses, a high-quality ski area (at 4,000 – 5,000 feet) with downhill skiing, cross-country skiing, ski touring, snowshoes, sledding, etc.

Where to Hike
With its location next to the Jura and on the edge of Lake Neu-

châtel, this former trade hub is crossed by several historic routes, beginning with the Via Romana, the Via Francigena (known as the Grand Cultural Route of the European Council and used today by pilgrims travelling from Canterbury to Rome), the Via Salina (the salt route, where precious mineral was transported from the Royal Saltworks at Arc-et-Senans in France to Bern, the Swiss capital), and the Route of the Huguenots, Cluniacs, and Pedagogues. All these routes offer countless possibilities for hikes or cycling tours and most are well marked on the highly sophisticated Swiss Mobile system (*swissmobile.ch*), which allows you to plan your route at leisure.

The seven walks from Vaulion, seven from Romainmôtier, a path that crisscrosses the French/Swiss border, the Fritzo walk through the Bonvillars vineyards, Covatannaz Gorge, Orbe Gorge, a climb of Mount Chasseron (5,000+ feet), or Mount Suchet are also some of the most beautiful walks in the region. In the winter, snowshoe trails that start in Les Rasses provide unforgettable experiences.

What to Eat & Drink

Most restaurants serve filets of perch or houting (two lake fish). Gateau au vin cuit (literally "cooked wine cake," it's a sort of molasses made with slow-cooked autumn fruit) and almond and honey tarts are also some of our specialties. Some restaurants use our regional truffle (the Burgundy truffle), which can also be bought at the Bonvillars Truffle Market (held once a year in October). And, of course, you must try the wines: Bonvillars and Côtes de l'Orbe (Chasselas, Chardonnay, Garanoir, etc.). Small vineyards produce specialties you can buy from them directly or from the Grandson Maison des Terroirs.

Where to Eat & Drink (Favorite Restaurants & Bars)

The Yverdon-les-Bains region has nine restaurants that have received Gault Millau awards, 31 mountain chalets, and countless other charming restaurants. My favorites are La Vieille Auberge (at Route Romaine 2 in Valeyres-sous-Rances) for its truffles, La Table de Mary (at Route du Gymnase 2) in Yverdon for its inventiveness, and the Casbah, a very typical mountain chalet in Sainte-Croix, for its candlelit fondue.

Budget Tips

In Yverdon-les-Bains, the Double-R (at Rue du Collège 4) makes delicious and very reasonably priced homemade hamburgers. In the summer, you can enjoy wonderful dishes at Le Ranch (on Chemin des Bosquets in Yverdon), Restaurant Le Colvert (Avenue des Pins 34 in Yvon), and the swimming pool in Orbe.

Vallorbe Casino (at Place du Pont 3) serves delicious and affordable menus and the Restaurant Jura (at Rue du Jura 19 in Sainte-Croix) has a very cozy traditional atmosphere with unbeatable prices.

How to Fit In

Be cordial. Greet people and thank them. Respect the peace and quiet. Noisy people do not go over well in Switzerland.

How to Meet Locals & Make Friends

The locals are very friendly and helpful but are often shy, especially if they cannot speak a foreign language. That said, the region's inhabitants often speak or understand English or German and even Italian or Spanish. Since the cafés and restaurants are very popular, you can strike up a conversation with someone in one of these places. The Yverdon-les-Bains region is also lucky to have many small businesses in its town centers and villages, which are usually run by the owner. These are great places to strike up a conversation and get per-sonalized recommendations.

Best Places to Take a Photo

In good weather, the following spots have an extraordinary view of the landscape, the three lakes, the Alpine mountain range, and a good section of the French Jura: Hôtel du Chasseron (on Mount Chasseron), the terrace at Grand Hôtel des Rasses, Grandson Castle's esplanade and ramparts, the Le

Suchet mountain chalet, Orbe Castle's esplanade and round tower, and Auges mountain chalet above Romainmôtier.

Final Notes & Other Tips

The Fête EAU-Lac (Lake-Water Festival) in Yverdon-les-Bains at the end of June, the Mediaeval Festival at Grandson Castle at the end of August, the Terroir without Borders Festival in Sainte-Croix at the end of August, the Autumn Fair and Cowbell Market in Romainmôtier in the middle of October, the Truffle Market in Bonvillars at the end of October, and the LaMara cross-country skiing race at Les Rasses at the beginning of March are all events not to be missed.

Finally, ask the tourist office about truffle hunts in the region.

Find Dominique at yverdonlesbainsregion.ch.

LA CHAUX-DE-FONDS
Landscape, friendly people, & the world's best watch museum.

FIND WI-FI HERE: Hotels, trains, shopping centers, & restaurants.

LANGUAGE: French   **CANTON:** Neuchâtel

Wolfgang Carrier
Architecture & Art Guide. Outdoors & Culture Enthusiast.

About Wolfgang
I was born in Stuttgart, Germany, in 1943. After my engineering studies at the University of Stuttgart, I came to La Chaux-de-Fonds (LCF) to learn French for six months. After those months, I stayed for professional reasons. I was transferred to New York for a while but eventually made my way back to LCF, though I often worked in Hong Kong, Germany, France, and Italy.

After retirement, I became active as a guide in architecture, LCF watchmaking, town planning, and art nouveau, as well as in the museums. I spend my free time biking, cross-country skiing, and participating in cultural activities.

What to Do In LCF (The Basics)
First, visit the Musée International d'Horlogerie (International Watch Museum). Then, take a guided town tour to discover our hidden treasures. Then, visit our beautiful crematorium (built in local art nouveau style sapin—literally "pine-tree style"). Finally, hike in the summer and cross-country ski in the winter.

Hidden Gems for Seasoned Travelers
You'll find the rich history of watchmaking at every street corner (in our decorated staircases, stained glass windows,

balconies etc.). For a deeper look, visit a watch factory (like Corum). You can also visit the neighboring town of Le Locle, where most of world's most famous watchmakers originated.

Day Trips
I love Murten, Bern, Geneva, Neuchâtel, and Lake Geneva.

Where to Hike
There are many possibilities close to the town, like the Doubs River (on the border between Switzerland and France). There is a hiking trail from Basel to Geneva over the ridge of the Jura hills, which is also possible in part with cross-country skis.

What to Eat & Drink
Have a torree (special sausages cooked in the embers of a pine-branch fire) in the woods.

Where to Eat & Drink (Favorite Restaurants & Bars)
La Ferme de Brandt (at Les Petites-Crosettes 6) is a farmhouse from the early 17th century. It's worth a visit. Le Mont Cornu (at Mont Cornu 116) is another farmhouse-turned-restaurant where you get the best cheese fondue in town. And La Pinte Neuchâteloise (at Rue du Grenier 8) is a nice little bistro.

For a great view of the town and surrounding hills, try the bar at Espacite Tower. For budget-travelers, Le Faucheur (at Granges 5) is a popular and reasonably priced restaurant.

How to Fit In
Try to speak the local language (French) and do not expect everyone to understand English or German. Be patient and quiet, especially in restaurants.

Best Places to Take a Photo
Check out the top of our Espacite Tower for a view of the town and surrounding hills and visit the watch museum for interesting interior photos.

Final Notes & Other Tips

LCF is a UNESCO World Heritage Site as of 2009. It is famously the birthplace of Le Corbusier, Louis Chevrolet (who created the car company in the USA), and the poet and writer, Blaise Cendrars.

Find Wolfgang at his tour guiding service at Rue des Chevreuils 21. Phone: + 41 32 926 61 35.

COLOMBIER

Castles, Roman villas, peace, quiet, & nature.

FIND WI-FI HERE: Le Chalet Restaurant.

LANGUAGE: French   **CANTON:** Neuchâtel

Louis-Philippe Burgat
Owner of Chambleau Cellars. Wine Aficionado. Bicyclist.

About Louis-Philippe
My family has been in Neuchâtel for generations (since 1401!), so I was born and raised in the area. Now I live in the middle of my vineyard in Colombier, making a living as owner of Chambleau Cellars. I ride my bicycle in the Jura Mountains in the summer and ski in the winter. I also do some sailing on the lake.

What to Do In Colombier (The Basics)
Visit the military museum in the medieval castle, with its huge uniform collection spanning from the Middle Ages to present days and see the remains of the ancient Roman villa on which the castle was built.

Hidden Gems for Seasoned Travelers
Tour the wineries on Friday night or Saturday morning or go to the Neuchâtel county wine embassy in Boudry Castle. In the summer, it's also nice to visit the Auvernier beach. It's just a short walk from Colombier on the lakeside.

Day Trips
Visiting the Latenium Archeological Museum in Neuchâtel is like taking a walk through prehistoric times. And for water sports-lovers, I recommend a visit to Auvernier or Estavayer-le-

Lac on the lake. The latter has a sandy beach with lots of water sports, including water skiing.

Where to Hike
Walk down the Areuse Gorge or from Noirague to the top of the Creux-du-Van through the 14 turns. The wildlife here is fantastic.

Where to Eat & Drink (Favorite Restaurants & Bars)
My favorite bar is the Rodolphe Club (at Rue Pury 11 in Neuchâtel) and my favorite restaurants are Café des Arts (at Rue J.-L.-Pourtalès 5 in Neuchâtel) and Le Poisson (at Rue des Epancheurs 1 in Auvernier).

Budget Tips
In the summertime, stay at Camping Paradis Plage.

How to Meet Locals & Make Friends
Come to the wine festival on the last weekend in September. The whole town is out in force during those three days. The festival is my drug!

Best Places to Take a Photo
Go up to the Chaumont Mountain and climb the tower.

Find Louis-Philippe at chambleau.ch.

AUVERNIER
15th century houses & incredible charm.

FIND WI-FI HERE: Restaurant du Poisson, La Golée, Le Croquignolet, & Le Siam.

LANGUAGE: French   **CANTON:** Neuchâtel

Thierry Amstutz
Watchmaker. Novelist.

About Thierry
My family is from Sigiswil, a small village in German-speaking Switzerland, but I have always lived in Neuchâtel Canton. I am a watchmaker, specializing in clock-making and restoration of ancient and modern clocks and music boxes, and passionate about the mechanisms giving life to PLCs.

My novel, La Pendule du Souvenir (The Pendulum of Remembrance), published by Editions Slatkine in 2012, is an unusual story about characters from the early days of watchmaking. And I have been president of the Association of Neuchâtel and Jura writers (AENJ) since May 24, 2014.

In addition to my business, I regularly present at the Art and History Museum Neuchâtel (MAH) to viewers of all ages from all over the world.

What to Do In Auvernier (The Basics)
Walk along the shores of the lake, visit Place du Marché in Le Locle, and stroll the cobbled alleys of our old town. There are also some very interesting artist workshops here. One of my favorite things to do on my own days off is visit them.

Hidden Gems for Seasoned Travelers

Le Musée d'Art et d'Histoire (the art and history museum) in Neuchâtel, le Musée International d'Horlogerie (the international watchmaking museum) in La Chaux-de-Fonds, Le Château des Monts (another watch museum) in Le Locle, and many other museums show the rich history of this township. And a visit to the La Collégiale (castle) in Neuchâtel is never a bad idea.

Day Trips

The Creux du Van in the Val-de-Travers is beautiful, as is La Vue des Alpes. And the cities of La Chaux-de-Fonds (a UNESCO World Heritage Site) and Le Locle are worthwhile stops.

Where to Hike

The walk at Tourbières aux Ponts, with its mossy peatlands, makes for a beautiful day.

Where to Eat & Drink (Favorite Restaurants & Bars)

In Auvernier, I love the Restaurant du Poisson (at Rue des Epancheurs 1), La Golée (at Grand-Rue 36), and Croquignolet (on Place des Perchettes). For good Thai food, try Siam (at Route de la Gare 36).

How to Meet Locals & Make Friends

In the evenings, head to the Neuchâtel Casino.

Find Thierry at aucarillondor.ch and aenj.ch.

VALAIS CANTON

VERBIER
Some of the best skiing in the world.

FIND WI-FI HERE: W Living Room, Pub Mont Fort (downstairs), Harold's Hamburgers, & Internet Cyber Café (at Place Centrale 4).

LANGUAGE: French   **CANTON:** Valais

Olly Norris
Ski Instructor. Sailor. Outdoor Enthusiast.

About Olly
I am a passionate skier and sailor and, from the age of 16, started to work professionally in both industries. I now work as a yacht skipper and coach in the summer months and as an alpine ski and telemark instructor during the winter months (for the École Suisse de Ski Verbier). During my early days as a ski instructor, I fell in love with Switzerland, both for its beautiful landscape and for the amazing people that live here, which is why I moved from England to base myself here permanently.

I spent six years living in Crans-Montana before moving to my current home in Verbier. My work has taken me throughout the Valais Canton and I have skied almost every resort in the region, from small gems like La Tzouma and Ovronnaz to the well-known resorts of Saas-Fee and Zermatt. On the rare occasion that I have some free time, I love nothing more than heading up the mountain with my friends, skiing in the winter or hiking and climbing in the summer.

What to Do In Verbier (The Basics)
Verbier is first and foremost a skiing destination. Get yourself a lift pass and explore the endless terrain. I recommend, even for the most accomplished skiers, employing the services of a

253

local guide or instructor to see the best the resort has to offer and, of course, brush up on your skills. On my days off, I'll often head up with a true local to explore new routes. I'm always delighted by the new routes and descents they show me.

Verbier is just as beautiful in summer and this time of year can often represent much better value. If your dream to visit the mountains doesn't rely on the opportunity to hurtle downhill on a pair of skis, then book your trip in summer and enjoy hiking, climbing, golf, quad biking, and paragliding.

Hidden Gems for Seasoned Travelers
Switzerland is home to some incredible thermal baths. A trip to Lavey-les-Bains, just a short drive or train ride away, is the perfect way to wind down and relax those muscles after a day spent skiing, mountain biking, or hiking. You are guaranteed to wake up the next morning feeling completely refreshed!

Where to Stay
Verbier is a world-renowned party destination and, if that appeals to you, finding accommodation as close to the center of town (Place Central) is essential to ensure an easy stroll home in the early hours. For those that want a slightly quieter experience, stay somewhere near the Savoleyres ski lift, which boasts stunning views of the town and mountains.

Day Trips
Only an hour away by car (or 1.5 hours by train), the resort of Crans-Montana is well worth visiting. It has a completely different atmosphere to that of Verbier, sitting on a sun-kissed south-facing plateau, which offers unrivaled views of the mountain ranges of Valais. Locals claim that it is the sunniest place in Switzerland (a bold claim but, based on the six years I spent there, a believable one).

Where to Hike
Verbier offers an array of trails. My personal favorite is the walk up to the summit of Pierre Avoi (just over 8,000 feet). It offers an

incredible 360-degree panoramic view, including Verbier, the Mont Blanc Massif, and the Rhône Valais. You can start your walk from the village (about a three hour round trip) or, if you're strapped for time, take the Savoleyres lift up the mountain and walk from there (about an hour round trip). The final stretch to the summit is quite steep, but there are some ladders and handrails in place to help you. If you have any doubts, hire a guide for the day to show you the way and make sure you're safe.

Where to Eat & Drink (Favorite Restaurants & Bars)

Cabane Mont Fort, situated at about 8,000 feet in the mountains above Verbier, is a quintessentially Swiss experience, with local food served at altitude on the side of the piste. It is open in the evenings, which means you can have the pistes to yourself (though a guide/instructor and head-lamps are essential for the ride down).

Le Rouge (at Rue de Ransou 37) is my favorite place for a long lunch or après ski, with a great atmosphere from lunchtime onwards. Before you know it, you'll be dancing the night away. And Borsalino (at Route des Creux 3) is a quiet and simple Italian restaurant run by lovely people. Go enjoy a pizza with friends away from the bustle of the rest of town.

Budget Tips

My top tip for dining out is to always ask about the menu du jour. This is a set menu that is either two or three courses and often includes a coffee/tea as well. Meals are composed of fresh seasonal ingredients and always offer excellent value. Traditional plates such as raclette, croûts (sauerkraut), and fondue, whilst brilliant, will often demand a high premium.

How to Fit In

The French-speaking locals are wonderful people and extremely welcoming of travelers and foreigners (like myself) who choose to settle in their country. Verbier is known as an English-speaking enclave and this does annoy the locals a little. Making the effort to learn a few French phrases is essential. A simple, *bonjour, ça va? Vous parlez anglais?* (hello, how are you? Do you speak English?) is all it takes to win them over.

How to Meet Locals & Make Friends
The most international and social communities in both Verbier and Crans-Montana are, in my opinion, the Swiss ski schools. Join your instructor for an apéro after skiing and you will be sure to meet a diverse community of people who are passionate about their work and the area in which they live.

Best Places to Take a Photo
The Savoleyres side on the way to La Tzouma offers beautiful views of both the Grand and Petit Combin, as well as the Glacier de Trient and the Massif du Mont Blanc, including Mont Blanc itself (Europe's tallest mountain). All offer stunning back-drops for your photo. If this isn't breathtaking enough, take to the air with a paragliding instructor and take the ultimate selfie as you fly above Vebier.

Find Olly at ollynorris.com.

Kent Berglund
Ski School Manager. Outdoor Enthusiast.

About Kent
I came to Verbier 20 years ago from Sweden (where I grew up). I run a ski school called Performance Verbier and in my free time, I hang out with family and do a lot of ski touring.

What to Do In Verbier (The Basics)
Well, as we are the third largest ski area in the world, you pretty much have to ski if you come here. In the summer, the mountain biking (both trail and downhill) is world-class. And, of course, hiking is a popular pastime.

One of the first things you'll want to do is head to the top of Montfort, where you'll see both the Matterhorn and Mont Blanc, as well as Lake Geneva on a clear day.

Hidden Gems for Seasoned Travelers
To get off the beaten path, get out of the main ski area and explore the four valleys. Nendaz and Veysonnaz are both amazing places. Le Chable (at the bottom of the mountain) is really up-and-coming, with good bars and restaurants.

Where to Stay
My picks are Le Chable or Verbier itself.

Day Trips
If you're not skiing, Chateaux Chillon (the island castle on Lake Geneva) is very nice...and there you have Montreux, as well. Aosta in Italy is about an hour away and (as always in Italy) it has great food and good shopping. For skiing, I love Les Diablerets, Champex Lac, or La Fouly.

Where to Hike
The area around Bruson is lovely, especially toward Mont Rogneux. And there are some stunning routes around the Mauvoisin Dam.

What to Eat & Drink
Raclette originated from our valley, so that's a must-try. The cheese-makers here (I think there are 16 of them) are allowed to put an A.O.C stamp on their cheeses, which means they're incredibly authentic and worth trying. Cheese fondue with an assiette valaisanne (local meat platter) is a must. And the local wines are really good (try the white Petite Arvine or Johannisberg and the red Humagne Rouge or Pinot Noir).

Where to Eat & Drink (Favorite Restaurants & Bars)
For a beer, try Pub Mont Fort (located at Chemin de la Tinte 10), The Loft (on Rue de Poste), and Fer a Cheval (at Rue de Médran 18). For cocktails, check out Nevai (at Route de Verbier Station 55), The Living Room at the W Hotel (at Rue de

Médran 70), or Farinet Lounge (in Place Centrale). For food, I like the Nevai Sushi Lounge (at Route de Verbier Station 55), Le Bec Brasserie (at Rue de Médran 77), and Le Caveu (at Place Central) for cheese.

Budget Tips
Check out happy hour (every day between 4 and 5 p.m.) at Pub Mont Fort for half price drinks. Chex Martin is great for families (the meat fondue is a fixed-price all-you-can-eat option). And it's always free to walk up to the little chapel of St. Christoph, where the views are stunning.

How to Fit In
Learn a little French (*bonjour* and *merci* will take you far). And know that everything here happens over a glass of wine.

How to Meet Locals & Make Friends
Have a glass of wine in Le Chable at Gietroz (at Route de Verbier 9) or Le Chat Bleu (at Route de Clouchèvre 24).

Best Places to Take a Photo
The Bruson ski area offers the most amazing view over Verbier.

Final Notes & Other Tips
Valais (the Swiss canton where Verbier resides) is the biggest wine producing area in Switzerland. The Rhône River runs through the valley before it goes into France. This makes for some really good wine. The reason not many people know about our wines is because nothing gets exported; they are simply not making enough, so everything is consumed locally.

Find Kent at performanceverbier.com.

VALAIS CANTON

SAAS-FEE
"The pearl of the Alps."

FIND WI-FI HERE: Coffee Bar (Obere Dorfstrasse 38).

LANGUAGE: German   **CANTON:** Valais

Fabian Zurbriggen
Ski Instructor. Hiker. Photography Hobbyist.

About Fabian
I was born and raised in Saas-Fee, which is a small, traditional village in the Saas Valley in southern Switzerland. After living abroad and in Zürich for a few years, I came home to Saas-Fee, where I now work as a ski instructor. I like to go hiking and take photographs in my free time.

What to Do In Saas-Fee (The Basics)
People come here to enjoy the impressive scenery. One nice way to discover the village is by walking up the one-hour chapel trail from Saas-Grund (a village on the way to Saas-Fee) to Saas-Fee. In 1938, the author Karl Zuckmayer walked this path and wrote about it in his book, A Part of Myself.

Other main attractions are the view at the world's highest revolving restaurant in front of the Allalin peak, the glacier and mountain view at Längfluh, and, in the summer, the very cute marmots at Spielboden, which sometimes come close and eat carrots or peanuts out of your hands.

And, of course, in winter, most people come to ski and in summer they come to hike and climb. The beautiful scenery and the relaxing spirit of the village attract visitors year-round.

259

Usually around mid-October the larch trees turn yellow, which is lovely to see.

Hidden Gems for Seasoned Travelers

If you can make it in winter during a full moon, go out for a midnight walk. The Alpine amphitheater-like setting of the valley and its surrounding mountains covered in white and calmly reflecting the moonlight is one of my favorite things in the world.

In summer, I like to hike up Hannig hill. There is also an easy hike through Bärenfalle to Melchboden, where you'll find a small hidden lake in the larch forest. From there, you can either walk past Hohnegg back to Saas-Fee or continue up to the cozy Restaurant Alpenblick for a break and to taste their delicious homemade pastries or dishes against a pretty excellent backdrop. If you continue up the mountain, you will come out of the forest and pass a few gnarled old larch trees. Further up, there is another restaurant offering a wide variety of local foods and dishes and a fantastic view. A cable car will take you back to the village.

The chapel Zur Hohen Stiege is also definitely worth seeing.

Where to Stay

I prefer the calmer and more relaxed back of the village, which is only a 10-minute walk from the center.

Day Trips

I recommend Mittelallalin—an alpine summit just below Allalin-horn. The Metro Alpin (an alpine subway) will take you there.

The neighboring villages also offer a variety of different attractions. In Saas-Grund, you should see the view from Kreuzboden. In Saas-Balen, there is a beautiful waterfall. And in Saas-Almagell, there's Furggstalden, a charming small settlement of old traditional houses.

The world-famous Matterhorn peak is also nearby. On public transport, you can be there in just an hour and a half.

Where to Hike
Hannig has a lot of beautiful trails and on the opposite side of the mountain, you'll find Plattjen, where you'll hike past large rocky fields, pine trees, alpine flowers, great views of the Dom peak, and, in July, the alpenrose (a type of rhododendron).

Spielboden/Längfluh is the area where you're likely to see some marmots and the glacier is close. There is a spectacular view and easy hike at the little lake in Kreuzboden (in Saas-Grund). And the Mattmark area has an easy hike around the lake (and if you're up for a longer hike, you can walk to Italy from there).

Where to Eat & Drink (Favorite Restaurants & Bars)
I often take visitors to Restaurant Alphitta (at Wildstrasse 72) for traditional-style ambience and food (plus, I like the walk through the village). Besides that, two of my favorite restaurants are Zur Mühle (at Dorfstrasse 61) and Chüestall (at Stadel-weg 23).

On the mountainside, I like the Alpenblick (mentioned above), Hannig (on Hannig hill), and Gletschergrotte (at Talabfahrt Gletschergrottenpiste 4b). And for a beer in the evening, I prefer the Happy Bar (at Lomattenstrasse 26). Popcorn (at Obere Dorfstrasse 6) and Poison (at Obere Dorfstrasse 22) are good places for a long night out.

Budget Tips
In the summer, most (though not all) accommodations in the Saas Valley offer a guest card that allows you to use most cable cars for free. Ask your host about it or stop by the tourist office.

Best Places to Take a Photo
Near the post office, there are some great scenery shots, including old traditional barns. The Gletscherbrücke has a

good view of the village and mountains. At Längfluh and Mitt-elallalin, there are some beautiful shots of the Allalin peak and the glacier scenery. And from Kreuzboden, the view of the Mischabel Mountains is great.

Final Notes & Other Tips

Long ago, people here used to make a living with agriculture and handcrafts, but now the valley is a tourism hub.

Surrounded by several 13,000+ foot mountains, the Saas Valley first attracted British alpinists to conquer the mountains. Later we started to have tourists in winter as well, and Saas-Fee became one of the most attractive ski resorts in Europe (we offer the best snow conditions and a very long ski season). Even in summer our ski pistes on the glacier open up for ski experts (and maniacs).

Saas-Fee, with its amphitheater-like setting (the village is surr-ounded by massive mountains), wide glacier fields, car-free village, and larch and pine forests, is called the pearl of the Alps. The landscape is certainly one of the most beautiful in the Alps. Plus, life is simpler here. I feel content in Saas-Fee and I wonder if you might feel the same.

ZERMATT
That car-free village overlooking the famed Matterhorn.

FIND WI-FI HERE: The train station & most accommodations.

LANGUAGE: German   **CANTON:** Valais

Ashley Wyss
Entrepreneur. Hiker. Skier. Climber. Traveler.

About Ashley
I'm originally from England but have been living in Switzerland for over 20 years. I run my own company renting out self-catering apartments in Zermatt. And in my free time, I do a lot of jogging, skiing, hiking, climbing, and travelling.

What to Do In Zermatt (The Basics)
In winter, it's a must to ski on the three ski areas here, which are all connected. It's also a must to ski into Italy. The more popular Cervinia and the less popular Valtournenche are both gems.

For the more adventurous, a heli-skiing trip is fabulous and easy to organize, as we have a heliport here and numerous mountain guides.

In summer, there are over 275 miles of hiking trails. One of my favorites (though a bit long) is from Trift across the Hohbalmen into the Zmutt valley. You can also hike to the Fluhalp and enjoy an amazing lunch.

Hidden Gems for Seasoned Travelers
Start with a hike up to the Mettelhorn (11,000+ feet), which is about four hours from the village through Trift. Stay overnight at

the Fluhalp (in summer); enjoy a great dinner and good wine and go upstairs to bed. Book ahead at *fluhalp-zermatt.ch*.

Where to Stay

Zermatt is a small village, so everywhere is good. Some guests like to be right in the center of the village close to shops, restaurants, and night life, while others prefer to be a little bit outside the center, where they can enjoy the peace and quiet. It's very much personal choice.

Where to Eat & Drink (Favorite Restaurants & Bars)

The new Gees Bar (at Bahnhofstrasse 70) has live music every night after 10 p.m. The Hotel Post's Brown Cow Pub (at Bahnhofstrasse 41) is always lively. And the Chämi Bar (at Bahnhofstrasse 28 in the Hotel Pollux) is cozy.

Budget Tips

It helps to pre-purchase a train pass. If you're just going from the airport to Zermatt and back, a Swiss Transfer Ticket is best.

Best Places to Take a Photo

Shots of the Matterhorn, of course!

Find Ashley at zermattvacations.com.

GRÄCHEN

A small mountain village surrounded by beautiful walking paths.

FIND WI-FI HERE: A public connection in the town center.

LANGUAGE: German   **CANTON:** Valais

Hannes Schalbetter
Restaurant Owner. Skier. Hiker. Hunter.

About Hannes
I grew up in Grächen and now run a restaurant and bar here. In my free time, I ski and hike. And in autumn, I dedicate myself to hunting.

What to Do In Grächen (The Basics)
Grächen is a small mountain village with a well-preserved center. It's excellent for families and has a good number of restaurants and bars for the younger crowd. In summer, you can take relaxing walks along the irrigation channels. In winter, there is a small but beautiful ski resort that offers both beginner and advanced slopes.

Hidden Gems for Seasoned Travelers
We have a small museum in Grächen that tells the story of Tomas Platter (the famous humanist, born here). And in just one hour by car or 1.5 hours by bus, you'll be in Salgesch/Varen, where you'll find scores of vineyards. The area is famous for its Pinot Noir.

There are also two night ski shows in the winter and they're worth seeing.

VALAIS CANTON

Day Trips
Start with Zermatt and Saas-Fee, two internationally known ski resorts in our immediate vicinity. Then head to the thermal baths of Leukerbad and Brigerbad, which can be reached in under an hour and are well worth a day trip.

Where to Hike
The Europaweg (Europe Trail) from Grächen to Zermatt is an excellent choice. It takes about two days. And for the experienced, advanced hiking crowd, the Tour Monta Rosa is a popular and solid choice. The whole tour is about 100 miles and passes through Zermatt, as well as Saas-Fee and Grächen.

Where to Eat & Drink (Favorite Restaurants & Bars)
In addition to my own bar and restaurant—Sigi's Bar and Restaurant Walliserkanne—I like the Tenne Bar (on Dorfstrasse), Restaurant Bargji Alp (at Bärgji-Alp 570), and Restaurant Hannigalp (at Heiminen 468).

Best Places to Take a Photo
The very best photos come from Hannigalp, where you'll find a very beautiful panorama of the surrounding mountain peaks.

Find Hannes at walliserkanne-graechen.ch and sigisbar.ch.

VALAIS CANTON

VISP

A tiny old town & great location for exploring Valais.

FIND WI-FI HERE: The tourist office, the train station, the two hotels in front of the train station, & McDonald's.

LANGUAGE: German   **CANTON:** Valais

Peter Salzmann
Hiking Guide. Storyteller.

About Peter

I'm a Visp local who has been working as a hiking guide for 10 years. In winter, I offer snowshoeing and walking tours in nearby towns and every Thursday evening I weave tales of astronomy and mythology at the Gornergrat Kulm Hotel (located on Zermatt at about 10,000 feet) under the stars.

In summer, I take hardcore hikers on grand tours of the Alps (like the eight-day tour around Monte Rosa and the nine-day tour around the Matterhorn). On summer nights when I'm not on a tour, I organize whisky nights with crime thriller readings in the peat bog on Moosalp/Törbel.

In spring and autumn, I organize cultural hiking trips on historic trails like Via Sbrinz (a cheese trail), Via Salina (the salt trail) through the Jura Mountains), Via Cook (the first-ever official tour route in Switzerland), and through the Valais vineyards for wine tasting.

Before becoming a guide, I studied advertising and marketing, worked as the director of a small theater, and then worked as a tourism director in Valais.

VALAIS CANTON

In my free time, I like to read about nice places and seek out the best hiking trails for future tours.

What to Do In Visp (The Basics)

For more than 100 years, Visp has been an industrial city. Visitors who have heard of it imagine that it is an ugly small town in a narrow alpine valley. So when they visit the small 800-year-old town center, they are pleasantly surprised.

Like most Swiss towns, the emotional center is the old church—a real gem. It's dedicated to the three kings who visited the baby Jesus and is a powerful, quiet place with a Roman crypt. The surrounding architecture is influenced by Italy, whose border is about 20 miles away and the plants and fruits are Mediterranean.

Hidden Gems for Seasoned Travelers

Every Friday evening, we have a small farmers' market in the old town. There you'll find a stand with local wine, another stand with warm cheese specialties, and a barbecue stand. As we live in the driest place in Switzerland, most Fridays are sunny and perfect for browsing.

Day Trips

Most visitors already know the Matterhorn/Zermatt (the best skiing area in the Alps with a panoramic view of 29 summits over 13,000 feet) or the Aletsch Glacier (the largest in the Alps) —both of which are just an hour away from Visp.

Less than half an hour away, though, we have Moosalp—a wonderful panoramic terrace at 6,500 feet above sea level with perfect restaurants. And in just 10 minutes by car or bus, you can visit the brand new hot springs in Brigerbad, which has the largest natural warm water surface in Switzerland.

Where to Hike

Start outside the railway station in Visp and walk along the irrigation channels that transport water out of the next valley, crossing steep mountain slopes to the meadows, fruit orchards and vineyards in the area. Those channels were built 700 years ago and hiking these nearly flat hiking trails is calming and refreshing in summer.

The channel walks are called suonenweg (literally "way of atonement") because in the past when someone in the village had sinned, he was sent up to do the dangerous irrigation repair work along the steep cliffs.

If you are a hardcore hiker, I recommend the trails between 6,500 and 10,000 feet above sea level, including the 373-mile Swiss Alpenpässe-Weg #6 from Chur to Lake Geneva, which passes through Simplon Pass, Visperterminen, Saas-Fee, and Zermatt.

What & Where to Eat & Drink

To taste real local food, I recommend the Terrasse Restaurant (at Sankt Martinistrasse 1). They offer a real Valais menu with a jerky carpaccio (as we live in the driest area of Switzerland, we dry the meat instead of fumigating it), raclette from four different mountain pastures, and, to finish, an apricot sorbet with a delicious apricot brandy (more than three quarters of Swiss apricots are harvested here in Valais).

In Visp, you are in the epicenter of a relatively unknown wine region, just a couple miles from the highest vineyard in Europe (3,600 feet above sea level), which is known for its Heida Wein, a Savagnin Blanc that is the father of Savagnin Blancs. Believe it or not, Heida Barrique 2012 from St. Jodern of Visperterminen won the international trophy of the British Wine Magazine Decanter in 2014 as best in show for white single varietals. So you've got world-class wine right next door.

Finally, I take my morning coffee in Tiziano's (at Bahnhofstrasse 2). I adore eating at the delicious-but-not-cheap modern 600-seat theater turned restaurant, La Poste (at La Poste Platz 2). My son meets his friends in the P2 bar (at Bahnhofplatz 7). And every second Friday in the winter, there is live jazz at Jazz-Chälli (on Fuelagasse).

VALAIS CANTON

Budget Tips

A mini glass of wine at the farmers market is three francs and a raclette is just four. People come all the way from Bern to shop at our farmer's market for these kinds of prices (and quality).

How to Fit In

We speak one of the oldest German dialects in the upper Valais because our language has been protected for over 1,000 years by high mountains on both sides, the Italian border in south, and the French language of lower Valais. So, while we are part of the German region of Switzerland, our German is different. In Zürich, for example, they say *grüezi* for hello. Here, we use *grüezi* as an insult. Nasty Swiss Germans are, in our dialect, *grüezini*. So if you want to say hello to us in a correct way, do not say *grüezi*. Instead, say *guetntagwoll* (pronounced "guten-tahg-voll"). And if that's too complicated, just say *tag*, which means "I wish you a good day."

How to Meet Locals & Make Friends

Come to the farmers market, drink a glass of wine with us, and have a raclette on Friday evenings at 5:30 p.m. This is the best way to become one of us.

Best Places to Take a Photo

Professional photographers take wedding parties into the alleyways in old town near the churches, so I'd suggest there.

Final Notes & Other Tips

Make sure to visit the Pfammatter butcher in the pedestrian area in front of the railway station. He offers a large range of the best local foods: the best spicy jerky in Valais, different dry flavorful sausages, a large range of tasty Alp cheeses, two different rye griddle cakes (the famous Valais bread), and a small range of delicious wines, including the Heida wine.

Find Peter at alpevents.ch.

VALAIS CANTON

BRIG

Adventure sports, protected forests, long glaciers, & high mountains.

FIND WI-FI HERE: The library.

LANGUAGE: German   **CANTON:** Valais

Kathrina Erdin
Outdoor Enthusiast.

About Kathrina
I grew up in Rheinfelden in Aargau (northwestern Switzerland), which is where they brew Feldschlösschen beer. And now I live in Brig-Glis, right at the heart of the mountains.

I work as a snowboard instructor in wintertime and in a rope park as security, support, climbing teacher, and mountain biking guide in summertime (when I'm not traveling, that is).

In my free time, I love everything outdoors. That's why I moved to Glis when I was 16 and that's why I stay. I snowboard, ski, hike, bike, climb, surf, kite surf, and wakeboard. And I love exploring nature both at home and abroad. For me, hiking to places where not many people go is one of the most magical things a person can do.

What to Do In Brig-Glis (The Basics)
It's a small town but we have a castle called Stockalperschloss and it has some really nice green gardens, where we often enjoy the sun in summer. It's also a cute place to have a beer or some food after a long hike in the mountains.

The most impressive thing about Brig-Glis, though, is its position in the center of so many beautiful mountains. During the day, you should really go and explore the landscape around town.

If you arrive in the afternoon and have little time, follow a small river called Saltina into its valley. It's a one to three hour walk round-trip and it's beautiful. If you want, there are even places along the way to have a BBQ. You don't need to be extremely sporty to go there and don't need much time, but it's an amazing place to feel like you're far away from the town, even though you're not.

Hidden Gems for Seasoned Travelers
In summer, if you're a climber, this is the place for you. There's a climbing guide—an entire book—dedicated to just this region. You can find the book in our local library and have a look.

For non-climbers, hiking, biking, and paragliding are the things to do here in the summer, spring, and autumn. Baltschiedertal is an especially nice short hike (start from Ausserberg and either loop back to Ausserberg or end up in Eggen). Bellwald is amazing for downhill biking, as is Fiesch.

In winter, it's time to ski or snowboard in some of the smaller ski resorts like Aletsch, Bellwald, Belalp, Rothwald, or Rosswald, which are all about an hour away.

Where to Stay
The old town center is where the restaurants and bars are. And it's a pretty small town...the farthest away you can stay is about 15 minutes on foot.

Day Trips
Zermatt is the popular place to go, but it's over-crowded and much too expensive, in my opinion. So, instead, I recommend going to Eggishorn, where you can enjoy massive mountains and the Aletsch Glacier. To get there, take the train to Fiesch and then two cable cars up to Fiescheralp - Eggishorn. It's amazing in both summer and winter, and you can see the

famous Matterhorn (which is even more beautiful from afar) from up there as well.

After that, take the train up to Oberwald. It goes all the way up the Oberwallis Valley and every little village on its way is worth a visit for their village life, small shops, original restaurants, many hiking trails, and cross country skiing.

Where to Hike

For something not too difficult or exhausting, try the Lötschberg Südrampe hike from Hohtenn to Brig, the walk from Riederfurka to Moosfluh, or the walk up the Bettmerhorn. The only downside to these hikes is that they're really popular.

If you'd like to be in the mountains overnight, take the two-day hike from Belalp to the Oberaletschhütte (where you can sleep and eat during the season; book ahead at: *oberaletsch.ch*). This is a difficult hike, but it's totally worth it if you are a fit and experienced hiker. If you want, you can stay there more than one day and go climbing around the hut.

All the trails around the Simplon Pass are also beautiful. The easiest one is the Stockalperweg. It leads from Brig all the way to Gondo, but the Simplon-Pass-to-Brig portion is unique and beautiful. It follows a stream called Saltina and crosses it via several small, handmade wooden bridges.

A more difficult hike is from the Simplon Pass to the Glishorn and from there down to Glis. The view around the Glishorn is unique, but it's a really long and steep hiking trail. Also, there aren't many landmarks and almost no tourists go there, so you should ask a local to guide you. Or, if you decide to go it alone, make sure you are in good health and have good shoes, enough food, and a map.

What to Eat & Drink

You absolutely have to try cholera (no, not the malady—the potato, leek, onion, cheese, and apple tart!). It's delicious. Gsottus is another regional specialty with boiled meat, beans, carrots, and potatoes. You can try some in Naters (a nearby village) once a week at Dorf Pinta Trächa (address: Landstrasse 14).

You should also try Swiss beer (Quöllfrisch, Blonde, and Feldschlösschen Bügel are really good) and wine. The highest vineyards in Europe are just 20 minutes away in Visperterminen, where they make mostly Heida wine (which is really tasty).

Where to Eat & Drink (Favorite Restaurants & Bars)
First, try Restaurant De la Place (at Alte Simplonstrasse 29); if you order the set menu there, you get a Quöllfrisch beer and a flämmli (a small glass of Schnapps and espresso). Ask the bartender how to drink it.

For nice concerts, try the Perron1 club at Bahnhofplatz 1.

For Italian food in the heart of Brig (with the best pizza and pasta in town), try Restaurant Commerce at Sebastiansplatz 2.

If it's steak you're after, Restaurant Pöschtli in Naters (at Belalpstrasse 18) and Eidgenossen in Brig (at Schulhausstrasse 2) won't disappoint.

And Bäckerei/Tea-Room Rafji, near the station (Rhônesandstrasse 15), has delicious bread, cakes, and coffee. Plus, you get a croissant for free with your coffee before 10 a.m.

Budget Tips
For coffee and bread, check out the tearoom mentioned above. And check out Käserei in Glis for affordable local cheese (schaukäserei-rhône.ch).

How to Fit In
The Swiss are very polite, so always say please and thank you and ask nicely when you're ordering something in a shop.

VALAIS CANTON

How to Meet Locals & Make Friends
Go to Restaurant De la Place (at Alte Simplonstrasse 29) and order a menu. And if you go snowboarding, climbing, or hiking, everybody always talks to everybody.

Best Places to Take a Photo
Try Eggishorn for a picture of the area and Glishorn if it's summer and you love long hikes. If you go up to the Belalp, you'll have a nice view over Brig and Glis, too. And the Stock-alperschloss and the Sebastiansplatz are good places to take a picture in town.

Final Notes & Other Tips
This is not the place to visit if you are looking for a shopping adventure. It's just a small town with nice people in the middle of unique mountains with beautiful nature.

LEUKERBAD

Calming landscapes, fresh air, friendly people, & thermal baths.

FIND WI-FI HERE: Restaurant Bodmenstübli.

LANGUAGE: German   **CANTON:** Valais

Sara
Freelance Architect. Vegetarian. Traveler.

About Sara

Hi, I'm Sara from Savièse and Leukerbad. I work as an architect in Sion and around the canton. In my free time, I love to travel and spend lots of time in my apartment in Leukerbad, which I just renovated. When I'm not there, I rent it out via Airbnb.

What to Do In Leukerbad (The Basics)

Take the cable car to the Gemmi Pass, which connects Leukerbad with Kandersteg. The landscape is beautiful and the rösti at the Gemmi Restaurant is the best! If you're sporty, you can walk up instead of taking the cable car. It takes about an hour and a half. After that, take a walk in Leukerbad's old town, which is a very typical Swiss village.

Hidden Gems for Seasoned Travelers

On the road to Leukerbad, there are several spots where I always stop for a picnic or just to observe the beautiful scenery of lower Valais. There are not many people who benefit from all the nice places along the road (which is too bad for them but lucky for us—as they remain quiet and beautiful).

VALAIS CANTON

Where to Stay
The most typical Swiss architecture is in the Leukerbad old town. Or, for something different, go to Zermatt. It's wonderful.

Day Trips
In winter, for ski enthusiasts, there are beautiful ski slopes in Torrent Horn. The scenery is spectacular. In summer, there are a lot of treks to do, including a one-hour walk to Bodmenstübli Restaurant, whose food is very tasty...and a real relief after a good hour of walking!

Where to Hike
For nature lovers, I recommend Daubensee (around the lake at the top of the Gemmi Pass). For the more adventurous among us, there is the walk from Gemmi across to Kandersteg in the Canton of Bern. For incredible views, trek from Montana to Leukerbad (a seven-hour walk).

Where to Eat & Drink (Favorite Restaurants & Bars)
The coolest bar in town is the Chinchila (at Kirchstrasse 12). The people are nice and the bartenders are cool. Altitude 1411 (at 1,400 meters above sea level) is a great place to have a drink while enjoying views of the Gemmi Pass. Tom's Saloon (on Haus Fortuna) is a little kitschy but full in the winter season and perfect for socializing.

How to Fit In
Switzerland is known for being clean and pure. Please do not throw your waste on the ground after your walks in nature.

How to Meet Locals & Make Friends
Swiss people love being out at the local bars for a drink or two—so head on over and say hi.

Best Places to Take a Photo
On the top of the Gemmi Pass when the sky is clear.

Find Sara at airbnb.com/rooms/2144427.

ST. MARTIN
Authentic heritage & extraordinary landscapes.

FIND WI-FI HERE: La Promenade tearoom.

LANGUAGE: French   **CANTON:** Valais

Patrice Gaspoz
Tour Leader. Nature-Lover.

About Patrice
I was born and raised here in St. Martin and currently work as a tour leader (also responsible for security and rescue). In my free time, I get out in nature—hiking, skiing, mountaineering, and painting.

What to Do In St. Martin (The Basics)
Visit the Val d'Hérens—an Alpine valley formed by a glacier—and explore the chimney-like formations known as the Pyramides d'Euseigne, the glaciers, the alpine meadows (full of cows), and the Grande Dixence Dam.

In Saint-Martin itself, which is a very authentic hamlet, wander the streets, explore the irrigation channels (which form an easy and pretty hiking trail), and check out the Agrotouristique d'Ossona—a working farm with restaurant and B&B.

Hidden Gems for Seasoned Travelers
I love Vallon de Réchy (a beautiful nearby nature preserve).

VALAIS CANTON

Where to Stay
The Agrotouristique d'Ossona—a working farm, inn, and restaurant—is located outside town on an easy hiking trail. (And if you continue on the trail past the farm, it will take you to the village of La Luette.)

Where to Hike
Stroll among the Saveur des Alpages path, located 2,800+ feet above sea level at the upper edge of the forest. This walk offers exceptional views and allows you to taste local products and typical local meals at restaurants/dairies along the way.

The recently constructed metal bridge (passelle), which leads to La Luette and the Les Prixes peaks, leads to an easy hike, appropriate for all ages and skill levels. Halfway up this hike (before the bridge), you'll find the inn mentioned above.

Another favorite is the Maurice Zermatten trail, which leads to a mountain hut called Becs de Bosson at the top of the Vallon de Réchy. This is a good place to see marmots and eagles.

What to Eat & Drink
The Tsarfion—a pork and cabbage dish—is a typical St. Martin recipe. Wines from the Cave du Paradou (Paradou cellars) are also worth trying. Some of the vineyards are at an altitude as high as 3,280 feet.

Where to Eat & Drink (Favorite Restaurants & Bars)
I'm a fan of L'auberge d'Ossona (phone: +41 79 467 1143), Restaurant Le Trappeur (at Route du Village 22 in Mase; phone: +41 27 281 2828), Le Refuge (on Route de Lannaz in Evolène; +41 27 283 1942), and Pas de Lona (at Rue du Lagec 3 in Eison; phone: +41 27 281 1181), where you'll find great tsarfion.

Best Places to Take a Photo
If you like hiking, go up to the Becs de Bosson mountain hut. From up there, you can see 24 of our tallest peaks.

Find Patrice at saint-martin-tourisme.ch.

MARTIGNY
Vineyards, orchards, mountain passes, & gastronomy.

FIND WI-FI HERE: Casino Cafe.

LANGUAGE: French   **CANTON:** Valais

Masal Bugduv
Philosopher. Dancer. Runner. Skier.

About Masal
My main interests are running, skiing, dancing, reggae, dance-hall music, and philosophy.

What to Do In Martigny (The Basics)
The Gianadda Museum is the town's most famous attraction. Another place that people should go is Le Musée et Chiens du Saint-Bernard (the Saint Bernard museum), though I've never been personally.

What I personally love about Martigny is its proximity to an apparently endless amount of trails. A 15 - 20 minute drive will bring you up about 3,000 feet in altitude. If you want to go hiking, your best bet is to find a local to go with you, but failing that you can map your own trails at *wanderland.ch* (which has a 25-franc subscription fee but is well worth the money). If you are looking for an easy trail, I recommend Les Gorges du Dailley from Les Granges just above Salvan (you leave from the parking of l'Hôtel Balance by foot).

Where to Eat & Drink (Favorite Restaurants & Bars)
Le Café du Midi (at Rue des Marronniers 4) is well known for its fondue and raclette and its casual atmosphere. The prices are

average for Switzerland (about 25 francs for the main course).

Café des Alpes (at Rue des Marronniers 2) is a cool, laid-back bar. Sunset Bar (at Rue du Léman 15) looks a bit tacky from the outside, but there's a cool, young atmosphere inside. Les Caves du Manoir (at Place du Manoir 1) is the only cool club in Martigny. It is, alas, rarely open. They pick and choose their weekends and are overly fond of metal-rock for my taste.

Budget Tips

I cannot emphasize enough how important it is, as a foreigner, to know the price of everything before making a purchase. Don't assume anything. The only relatively cheap place to eat is Chez Giusi's near the church, just off the square. Her pizzas and focaccia are delicious (at about 8 francs for a large slice) and you can have a sit-down meal. There are no dogs allowed, which is unusual for Switzerland.

How to Fit In

There are 1001 things that we do that the Swiss find strange—and vice versa. The list is too long to get into here, but if you're really interested, read *Swiss Watching* by Diccon Bewes. One thing I do warn visitors about is pedestrian crossings (if you're driving). Often, the Swiss do not look up before crossing them.

How to Meet Locals & Make Friends

Join a club—running, skiing, mountaineering, dancing, etc.

Best Places to Take a Photo

Walk up to le Chateau de la Bâtiaz. It is a lovely walk and you'll get a panoramic view of Martigny.

Final Notes & Other Tips

Le Bâtiaz has a reputation as a hot/dangerous area, due in part to the number of brothels and associated bars that were there in the past. This is no longer the case and it is now a nice, tranquil part of town. Also, there is a very strong wine culture in Valais if that's your thing.

VALAIS CANTON

SION
Land of castles & charming buildings from the Middle Ages.

FIND WI-FI HERE: There's a city-wide free Wi-Fi network.

LANGUAGE: French   **CANTON:** Valais

---

100 LOCALS

Fanny Corvaglia
Tour Guide. History, Architecture, & Art Buff.

About Fanny
I was born and raised in Sion and still live here to this day. I work in the tourism office running guided tours of the city. I find the city's history, architecture, and art incredibly fascinating.

What to Do In Sion (The Basics)
First, visit the town and follow the Discovery Walk route (you can get directions and a map at the tourist office). There are numbers situated throughout the town and for each number there is an important monument or place to see. Panels are written in French, German, and English and explain the history or the architecture of each sightseeing point.

Hidden Gems for Seasoned Travelers
Walk along the Bisse de Clavau (an irrigation channel) for a beautiful view of both castles and the plain of the Rhône.

The Domaine des Îles park is an excellent spot in the summer. Walk around the lakes, go for a swim, or enjoy the open-air sport and leisure center amenities, including mini-golf, a little train and play area for kids, tennis courts, and a climbing wall.

VALAIS CANTON

Where to Stay
The mountain villages of Evolène, Derborence, and Nax are picturesque places and good starting points for beautiful walks.

Day Trips
First, check out the haut-Valais (the upper, German-speaking part of Valais), where you'll find Zermatt, Saas-Fee, a number of gorgeous villages, and the Alestch Glacier.

What to Eat & Drink
Don't miss the local white wines—Fendant and Petite Arvine.

Where to Eat & Drink (Favorite Restaurants & Bars)
My first choice is Relais de Montorge (at Route du Sanetsch 99). Second, try C'est Ça (Place des Tanneries 9). Finally, I love Cafétéria de Valère (at Colline de Valère inside the castle).

How to Fit In
To fit with the culture, drink one more glass of wine. Ours is a drinking culture (though not a drunk culture).

How to Meet Locals & Make Friends
Try the bars, exhibitions, and festivals.

Best Places to Take a Photo
Without a doubt, the Bisse de Montorge!

VALAIS CANTON

GRIMENTZ
Simplicity, authenticity, beauty, & skiing.

FIND WI-FI HERE: Bar Domino, Alpina, Becs de Bosson, Cristal, Moiry, Bendolla, & Le Country.

LANGUAGE: French   **CANTON:** Valais

Christine Torche
Ski Instructor. B&B Owner. Mountain Lover.

About Christine
I was born in Geneva and moved to Grimentz with my husband in 1984. We came because we love skiing and mountains and knew we'd be happier outside the city. Our friends thought we were crazy to quit our jobs and move to such a remote place...but now everybody envies our life and we are really happy we made that choice.

For 25 years, I worked for the Swiss ski school as an instructor and for the last five years I've been an independent instructor, which I love.

Since our two boys left home, I've also been running a little one-room B&B, Altitude Attitude, out of our home. We are right in the heart of the old village and people are crazy about it.

What to Do In Grimentz (The Basics)
Take a stroll through the pedestrian walking area of the old village and enjoy the feeling that time has stopped. Take time to enjoy the old wooden houses, which are full of interesting architectural details. Then stroll through the garden behind the

church, which is the cemetery, where you'll find a simple plot of land covered in wooden crosses.

Hidden Gems for Seasoned Travelers
The *via ferrata* (self-attaching climbing route) on the side of the Moiry Dam is absolutely magnificent. If you're lucky, you'll see edelweiss flowers and *bouquetins* (ibex) along the way.

In wintertime, the special thing to do is full-moon ski. You have to book in advance (at *tinyurl.com/pkgtwp3*) and, of course, it only happens once a month during the full moon. When we go, we start with a fondue in the Bendolla Restaurant, which has good ambiance and better music. Every time we go, there are about 200 people there enjoying themselves. Then, after eating, when the moon comes out, we all go up to the panorama at Orzival and we ski down.

Where to Stay
Stay in the old village area, where you'll find plenty of hotels, apartment rentals, and B&Bs.

Day Trips
In spring or late autumn, head to Lac de Moiry for some spectacular natural beauty. In the summer, try Moiry hut for a taste of the glacier and high mountain scenery. It's about a two-hour hike and you'll need good shoes.

You can also take the Telephérique Grimentz Zinal (cable car) and walk up to Corne de Sorebois, then down to Lac de Moiry and back to Grimentz. This takes about four hours. And if you want to extend your hiking time, before you head back to Grimentz, you can follow signs for Chemin des 2500 (an extra four hours of hiking to a large lake) or Le Tour du Lac (an extra 2.5 hours, also around a lake).

For the less hiking-inclined, I recommend a visit to some of the less touristy villages of the valley, like St. Jean, Pinsec, Mayoux, Mission, Ayer, Chandolin, and Vissoie. You can get cheap and interesting guidebooks for each one at the tourist office.

VALAIS CANTON

Zermatt, Sion, and the hot springs in Loèche les Bains or Saillon are also worth a visit, as are the great museums of Gianadda in Martigny and La Fondation Arnaud in Lens.

Where to Hike
There are so many possibilities...You can hike to and sleep in our mountain huts (Becs de Bosson hut, Moiry hut, Traduit hut, Arpitetaz hut, or Grand Mountet hut). You can do some mountaineering (if you're a beginner, hire a mountain guide). Or you can climb Bishorn—a 13,000-foot mountain that requires no mountaineering knowledge, just a mountain guide and good fitness.

What to Eat & Drink
In the summer, ask for sérac, a soft cheese made from buttermilk. For wine, visit the bourgeoisie house to taste the famous Vin des Glaciers. Finally, try viande séchée (dried meat) and sausages made in the valley.

Where to Eat & Drink (Favorite Restaurants & Bars)
For après ski, stop at Florioz (at Route des Rahas 20) at the end of the slope for a beer and a flamkuchen (thin bread with cheese and toppings).

Have a raclette au feu de bois (wood-fired) or fresh game during hunting season at Moiry Restaurant (on Rue du Village).

I also love the Écurie a Buvette, which is reached via a beautiful one-hour walk outside town. Try the flamed rösti. (*buvette-ecurie.ch*)

Restaurant du Lac de Moiry is also wonderful, with a great location, cozy interior, and good food. (*moiryresto.ch*)

Bendolla, at the top of the Grimentz gondola, is the best altitude restaurant I have ever visited. The *plat du jour* (plate of the day) is always unique and if you're a dessert lover, don't miss the milles feuilles (napoleon pastries).

Budget Tips

In the summertime, you can camp for free just 10 minutes outside the village (on foot). The place is called îlot bosquet and offers toilets (though no showers). All you have to pay is the tourist tax (2.50 francs per night per person). Paying the tourist tax gets you an access card that gives free access to the yellow post buses and the cable car and reductions on the swimming pool and tennis courts.

How to Meet Locals & Make Friends

Be friendly, be curious, spend time here, come again, and participate in the firong (small market) in the old village on Fridays in the summertime.

Best Places to Take a Photo

Anywhere in the old village, on Lac du Moiry (where the landscape is always changing), or on top of the Téléphérique Grimentz – Zinal in the heart of the Alps surrounded by 13,000+-foot peaks.

Final Notes & Other Tips

Don't discount the off-season. Autumn is stunning—from October to early November, there's great light, beautiful colors, and a serene quietness. It's my favorite season.

Find Christine at grimentz-ski.net and tinyurl.com/our96z4.

TICINO

LOCARNO
Good weather, Italian food, & lovely natural spaces.

FIND WI-FI HERE: McDonald's, Manora, the train station, Piazza Grande, & the supermarkets.

LANGUAGE: Italian   **CANTON:** Ticino

Marco Luigi Regina
Hiker. Traveler. Sports Enthusiast.

About Marco
I'm a bit complicated. My father is Italian and my mother is Polish, but I was born and have always lived in the Italian part of Switzerland, except for a year in New Zealand and two years in the French part of Switzerland.

I'm a mechanical technician, but I'm about to start a new adventure as a trip leader for a coach company that does trips around Europe.

In my free time, I used to enjoy skydiving, BASE jumping, free-diving, and hiking, but since May I've been dedicating most of my free time to physiotherapy due to a BASE accident. Right now, I'm mostly reading, cooking, and traveling.

What to Do In Locarno (The Basics)
To start, leave your luggage at the train station in the blue lockers (they're easy to find) or drop it at your hotel/hostel/apartment and enjoy a walk by the lake, which is only three minutes from the station. The area is full of small bars and

288

restaurants where you can enjoy a cold beer in summer or a lovely cappuccino in winter.

Hidden Gems for Seasoned Travelers

An interesting place to see is the Verzasca Valley (Valle Verzasca), where you can follow a mountain road by car, motorbike, or bus. At the beginning of the valley, there is a huge dam that was featured in the James Bond movie *GoldenEye*. Brave souls can book a bungee jump from it.

This region is a mix of Swiss mountains, Italian food, and tropical environment (palm trees!). The most important thing is to get out and enjoy it all.

Where to Stay

A good way to enjoy this area is camping. There are plenty of campgrounds all around the region, from cheap to pretty expensive (depending on the number of stars). Another great option is rental apartments. Private people are renting rooms with kitchens and everything else you need.

Day Trips

Cardada-Cimetta is an amazing location that offers a breathtaking view of Lake Maggiore. It is reachable from Locarno by public transport. There's a little funicular that goes up to Orselina, where a cable car will bring you up to Cardada. From there you can hike for about an hour to Cimetta or take a chairlift. There are a few restaurants and nice spots at the top of the mountain and along the hike, as well as a panoramic platform and a horse farm. It's also a famous location for paragliding (for both beginners and experts) and a tandem flight on a sunny day is a must.

In winter, this is a lovely ski resort for those who want to learn how to ski or snowboard.

Monte Tamaro is another great place, similar to Cardada-Cimetta but a bit farther south. There is a cable car from Rivera and at the top there are a few cool activities.

TICINO

As mentioned before, in the Verzasca Valley you can enjoy a beautiful drive alongside the artificial lake (where people BASE jump from the dam) and then a river. Eventually, you'll come to the amazing Roman bridge at Lavertezzo, where the beautiful green water will capture your heart.

Gordevio in the Maggia Valley (Vallemaggia) and the Verzasca Valley are well known for canyoning. And we've also got one of the world's top skydiving centers at the Locarno Airport.

If you're a fan of history and architecture, the windy city of Bellinzona is a must-visit. It's famous for its castles and the wall from the Middle Ages that still crosses part of the city.

Where to Hike

You can find hiking trails pretty much everywhere. For experienced hikers, there are two specific trails that will take you on a stunning week-long journey (though you can always stop by descending other trails into some amazing locations). The first is the Via Alta Vallemaggia (*vialtavallemaggia.ch*) and the second is Via Alta Valle Verzasca (look it up at *verzasca.net*).

Another beautiful hike is the route around the Basodino Glacier. Start from Robiei, which is reachable by cable car from San Carlo in the summer, or Piano Delle Creste, which is reachable from San Carlo on foot.

You can find lovely heated shelters with kitchens, beds, toilets, and showers on pretty much every mountaintop here in Switzerland. A friendly local is normally there to help.

Where to Eat & Drink (Favorite Restaurants & Bars)

Start with Ristorante Pizzeria Bellariva (on Via Cantonale in Gordevio). This place has some of the best pizza you'll eat in your life. They also serve every kind of pasta and other tasty seasonal dishes. Call ahead to book a table: +44 091 753 1965.

Another favorite is Ristorante Campanile (at Centro Intragna in Intragna). It's a lovely place where you'll find a different menu for every season. Try the fresh, homemade pasta with fish, vegetables, or meat. Wild game is also very typical. The sella di capriolo (a venison dish) is simply amazing.

My third pick would be Ristorante Pizzeria Gnesa (at Via San Gottardo 80 in Gordola). This place also offers seasonal dishes and good pizzas. If you like prawns, linguine alle code di gambero is what you want. That's what I always eat there.

Budget Tips
Avoid restaurants/bars in touristy places (near the lake, airports, train stations, etc.). The better prices are a little outside these areas.

In Switzerland, it is legal to drink alcohol in the street, so don't worry if you want to buy a beer at a grocery store to save money; you can enjoy it sitting at the beach or another nice location around town. There are very few areas where you are not allowed to drink, and they are well marked.

How to Fit In
If you're Russian, don't drink too much. If you're American, don't shout too much. If you're Italian, don't talk with your hands too much...But I jest...Respect the local rules and customs and don't be too noisy or litter, especially in small villages.

How to Meet Locals & Make Friends
In the summer, there is a movie festival in Locarno, as well as an event called Moon & Stars, where stars like Pink, Santana, REM, Green Day, etc. perform. During these events, you can meet people from around the world.

In wintertime, there's an event called Locarno on Ice where they set up a rink surrounded by bars with hot wine, local food stands, and a little Christmas market. There is live music.

TICINO

Best Places to Take a Photo

Lungolago di Ascona, Cardada-Cimetta, Piazza Grande Locarno, and everywhere in the mountains and nature.

Final Notes & Other Tips

Maybe avoid November, which tends to be rainy, but do come in autumn. The fall colors in this area are something magical to behold.

BELLINZONA
Ancient walls, three (yes, three) castles, & lovely views.

FIND WI-FI HERE: Manor Appunto (café) & the train station.

LANGUAGE: Italian   **CANTON:** Ticino

Miriam Moretti
Yogi. Reader. Music-Lover.

About Miriam
I was born and raised in Bellinzona and I just moved to Fribourg to study nursing. In my free time, I like listening to music, practicing yoga, reading, and spending time with my family.

What to Do In Bellinzona (The Basics)
Well, first you have to see the castles. There are three of them: one is very big and in the middle of the town, the second has typically medieval characteristics, and in order to see the third castle, you have to walk 30 minutes up the mountain.

Also, every Saturday, there is a traditional market in the historical center where you can buy all sorts of local products and see people come together in a festive atmosphere. It's absolutely worth seeing.

Hidden Gems for Seasoned Travelers
One really special thing is our Carnevale festivities in February. Bring your mask or costume, get in a good mood, and participate in the afternoon show or go partying all night long.

For those coming in spring, summer, or fall, there are a lot of nice hiking trails near the river in a region called Golena. Or you can even make your way up to the top of the mountains

293

and spend the night in a hut, enjoying the energy of the mountains for more than one day at a time.

In winter, it's nice to go snowshoeing.

Where to Stay
In the city center, there is a beautiful youth hostel or you can look for a room in the area around the town municipal building, the train station, or the Ravecchia neighborhood.

Day Trips
Start with Locarno, which is a small city facing a beautiful lake (Lago Maggiore); it's only 20 minutes away by train. Personally, I think the best way to go to Locarno is to take the train to Tenero and walk along the lake to Locarno (which takes about an hour). And if you visit in the summertime, there are some great jazz and rock festivals and an international film festival (the biggest in Switzerland) there.

If you come in winter or spring, you'll find both classical and rock concerts in nearby Lugano.

Where to Hike
First, I recommend picking up a hiking map at the tourist office. For adventurous hikers, the journey to the Pizzo di Claro is a great challenge. A trip into the Valle di Blenio (approximately 30 minutes from Bellinzona) is also a nice idea. For something less daunting, you can walk up to a hut (there are several in the area), have a drink, and come back down.

What to Eat & Drink
The culture in Ticino is closer to Italian culture than the Swiss and our food reflects that similarity. Local restaurants and grottos (small restaurants only open in the warm season) offer a variety of pastas, pizzas, gnocchi, polenta e spezzatino (cornmeal and red meat), salametti (local sausages), and, of course, seasoned or fresh Alp cheese, which comes directly

from the mountains. If you like coffee, we have good espresso and cappuccino as well.

Where to Eat & Drink (Favorite Restaurants & Bars)
Il Ristorante del Popolo (at Viale Stazione 31) is cheap but really good. Il Corona (at Via Camminata 5) is known for amazing pizzas. And Osteria Mistral (at Via Orico 2) is a bit more expensive but offers creative dishes with the best local products.

How to Fit In
Respecting our language will always make us happy. Speak Italian or English to us and forget about German or French (just because we live in Switzerland doesn't mean we know all the national languages).

How to Meet Locals & Make Friends
You'll have a lot of success just taking an interest in our culture. After all, people love their habits. Also, go for a hike and you are likely to meet open-minded people (especially at the huts) or go to some international summer festivals.

Best Places to Take a Photo
In the historical center or at one of the castles.

Final Notes & Other Tips
Most people think that Ticino always has nice weather. Although it's true that we have a bright and warming sun, I advise you to pack an umbrella and some good shoes, as it can sometimes pour for four or five days in a row. Finally, you can find the tourism website at *bellinzonaturismo.ch*.

TICINO

LUGANO
Lake Lugano, Monte San Salvatore, & a sunny Mediterranean climate.

FIND WI-FI HERE: At Manor & via Boingo around town.

LANGUAGE: Italian   **CANTON:** Ticino

Nicole Ebenhack
Fitness & Nutrition Coach. Skier. Hiker. Entrepreneur.

About Nicole
I was born and raised in Denver, Colorado, but after school and about five years in my career in the central U.S., my husband and I moved to Lugano. I always wanted to travel but didn't have the resources growing up. I've worked hard to change that over the years and living and working in Switzerland is the fulfillment of a life-long dream.

After moving to Lugano, I used in-home fitness programs to lose 25 pounds and get into the best physical and mental shape of my life, so now I pay it forward as the CEO of my own online fitness and nutrition coaching business helping people accomplish their goals and create time and financial freedom so that they, too, can enjoy healthy, fulfilling lives.

In my free time, outside is where I prefer to be, so you'll find me skiing, hiking, and exploring new places on foot every chance I get! My current goal is to summit the Matterhorn in Zermatt, so right now I am focusing my attention on training for that.

What to Do In Lugano (The Basics)
The first thing anyone notices about Lugano is, of course, the lake. It is big and gorgeous and the focal point of the entire

city. Start your time here with some gelato from La Fredda Tentazione (address: Via Pietro Peri 2). From there, walk toward the lake and take a right when you get there to follow the footpath for a breathtaking panorama of the valley Lugano sits in. Then, make sure to retrace your steps past the city center and to Parco Civico-Ciana, where you'll find the quintessential view over the lake. Lots of people miss the walk back, but it's a very different experience with different views.

Along the way, you'll find a boathouse with chairs and tables available for sitting and relaxing. Continue on the footpath to its very end, where you'll find a boardwalk and can sit, relax, and soak up some sun. There's also a fantastic playground.

If you are in the mood for coffee, there is a little café called Café a Porter (address: Via Pasquale Lucchini 1) near one of the Parco Civico-Ciana entrances. It's a nice place to grab a take away cappuccino—particularly before Lugano wakes up (around 8 a.m.) and the hustle and bustle begins. It's so peaceful and beautiful to be alone in the park.

From the park, you can walk outside the city and catch the funicular (at Via Ceresio di Suvigliana 36 in Ruvigliana) up to Monte Bre for a drink and to take in the sprawling view of Lake Como to your left, Lago Maggiore to your right, and Lake Lugano straight ahead.

Alternatively, past the end of the lake's footpath at the fountain (on the opposite end of the footpath from the park), you'll find Monte San Salvatore. You can also take a funicular (at Via delle Scuole 12) up and down the mountain for views and a drink—or you can pack a bag and hike it.

Finally, on a nice, calm day, you should definitely rent a paddleboat from Pedalo Rivetta Tell (at Palazzo Rivetta Tell). This is one of my favorite things to do.

The Lido di Lugano (at Via Lido), with an Olympic sized pool, a smaller, heated pool, a diving pool, a paddling pool, a lake beach, and a restaurant/bar, is also a nice place to be.

TICINO

Hidden Gems for Seasoned Travelers

The area of Ticino is known for its grottos (stone homestead ruins turned into restaurants). They are characterized by their outdoor grills and sprawling terraces, which are always tucked back into the trees and away from the cities. Grotto del Cavicc (at Via ai Canvetti 19a in Montagnola) is my favorite and is a must for anyone who wants to get away from the hustle and bustle of the city (and for the foodies). Hermann Hesse—a famous Swiss writer—spent a lot of time eating, drinking, writing, and socializing there.

Go with a friend and order a half or full liter of the *nostrano rosso* (the house red), which is a Tichinese Merlot typical of the region. Drink your wine out of the striped ceramic bowls like a local instead of with a wine glass. And as for food, start with the selection of cold meats and finish with the pork ribs, dry-rubbed, grilled, and oh-so-delicious with a side of rosemary potatoes! Menus are available in English and Taxi Lugano (*taxilugano.ch*/+41 79 836 5738) can get you there and back.

After dinner, walk to Church of Sant'Abbondio (address: Casella Postale 339 in Gentilino). It is a magnificent building with a domed bell and clock tower and a cypress-lined walkway next to the Gentilino cemetery where Hermann Hesse is buried.

Where to Stay

The most convenient and logical place to stay is at the Hotel Lugano Dante (at Piazza Cioccaro 5), which is right in the middle of the city center. From there, everything you'll want to see and do is within walking distance.

Day Trips

For a really special day trip, head north to Sonogno and hike along the river to Lavertezzo (about a 2.5 hour walk), where you will encounter a gorgeous Romanesque arched bridge called the Ponte dei Salti. Here, you can spend some time swimming and diving in the canyon before hiking the Verzasca Valley to Maggia (an overnight hike).

It's also easy to get to Locarno and Bellinzona, which are north of Lugano, or Milan and Como, which are about an hour south (in Italy).

Where to Hike

Lugano is surrounded by several local mountains that can all be hiked: Monte Generoso, Monte Bre, Alpe Bolla, Denti della Vecchia, Monte Bar, Monte Lema, Monte Tamaro, and Monte San Salvatore. The paths here are all well marked and taken care of and Switzerland (as a whole) has created incredible resources for hikers and made them available online (at *myswitzerland.com* and *lugano-tourism.ch*).

That said, the quintessential local hike to take would be up Lugano's home mountain, Monte San Salvatore. The trailhead is easy to access by foot from the city center and, while planning is a cinch, the hike itself is both challenging and rewarding. The 360-degree view of the Alps and Lake Lugano from the rooftop of the church that sits atop Monte San Salvatore is sure to take your breath away (it's where my husband proposed—that's how beautiful it is).

The trailhead is just past the Scuole Paradiso bus stop, near the funicular station at the base of Monte San Salvatore. Once you get to the summit, continue upward to the church and climb the staircase to the roof. From here, you have a few options. You can hike down the way you came. You can hike through Corona to Parco San Grato (a botanical garden with beautiful flora and views of the surrounding summits) and then down to Morcote where you can catch a bus back to Lugano. Or you can ride the funicular down. My personal preference, though I do not typically favor going back the same way I came, is to hike back down. Round trip, this takes an average hiker four to five hours and can be done early morning or mid-day with plenty of time to clean up, rest, and go out to enjoy your evening on returning.

Where to Eat & Drink (Favorite Restaurants & Bars)

My absolute favorite is Mojito Bar (on Riva Albertolli), which is an open-air bar open on the lake's footpath every summer. Mojito Bar is where everyone goes to enjoy the gorgeous outdoor Lugano nightlife. Order the signature mojito.

My next favorite is Bottegone del Vino (at Via Massimigliano Magatti 3), an absolutely charming hole-in-the-wall right next to the city center. The menu changes daily and is limited, similar to an Italian trattoria, and typical of the local establishments. The wine and desserts are fantastic here and the service is wonderful.

Finally, I like Grotto della Salute (at Via Madonna della Salute 10), which is near the train station. Although close to the city center and easy to walk to, this grotto is still tucked away in some of the most incredible trees you will ever lay eyes on. I want to climb them every time I'm there. The menu is more sophisticated than at other Tichinese grottos and changes seasonally. There's also a special daily menu.

How to Fit In

There is a bike kiosk in town, but the city is not well equipped for cyclists, so I recommend ignoring it. Trust me when I tell you that you will not get anywhere fast on a bike in Lugano and you won't enjoy trying either. (I should know...I brought a bike over from the states and attempted to use it as my primary mode of transportation for quite some time before it became abundantly clear to me that walking is much more enjoyable). If you choose to ignore me on this and rent a bike, please do not ride it on the sidewalks. It's illegal and dangerous for pedestrians.

If you order a cappuccino here (and you should), make sure you order it before 11 a.m. Cappuccino after 11 a.m. will make you stand out right away.

Finally, Swiss people have unspoken quiet hours from 10 p.m. to 8 a.m. And, of course, you'll want to be polite and considerate of the people that you come into contact with. Other than that, though, there is not a lot you can do to upset people in

Lugano, since Italian culture is pervasive here and Italians like to just go with the flow.

How to Meet Locals & Make Friends

If you are coming to Lugano from another part of Switzerland, you'll notice an immediate cultural difference. In the French and German parts of the country, people keep mostly to themselves and are much more reserved. In Lugano, the people are friendly, outgoing, talkative, and approachable. When you are out and about, just strike up a conversation with anyone around you and they will be happy to talk to you. (That said, in Lugano, very little English is spoken, so if you do not speak Italian, you might have to try your luck a time or two to come up with an English-speaker.)

You can also use social media to network before you arrive. There are Lugano groups on Facebook, MeetUp, InterNations, and Couchsurfing.

Best Places to Take a Photo

A picture in front of Lake Lugano and Monte San Salvatore next to the wrought iron gate in Parco Civico-Ciani is the most quintessential view there is, but the photo ops from atop Monte Bre and Monte San Salvatore are even more impressive if you ask me.

Final Notes & Other Tips

My favorite summer activities are Pardo al Parco, which is a miniature version of the Locarno Film Festival held in Parco Civico-Ciani and Estival, which is an open-air jazz festival.

In fall and winter, Lugano is a bit sleepier. So if it's events you crave, come in summer. That said, there is an autumn market and a Christmas market here every year and both are lovely. Make it a point to have chocciolatta densa (Italian hot chocolate) if you're here in the winter months. It's so thick you almost need a spoon to drink it. The best one is at Munger (at Via Luvini 4), which is to the left of Manor in the city center.

TICINO

Finally, I'll leave you with a tip for the grocery store: You have to weigh your own produce here, so make sure you do that with any fruits or veggies you want to buy before heading to the cash register. You also have to buy your own grocery sacks here and bag your own groceries. When you get in line to check out, grab one of the foldable nylon grocery sacks that you see by the gum. One sack costs about two francs and is very handy to have when traveling!

Find Nicole at nicoleebenhack.com and facebook.com/ nicole.ebenhack.

MELIDE
An excellent home base for exploring the Sottoceneri.

FIND WI-FI HERE: Along the lake (a city connection).

LANGUAGE: Italian   **CANTON:** Ticino

Angelo Geninazzi
Traveler. Reader. Nature Lover.

About Angelo
I have always lived in Melide, I work for an economic association, and in my free time, I like traveling, reading, and outdoor sports.

What to Do In Melide (The Basics)
Start by exploring the area around the lake. In the past, the people of Melide made a living thanks to fishing and repairing fishing nets. The lake has always been central to the town's existence and today it is the most beautiful part of the village.

Melide is also an excellent home base for exploring the whole Sottoceneri (the part of Ticino that lies south of the Monte Ceneri Pass and which is less known to the tourist masses, although it contains a lot of hidden gems). So make sure to explore the region as well as the town.

Hidden Gems for Seasoned Travelers
There is one place in particular that I like very much: To get there, go up into the forest (which is above the whole village and the main road), follow the fitness path (vita parcour) for about 15 - 20 minutes (there is only one direction to go: straight ahead), then you'll see (on the left side) a small plain with less

TICINO

trees and from there you'll have a spectacular view of the lake below, the mountains in the background, and the neighboring villages. There's also a little fire-pit for BBQs and not many people come up there, so you'll probably have it to yourself.

For a more relaxing activity, I suggest a boat trip to the small typical villages around the lake.

Day Trips
One nice option is the neighboring village of Morcote, about 10 minutes away by car. Morcote has a lot of curiosity/corner shops and it's a great place to eat a delicious gelato and enjoy the nice view over the lake and Italian villages on the opposite bank. Also, at the end of Morcote, there is a beautiful garden called Scherer Park full with subtropical vegetation and works of art. Walking through that garden is like being inside a fairy tale.

A bigger excursion you can do is to top of the hill (Alp Vicania) above Melide and Morcote. There are hiking trails (both short and long) that lead through the forests there. And when you get hungry, the Alpe Vicania restaurant will be happy to offer you some typical Ticinese foods.

Finally, I recommend a visit to Monte Brè and Monte Generoso —two beautiful mountains that you can reach on foot or via public transportation. At both peaks, you'll find drinks and food from spring to autumn.

Where to Hike
The whole area from Monte San Salvatore to Morcote is full of hiking trails for every fitness level and duration. If you like high Alpine hiking, I recommend Monte Bar—the mountain behind Lugano, which is almost 6,000 feet high—and the area around Monte Generoso (with an altitude of about 5,500 feet).

The route between Monte Tamaro (about 6,500 feet) and Monte Lema (about 5,300 feet) is a very famous excursion that you can do by mountain bike as well as on foot. If you are lucky and have a clear day, you can see all the way to the Bernese Alps.

What to Eat & Drink
If you're here in fall/winter, try our chestnuts. You can even collect some on your own in the forest in September/October.

Where to Eat & Drink (Favorite Restaurants & Bars)
One of my favorites is Hotel and Restaurant Al Boccalino (at Via Borromini 27, phone: +41 91 649 7767). It's a small restaurant near the lake with a few rustic rooms. The atmosphere is casual and personal and you can eat outside under the pergola (a shaded terrace).

Another favorite is Hotel and Restaurant Del Lago (at Lungolago Motta 9, phone: +41 91 649 7041). It's a designer hotel at the lakeside with an excellent fish restaurant.

How to Fit In
In Ticino, it's important to be open and friendly. It is normal to chat with a person you see for the first time on the bus.

If you are invited to eat with some locals, make sure to bring a little gift. When eating, taste a little bit of everything before saying you don't like something, because to be hospitable is very important to locals and you might offend them by refusing to taste what they offer you.

How to Meet Locals & Make Friends
One way to meet locals is to participate in the numerous local events, which start in the spring and end in the fall. For example: the gastronomic walk through the narrow streets of Melide, the summer market at the waterfront, or the castagnata (a mini chestnut and wine festival in the square). You'll meet a lot of locals at these events.

Another way, especially for parents, is to go to playgrounds with your children, where you always will find parents standing around chatting.

For young people, I recommend visiting the summer markets, street art shows, and concerts in parks or going ice skating on one of the area's many rinks in the winter. Here in Melide, you'll find ice skating (as well as mulled wine and snacks) in the village square from late November to early January.

Best Places to Take a Photo

The best place to get a memorable photograph of Melide is along the lake, especially in the sunset light or when it is dusted with snow (which is rarely, but if you can catch it, it's stunning).

Final Notes & Other Tips

Check out the Swissminiature Park, where you can admire more than 120 models (at a scale of 1:25) of the most important buildings, monuments, and transportation infra-structure in Switzerland.

LAVERTEZZO
The green heart of Ticino.

FIND WI-FI HERE: Campsites & most public areas.

LANGUAGE: Italian   **CANTON:** Ticino

Alan Matasci
Manager, National Sports Center.

About Alan
The family has deep roots in the Sonogno area, where I grew up and still live, now with a wife and three children. I work as a manager at the National Sports Center of Tenero. And in my free time, I work on local development projects with the Foundation Verzasca, the tourist board (OTLVM), and the regional development agency (ERS).

I am an avid sportsman, frequenting the mountains in all seasons. And I love reading and traveling.

What to Do In Lavertezzo (The Basics)
Lavertezzo is often associated with a particularly beautiful and unique stretch of the river Verzasca. It's a stretch with large puddles, boulders polished over the centuries by the emerald waters, and an ancient bridge with two arches (called Ponte dei Salti—literally "jumping bridge"). This is the postcard-perfect place that you absolutely must not miss.

The other must-see is a section of the Sentierone path, which runs from Sonogno to Gordola. Here, you'll pass through beech forests on the centuries-old path, built back when the nomadic life—moving up the mountain with the animals in summer and down into the valleys in winter—was essential to the survival of the Verzaschesi locals.

Hidden Gems for Seasoned Travelers

Even the most experienced travelers will be impressed by the charm of this landscape in every season, with its largely untouched nature and characteristic stone houses. Among my favorite little gems is the town of Corippo—the smallest town in Switzerland, with just 12 full-time residents. Another favorite is Castello Marcacci in Brione—a mansion-like castle with four corner towers. And a final favorite gem of mine is the newly restored ancient church of San Bartolomeo in Vogorno.

For those who love hiking and mountain biking, our peaks and mountain huts won't disappoint, particularly the Osola and Bardughée huts for families or the beautiful Starlarescio, Baron, or Cornavosa in general.

For those who love culture, there's also an interesting, easy, and well-marked trail called itinerari etnografici. It runs from Vogorno to Odro Bardüghè and features some sweeping views of both Verzasca Dam and Lake Maggiore. The hike typically takes around 5.5 hours.

Where to Stay

If you stay in a typical rustico (stone house) you definitely won't be disappointed.

Day Trips

I heartily recommend Sonogno, Corippo (the smallest town in Switzerland—mentioned above), Brione (with its interesting castle, church, and municipal house), and the Verzasca Dam (made famous by a bungee-jumping James Bond and perfect for an iconic area photo).

Where to Hike

The Sentierone Trail (mentioned above), which runs along the river, is a must. The beautiful valley walks from Osola to Brione or Vogornesso to Sonogno are easy for everyone. For more intense hikers, the most beautiful peaks are the Pizzo Barone, the Poncione of Alnasca, and Pizzo Vogorno. You won't need mountaineering equipment, but you will need to be very fit and very prepared for those daunting treks.

For mountain bikers, I recommend the new track between Sonogno and Brione with some deviations in the side valleys.

Where to Eat & Drink (Favorite Restaurants & Bars)

The Grotto al Ponte (phone: +41 91 746 1277) is one of the most typical and popular restaurants in the area. I also appreciate the Grotto Efra Sonogno (on Strada de Redorta in Sonogno; phone: + 41 91 746 1173), Sassello (on Permaioo in Gerra; phone: +41 91 746 13 09), Il Bivio in Corippo (phone: +41 91 746 1616), and Vittoria in Lavertezzo (phone: +41 91 746 1581), which all use local products and local recipes.

Budget Tips

If you are traveling by car, I recommend the convenient Parking Card (available at the tourist office, the kiosks, or the infopoints), which comes with a tourist map and allows you to park without any extra fees in 30 different areas.

Best Places to Take a Photo

Lavertezzo and the Verzasca Dam are some of the most popular. I'd also recommend the Verzasca River, the beautiful waterfalls in Sonogno or Gerra, any of our alpine lakes, and the sweeping views from the Alpe Bardughè or Val Osola.

The best photo I've ever seen personally was from Alpe d'Starlarescio looking toward Poncione Alnasca. It was the very definition of alpine environment.

Final Notes & Other Tips

In the summer months, there is a lot of "hit and run" style tourism, in particular to the river to cool off or for nature walks. First, I'd avoid this in-and-out approach. To really experience the valley, you'll need to stay a while.

Second, keep in mind that the summer is busy and the nucleus of everything is animated Sonogno. If you are after bustle, that's the time and place to pick. If, on the other hand, you're looking for a quiet immersion in nature and a real experience of the valley, come in spring or autumn.

Find Alan at www.fondazioneverzasca.ch or tenero-tourism.ch.

ST. GALLEN
A lovely city with a traffic-free old town & a famous library.

FIND WI-FI HERE: Starbucks, McDonald's, & most restaurants.

LANGUAGE: German   **CANTON:** St. Gallen

Kilian Schefer
Mountain Biker. Traveler. Software Engineer.

About Kilian
Hi all! My name is Kilian and I work as a software engineer, creating web applications. I moved to St. Gallen three years ago, to a suburb called St. Georgen just above the city on one of the two hills that flank the town. Originally, I'm from Goldach, a small village about 15 minutes from St. Gallen by car, right next to beautiful Lake Constance. In my free time, I like mountain biking and traveling.

What to Do In St. Gallen (The Basics)
Even though it's not the most famous destination in Switzerland, St. Gallen is a great choice for travelers. It's a comfortable size (you can reach most places in and around town by foot) but also has a lot to offer.

The city was founded in the 7th century and got its name from a monk called Gallus. The abbey and its famous library are a UNESCO World Heritage Site, so that's the low hanging fruit and a good first stop. If you go there by foot, you'll also pass through old town, which features rows of old buildings that, from a bird's eye view, actually form a circle. Make sure you pay attention to the artistic bays on most of the houses— they're all unique and proof of the travels that textile workers made in the 18th and 19th century.

EASTERN SWITZERLAND

Hidden Gems for Seasoned Travelers
In case you're the museum type or if the weather is too bad, I'd recommend the Textile Museum in the city center. Also special is the Criminal Museum, where they exhibit tools that have been involved in real crimes.

Another awesome spot is the City Lounge near the train station —a whole area covered in red, including furniture, a parked car, a fountain, and a vase.

Where to Stay
For a real taste of the city, find a hotel in the old town (for example Hotel Dom or Hotel Vadian). From there, most of the interesting places are just a few minutes away on foot.

Day Trips
Once you've hit the St. Gallen sights, check out Appenzell, a very traditional area nearby that is exactly what most people imagine Switzerland to be—green hills, farms spread all over the place, cows, and mountains. People there are very trad- itional and even young people walk around in traditional clothing for special holidays and events.

Appenzellerland is also a great area for hiking and, for the less energetic, there are several mountains (Säntis, Kronberg, Hoher Kasten) that you can reach by cable car.

In the opposite direction, a day trip could lead you to the shores of Lake Constance. It's the eastern end of Switzerland and, in the summer, there are paddleboats available for rent in Rorschach, Arbon, or Romanshorn. Make sure to take your swimming gear with you. Water temperatures in summer vary from 66° to 75° Fahrenheit.

Where to Hike
One favorite is the three lakes (Drei Weiheren), which you can reach either on foot or via train. It's a well-loved place for local people to relax and get in touch with nature. The top offers a

stunning view of the city. And behind the lakes, there's another hill with a great restaurant on top offering food like grandma did it back in the old days. There's also a little zoo with goats and a donkey.

On the other hillside, we have a wildlife park (called Peter und Paul) with animals that live in Switzerland (deer, marmots, forest cats, goats, and many more). There is no entrance fee, as the park is sponsored by local companies. Take the bus toward the park and get off along the way for a wonderful walk.

What to Eat & Drink & Where to Eat & Drink It
There is a little restaurant in the old town called Fondue Beizli (at Brühlgasse 26; phone: +41 71 222 4344) that does fondue well. It's a popular spot, so reserve a table if you're going for dinner.

You should also try OLMA Bratwurst, a famous local grilled sausage that can be bought from most of the butchers in town (Metzgerei Gemperli, Metzgerei Rietmann, or Metzgerei Schmid) as a take-out dish.

There are also a couple of wonderful cafés and a chocolate shop where you can try chocolate from Maestrani, a company that originally produced in the St. Georgen quarter.

My absolute favorite restaurant in town is Oya (at Schwertgasse 27). It's a small gem with a charming wooden interior. For lunch, they offer Scandinavian dishes. In the evening, they have local beers (Schützengarten Lager, St. Galler Klosterbräu) along with several Scandinavian beers.

For a lovely Italian lunch or dinner, try Ristorante Acquarello (at Davidstrasse 38). They have some wonderful lunch menus at pretty good prices.

And if you'd like to try local food, visit Restaurant Markplatz (at Neugasse 2). Right in the center of our old town, they offer rösti in different variations, which is definitely worth trying.

EASTERN SWITZERLAND

Budget Tips
There is a hidden gem called Gartenhaus (at Geltenwilen-strasse 8), where a lot of workmen go for lunch. The menu is tasty and the soup is great.

Best Places to Take a Photo
Take a walk to the monastery (Kloster) area for a shot of the impressive church with its two towers. Once in that area, you're very close to the cable car to the three lakes (Drei Weiheren) where you'll get an awesome view of the city.

APPENZELL
Cliffs, lakes, rocks, colors, & that quintessential Swiss mountain inn.

FIND WI-FI HERE: Ebenalpbahn Station & some mountain inns.

LANGUAGE: German   **CANTON:** Appenzell

Nicole Knechtle
Inn Manager. Nature Lover.

About Nicole
I grew up in Appenzell and, along with my husband, I own the Berggasthaus Aescher-Wildkirchli [Editor's note: This is the picturesque inn built up against a cliff constantly featured on Pinterest boards and magazine websites!].

What to Do In Appenzell
First, walk around the historic town of Appenzell. From there, you are already on the border of the Alpstein hiking area, which has well-kept trails and a lot of mountain inns to stay in.

A top tour for fit hikers is the Wasserauen-Aescher-Ebenalp-Schäfler-Säntis-Rotsteinpass-Meglisalp-Seealpsee-Wasserauen walk. It is at least a two-day tour and I recommend staying in mountain inns along the way. You can find a hiking map at *alpstein.ch*.

Where to Stay
I like mountain inns like Berggasthaus Forelle (alongside the Seealpsee lake), Berggasthaus Meglisalp (in a fabulous, small farm village in the Alps), and Berggasthaus Bollenwees (alongside the Fälensee lake). In all, the region boasts 27 mountain guesthouses.

Day Trips
Most people go to St. Gallen for the day, but Switzerland is so small you could hit most of the beaten tourist track—Zürich, Lucerne, Zermatt, Bern—in a week or so.

Where to Hike
From our front door at Berggasthaus Aescher, it takes one hour on foot to get to the wonderful Seealpsee lake down in the valley. And coming back up the cliffs from the valley floor takes about two hours.

What to Eat & Drink
Try höhlenmeringues (meringues with cream and ice cream), nussgipfel (a hazelnut pastry), and Appenzeller Locher beer.

Where to Eat & Drink (Favorite Restaurants & Bars)
My favorites are Berggasthaus Forelle (at Seealpsee 8), Berggasthaus Schäfler, and Berggasthaus Mesmer. All three are in the mountains and both Forelle and Schäfler are close enough that you could go for lunch from here.

How to Meet Locals & Make Friends
Sit with other people when you're at one of the mountain inns. Drink and enjoy and start up a conversation.

Best Places to Take a Photo
From the Aescher Cliffs or on top of Ebenalp. [Editor's note: Nicole's mountain inn itself is actually an iconic shot; just Google "Aescher Cliffs" and you'll find pages and pages of photos of the inn's iconic exterior.]

Final Notes & Other Tips
In this region, it's always good to have cash on you. In most of the guesthouses, you can pay by card but you never know.

Find Nicole at aescher-ai.ch.

316

SCHWELLBRUNN
A traditional village built on a hill.

FIND WI-FI HERE: B&B Gästehaus Rössli.

LANGUAGE: German   **CANTON:** Appenzell

Martin & Marie-Theres Sebastian
Nature-Lovers. Music Enthusiasts.

About the Sebastians
We are a multicultural couple. Martin (the husband) is a nature-loving Swiss guy and Marie-Theres (the wife) is a family-oriented Filipino lady. We speak English, French, German, Swiss German, and Filipino. In our free time, we go to concerts or take long walks in nature with our dog. For work, we run a B&B in a beautiful art nouveau building in the heart of Schwellbrunn. Our motto is "a place to decelerate."

What to Do In Schwellbrunn (The Basics)
First, take a walk through the historic village with your camera in hand. Then visit one of the nearby viewpoints (they're all wonderful).

Hidden Gems for Seasoned Travelers
The highest mountain in the region (Mount Säntis) is right outside our front door. It's over 8,000 feet above sea level and at the top hikers are treated to one of the most beautiful panoramas in Switzerland. Other wonderful peaks just around the corner include the Hohe Kastens and the Kronberg.

If you prefer a cozy and cultural experience, visit Appenzell (the region's main town) and explore a cheese house or a historical museum.

EASTERN SWITZERLAND

Day Trips
The picturesque town of Appenzell (located at the foot of the imposing Alpstein mountain) with its famous main street is a must-see. The Alpstein area is perfect for hiking (in all seasons), climbing, skiing, snowshoeing, sledding, or just relaxing at a viewpoint. Rest and relaxation is guaranteed. Larger centers like Herisau, St. Gallen, Wattwil, Will, Winterthur, and Zürich are also easy to reach from here.

Where to Hike
We have some very nice trails that lead toward Toggenburg through soft hills, past simple chalet-style restaurants, and to sweeping, open views of the region's many valleys. Alternatively, the famous Camino de Santiago passes through here.

What to Eat & Drink
World-famous local specialties include Appenzeller cheese, smoked meat, Appenzell biber (a special type of gingerbread cookie), Appenzeller beer, or our special soft drink, Appenzeller Flauder.

Where to Eat & Drink (Favorite Restaurants & Bars)
We like Restaurant Sitz (on a hill just outside Schwellbrunn; phone: +41 071 351 2405). A small footpath leads from the parking lot about 15 minutes up to the cozy house. There is a family ski lift in winter. And on Sundays they often have live traditional music.

Restaurants Ochsen and Harmonie (in the Schwellbrunn town center) are also lovely, with traditional food and friendly locals. And the Schnuggebock Restaurant in Teufen is a historic and interesting experience, located in a museum that showcases what life was like here 100 years ago.

Best Places to Take a Photo
Högg, Landsberg, Sitz, Risi, Geren, and Horst are all scenic.

Find the Sebastian family at roesslischwellbrunn.ch.

318

QUINTEN

A photographer's paradise with sheer cliffs & a blue-green lake.

FIND WI-FI HERE: Restaurant Schifflände.

LANGUAGE: German   **CANTON:** St. Gallen

Marcus Händel & Marc Nay
An Artist (Marc) & A Photographer (Marcus). Nature Lovers.

About Marc & Marcus

Marc: I'm an art historian teaching in Chur on subjects like medieval wall paintings, rural architecture in the Alps, and building activities in early tourism. I love the evenings down at the lake, singing and spending time with my friends. I settled in Quinten in 2011 because I love the quietness, the friendly community, and the beaches.

Marcus: I grew up in Sweden but have been living and working in Zürich for a long time now. I spend as many weekends as possible in Quinten with my family. I'm quite addicted to photography and have devoted my Instagram account to lake Walensee.

What to Do In Quinten (The Basics)

Quinten is divided into a few hamlets at the southern shore of Walensee. Every hamlet has its own charm. They are connected with a walking trail that offers a lot of wonderful views and places that invite the hiker to stay. The simplest way to explore is via the walking trail from Quinten-Dörfli to Au, where rocks from the steep cliffs fall directly into the lake. Combine your walk with a picnic at Knüsel (a clearing with a fireplace along the shore just east of Quinten). You'll also get a wonderful view if you walk 15 minutes from Quinten-Dörfli up to the

319

schützenhaus (club-house). On the way, visit the small chapel dedicated to San Bernardino.

Quinten is an archipelago with cliffs and steep meadows dividing it from the other hamlets. The walking trail from Quinten to Au is an exception; all other walking trails head steeply upward to the top of the cliffs, the end of the lake, and up to the rocks of the Churfirsten mountain range.

We also recommend taking a scheduled boat to one of the ends of the Walensee (Walenstadt or Weesen) and walking back to Quinten.

In summertime, you should also go for a swim at one of the beautiful beaches. For safety reasons, though, don't cross the lake unaccompanied. Swim along the rocks and don't forget your goggles, because the spectacular landscape continues under the surface of the water.

Hidden Gems for Seasoned Travelers
Skilled hikers should explore the steep slopes surrounding Quinten, including the path to Laubegg (where villages used to transport hay by sled to the Quinten shore).

Another insider tip is to visit of the Kublihus in Laui, where you can spend an evening enjoying a tasty meal or a glass of Quintner wine.

In the winter, I suggest a walk through the magical snowy forest. From December 1st to January 6th there's a very special advent calendar on the path between Au and Quinten-Dörfli. Each day, another gate along the path opens showing different animals from the area. If you're here in winter, keep your eyes open for avalanches in the distance. Avalanche spotting is a favorite local sport.

Day Trips
Since Quinten is only accessible by boat or on foot, you'll need

to head to Walenstadt or Weesen if you want to catch a train or rent a car. Once you're out of our little car-free hamlet, head to Sargans Castle (for its picturesque view), Walenstadt-berg (for views over Sarganserland and the lake), Weesen (a nice village at the lake with boat service to everywhere), Bad Ragaz' Tamina-Schlucht (a deep gorge with a walking path), Betlis (for its waterfalls), Murg/Murgtal (for excellent hiking), and the Flumserberg ski and hiking region.

On a good-weather day, take the funicular up to Pizol. From there, you'll have panoramic views of Germany, Liechtenstein, and Austria.

Where to Hike

The most popular hike is from Weesen to Quinten to Walen-stadt, which stretches from end-to-end across the entire lake and takes about eight hours to walk. The hike to the Murgsee lakes, which starts at one of the two parking areas at Murgtal (just above Murg), is also a nearby classic.

From May to October, the five-hour hike along five lakes in Pizol (known as the 5-Seen-Wanderung) is a must-do for the ambitious hiker and for any photographer. It offers the most stunning views at altitude between 7,000 and 10,000 feet.

Where to Eat & Drink (Favorite Restaurants & Bars)

Sagibeiz (at Alte Staatsstrasse 6 in Murg) is the place to be on the south side of the lake. In Unterterzen, the Resort Walensee (at Gostenstrasse 20) offers a picturesque setting on the lake with a backdrop of mountains. In Quinten, Seehus and Schifflände, are both worth a visit. And don't miss the terrace in front of Ürsel and Susanne's farmhouse, slightly above the Au wharf.

There's also a wine bar in the old post office and Maggie's Shop in the cellar of an old farmhouse (where she sells delicious specialties produced in house). Pro tip: Buy the mustard made with ficus for barbecues at the lake.

Budget Tips

We have this in common with Venice: all goods have to be shipped across the water. This means that if Switzerland is expensive, Quinten is even more so, and if you want to cook for yourself at all, you'll need to bring groceries over from Murg (we don't have a grocery store here).

How to Fit In

Don't litter, be friendly, and smile. You will get a smile back! Don't pitch your tent without asking the mayor for permission and always let the hay car pass when it crosses below the pergola down at Quinten Harbor.

How to Meet Locals & Make Friends

The best way to make friends is to help them with their work in the vineyards, meadows, and gardens. If that sounds like too much work, you can find some of the locals at break times and after work at the regulars' tables at Seehus and Schifflände. Toward dusk, you'll find people taking a walk at the lake or sitting outside enjoying the evening.

Best Places to Take a Photo

The public boat between Murg and Quinten is probably the best photo spot in the region. For knick-knack lovers, the gift shop in the old school is something special. For hikers, head up the rocks behind the village.

Final Notes & Other Tips

Quinten is a car-free town that can only be reached by boat or on foot. Behind the town, you'll find pure nature and summits. This means if you want groceries, you have to cross the lake. In nearby Murg, there is a small shop and you can, of course, find shopping centers about half an hour away.

Find Marcus and Marc at instagram.com/quintner and instagram.com/buentner.

WEESEN

Gorgeous lakes & mountains in a Mediterranean climate.

FIND WI-FI HERE: Most hotels (including the Flyhof).

LANGUAGE: German   **CANTON:** St. Gallen

Burkhard Zerlauth
Chef. Family Man.

About Burkhard

My name is Burkhard Zerlauth. I am a 45-year-old husband and father of two sons. I am originally from Austria but have lived in Switzerland since 1989. By profession, I am a trained chef and waiter. In February 2013, I rented the Flyhof hotel and restaurant, which I now run full-time. In my free time, I spend as much time as I can with the family.

What to Do In Weesen (The Basics)

We have a crystal-clear lake surrounded by a great forest and mountain region. The area is ideal for walking, cycling, swimming, climbing, diving, skiing, and pretty much any other outdoor sport you can think of. Nature lovers will find a lot to love here.

Hidden Gems for Seasoned Travelers

One particularly rewarding hike leads from the town Arvenbüel to Amden to the viewpoint Chapf (more than 4,000 feet above sea level), which has a stunning panoramic view of the Glarus Alps and the entire length of Lake Walen. The hike only takes about an hour.

Another rewarding hike is the forest trail that leads from the village of Betlis to a viewing platform overlooking the spectacular Seerenbach waterfall on the north shore of Lake Walen. It boasts a cascade height of almost 2,000 feet as it makes its way down to Betlis to join the waters of the Rin Spring.

The gorge where the waterfalls plunge into the depths is also incredibly impressive; the spring at the bottom is naturally lit up from the inside. At the beginning of the 20th century, researchers began to investigate the source of this light and discovered a large cave system underwater. About two miles from the cave entrance is a junction where water disappears inside the mountain. Where to? Well, so far no one knows. It may well remain a mystery forever.

Where to Stay
Weesen is on Lake Walen and is perfect for those seeking a lakeside view and Mediterranean climate. Amden is embedded in a mountain landscape. Both are worth visiting and both are nice to stay in as well.

Day Trips
One favorite day trip is the picturesque village of Quinten, located on the bank of Lake Walen across from Murg (where you'll find the train station). It's only accessible by boat or on foot and the term "traffic" is literally unheard of there. Being south-facing under the steep faces of the Churfirsten gives this place such a mild climate that it has become an excellent wine, fig, and kiwi-producing region.

Betlis, mentioned above for its waterfall (one of Switzerland's highest), is another special spot with a Mediterranean climate and almost 40 residents. The town is situated on the southern slopes of the Ammler Cliffs. The unique climate means the town grows grapes, figs, and palms. It's a wonderful little place to stay, where the world seems always seems to be in order.

Where to Hike
Both Amden and Weesen are inviting for hikers, especially in

the summer. I particularly recommend the walks from Walen to the Spear, Leistkamm, or Mattstock peaks. Those routes offer lots of views and a true Swiss hiking experience.

Where to Eat & Drink (Favorite Restaurants & Bars)

My favorite restaurants are Paradiesli (at Obere Betliserstrasse 12) and Strahlegg (at Untere Betliserstrasse 4) in Betlis. Both have wonderful locations overlooking the lake.

How to Fit In

Keep things tidy. Switzerland is a very clean and well-organized country, which says a lot about the people and their values.

How to Meet Locals & Make Friends

Just start a conversation with someone. The Swiss are very polite. They like to talk with people from all over the world. In Switzerland, there are four national languages and almost everyone speaks English, which says a lot, I think.

Best Places to Take a Photo

We are surrounded by mountains, so you'll find a lot of beautiful shots along the walking trails here.

Find Burkhard at flyhof.ch.

WALENSTADT
A lakefront paradise in the area known as "Heidiland."

FIND WI-FI HERE: Hotel Churfirsten (hotel & restaurant).

LANGUAGE: German   **CANTON:** St. Gallen

Thomas Kessler
Outdoor Sports Enthusiast. Business Owner.

About Thomas
I'm 37 and was born and raised in Murg on the shores of Walensee. I lived abroad for a while, then made my way home seven years ago with a plan to start an outdoor company called Outivity. Since I've always felt connected to nature, this seemed like a logical next step.

I spend my free time (as you'll have guessed) in the mountains climbing, mountaineering, paragliding, skiing, etc.

What to Do In Walenstadt (The Basics)
The first thing everyone should do is explore the lake. Walk around. Take photos. Enjoy.

After that, take a cruise on the lake to the wine village of Quinten. Enjoy a gondola ride up to Flumserberg for a hike. Or have fun on the summer toboggan run, FLOOMZER.

Hidden Gems for Seasoned Travelers
In the summertime, go up to the Schrina/Walenstadtberg viewpoint for sweeping views of the valley and the lake. You can get there by car or via public bus service to Walenstadt-berg/Hoehenklinik and then a 30-minute walk uphill to Schrina.

(You can also go in winter, but you have to walk up and pull your own sled for getting back down.)

Day Trips

Go to Flumserberg and have fun on the summer toboggan run (the FLOOMZER), spend an afternoon on the climbing tower (CLiiMBER), or just take the gondola up to Maschgenkamm and have a latte with a view of the surrounding mountains.

In the winter, Flumserberg is a mecca of skiing, sledding, winter hiking, husky rides, and snowshoeing.

It's also easy to get to Bad Ragaz to visit the Tamina Gorge and take a dip in the thermal bath (Tamina Therme). If you're going by car, you can continue from the Tamina Valley (Taminatal) up to the dam in the Calfeisental where you'll find a little village at the end of the lake called St. Martin. If you don't have a car, you can hike from Taminatal to St. Martin in about 2.5 hours. The town is a real gem.

Another fun option is to rent an e-bike in Unterterzen at the InterSport Walensee (intersportwalensee.ch) and explore the valley that way.

You could also easily visit the small country of Lichtenstein.

Where to Hike

In addition to the great hikes around Flumserberg (for which you can get a free trail map at the gondola station), I recommend the path from Walenstadtberg to Tschingla, just below the walls of the Churfirsten, or the beautiful walks around Murgtal's pristine lakes.

Where to Eat & Drink (Favorite Restaurants & Bars)

Try Neptun Restaurant (on the beach at Kasernenstrasse 10 and only open in summer), Boomerang Bar (at Stampfstrasse 78), and the tiny Ochsen Bar (at Seestrasse 8). Or take the boat to Quinten to enjoy the Mediterranean climate and go for a local fish menu in Restaurant Seehus.

How to Meet Locals & Make Friends

In the summertime, the place to be is Neptun. It's a strand bar/ bistro where you can get your beer while sunbathing along the Walensee. In the evenings, people may move to Boomerang Pub, a five-minute walk away.

Best Places to Take a Photo

At the lakeshore or high above town at the viewpoint in Schrina/Walenstadtberg.

Find Thomas at outivity.ch.

ST. MORITZ

Gliz, glamour, & an eclectic mix of cultures, activities, & lifestyles.

FIND WI-FI HERE: Most restaurants & cafes.

LANGUAGE: Romansh & German   **CANTON:** Graubünden

Reto Mathis
Foodie. Event Organizer.

About Reto
I was born in the Engadin and have lived here most of my life. For more than 20 years, I have been the head of seven different restaurants—including La Marmite, renowned for its truffle and caviar specialties—under the umbrella of Mathis Food Affairs.

I also organize events, including the St. Moritz Gourmet Festival, the St. Moritz Music Summit, and the ChefAlps International Cooking Summit. I also work as a caterer for companies and organizers of major events, such as Audi, FIFA, and the Snow Polo World Cup St. Moritz. And I distribute the Reto Mathis Delicatessen line with selected specialties for epicures.

When I'm not working, I hit the slopes in the early morning or bike into the Roseg Valley in summer.

What to Do In St. Moritz (The Basics)
In the winter, get up early to watch the Cresta riders sled the famous run or watch the sunrise with a morning coffee at the quattroBAR, followed by skiing.

In summer, golfing one of our two beautiful 18-hole courses is an excellent way to spend a day. And there is a pleasant nine-hole executive course at the Kulm Hotel.

I also recommend biking along the Corviglia Flow Trail. Go up with the cable car (it transports bikes) and enjoy the downhill run. Or take on one of our biking tour routes: St. Moritz – Bernina Pass – Alp Grüm – Pizzoccheri at the Hotel Bellavista – St. Moritz or St. Moritz – Rosegtal – St. Moritz.

Hidden Gems for Seasoned Travelers
One fun thing to do is have lunch at the Kuhstall in Furtschellas, then go up the mountain by ratrack (small tractor) and race down on a sled.

Where to Stay
Stay in the center of town (Dorf) to see and be a part of the city energy. Everything is walking distance, so it's easy to get around.

Day Trips
Skiing at Diavolezza/Lagalb over the glacier is definitely an experience. It's also easy to hop over to Livigno or Chiavenna in Italy for a change of scenery and Italian flair.

Where to Hike
I am a big fan of the nature reserve in Zernez. Bring binoculars and a guidebook and you are bound to discover something special. For experienced hikers, I recommend the hike up to Muottas da Schlarigna for fantastic views over the valley and then the trail over to the Hahnensee for lunch.

I also love the route from St. Moritz Bad to Alp Staz to Muottas da Schalrigna (where the 1,000-year-old Swiss stone pine tree population is the oldest of the valley) to the Alpine path toward Hahnensee and back to St. Moritz Bad and the route called Via Engiadina from Sils Baselgia to Grevasalvas to Maloja along the lake passing Isola and back to Sils.

What to Eat & Drink
Try the Engadin sausage with polenta or rösti and the bündner platter with air-cured beef, Alp cheese, and pickles.

Where to Eat & Drink (Favorite Restaurants & Bars)
For bars, try the Cascade Polo Bar (at Via Somplaz 6), the Carlton Hotel Lounge (at Via Johannes Badrutt 11), and the Sunny Bar at the Kulm Hotel (at Via Veglia 18).

For restaurants, visit Krone (at Via Tinus 9), Ecco on Snow (at Via Maistra 3), and La Coupole Matsuhisa (at Serlas 27).

Best Places to Take a Photo
In front of Badrutt's Palace Hotel, by the lake, or on the slopes.

Final Notes & Other Tips
The St. Moritz Gourmet Festival takes place the last week in January and offers 40 different events for gourmet fans at prices from 40 - 550 francs per person. For more than two decades, the festival has had worldwide cult status. Over the last 21 years, no fewer than 64,000 gourmet fans have come to the Engadin to be spoiled for a whole week by 181 international master chefs from over 30 nations.

Find Reto at mathisfood.ch, cascade-stmoritz.ch, delicatessen-rm.ch, stmoritz-gourmetfestival.ch, and chefalps.com.

AROSA
Guaranteed winter snow & great skiing.

FIND WI-FI HERE: Check with the tourist office for a list of options.

LANGUAGE: Romansh & German   **CANTON:** Graubünden

Andres Widmer
Chef. Climber. Mountaineer. Skier. Traveler.

About Andres

I grew up in a small dairy-farming village near Arosa called Langwies. In 2002, my parents moved us to Arosa to open a bakery (which has two locations in town and is my first recommendation for coffee, pastries, and baked goods).

After school, I served in the Swiss army as a chef for a time, which took me to 11 different bases, allowing me to see much more of my country and to learn French and Italian.

After the military, my brother and I took a six-month trip around the world. It had a huge impact on my life. Since that trip, I travel as much as possible. One highlight was crossing South America (from the Pacific to the Atlantic) by myself.

Now I'm working in Vaduz. I come to visit my family at least once a month, so I'm still connected to my hometown.

Since this is a mountainous area, my free time activities are climbing, mountaineering, ice climbing, skiing, and pretty much anything else that takes me up and down the peaks. I also love scuba diving and playing guitar.

What to Do In Arosa (The Basics)

The first thing to understand is that Arosa has drastic low and high seasons. In low season (between the summer and winter seasons), you can walk from the top of the village down to its bottom without seeing a single person. The best time to come is summer or winter—and the activities vary by season.

In winter, obviously, go skiing. Find a local to get you to the fastest cable cars and avoid the crowds. Last winter, they opened a cable car connection between Arosa and Lenzerheide, which means now you can go skiing in two different areas with one ticket. If you aren't into skiing, there are nice sled runs, beautiful viewpoints to explore on foot, and events every week.

In summer, hiking is the most obvious activity, but you can also go biking, swimming, or paragliding—and we have plenty of events, too. The biggest event in summer is the classic car race, which hosts 250 classic cars and more than 45,000 guests. There is also a music course here in town where you can improve your skills as musician.

Hidden Gems for Seasoned Travelers

If you enjoy nature, there are about 16 lakes hidden around the surrounding area, each one like a Bob Ross painting. My personal favorite is the Schwellisee. It's easily accessible on foot, not too crowded, and just below my second favorite lake, Älplisee. On the way, you practically step on a spring. I've always been fascinated by water and seeing water coming out of holes in the rock is something you usually don't just stumble over.

For hiking, I recommend Schiesshorn, which definitely has the best view of Arosa and the valley. Make sure you have good shoes. If you want to see a classic Alpine village, hike from the dam to Medergen or (a bit further) Sapün.

For the sporty, there are two hidden waterfalls for ice climbing, one of which is even good for beginners. There is a climbing garden (a rock outcrop with bolts for sport climbing) on top of the Weisshorn—and not many people know that. Also, in summer you can hike to the Ramoz hut, a small hut about two hours away from civilization in the mountains. Stay overnight and hike the highest peaks the next morning.

Day Trips

If you like beautiful landscapes, take the train to St. Moritz. If you want to go further, the Glacier Express train goes directly from Chur to Zermatt.

In summer, there are beautiful places to swim—like Crestasee or Caumasee near Flims—which are very hidden, mostly known only to locals but still crowded on sunny days.

In winter, you can cross the mountains by cable car to Lenzerheide and spend some time in the village or skiing.

In the valley (Schanfigg), there is a small skiing area called Hochwang. It is small and the cable cars are slow, but many people love it because it's cheap, faces south (which means a lot of sun), and offers nice landscapes and slopes and very few tourists. To get there, take the road up to Fatschel from St. Peter (there is a shuttle bus in winter).

Where to Hike

I love the trails leading from Arosa to Ochsenalp, Medergen, Strassberg, Pirigen, Matijschhorn, Schiesshorn, Rothorn, Hörnli, and the lakes I mentioned. There's even a trail you can walk all the way down to Chur if you are tough enough. All these trails are well marked. [Editor's note: You can get official maps at the tourist office, but Andres kindly sent some starter maps for his favorite hikes. Download them at *gigigriffis.com/arosa*, password: arosa.]

For Schiesshorn, there are two ways to reach the top, so you can hike up one side and go down on the other. They are both about the same distance. And the top gives you the perfect overview of Arosa. This is a one-day hike.

For Weisshorn-Hörnli, you'll need an all-inclusive card for Arosa to reach the top of Weisshorn by cable car. On top is a great view (you see the entire valley, including Chur). From there, walk to Hörnli. When you arrive, you can take the cable car back down. There are restaurants at both ends of the trail.

For Ramozhütte (the small hut I mentioned earlier), allow about two hours. The path goes trough a small, beautiful valley of pure nature. The hut is run by the Swiss Alpin Club (SAC) and for a small fee you can stay overnight, but you'll need to book ahead. The hike up there is great as it is, but if you want more, you can go to the Erzhorn saddle, cross to the mountain cabin, and hike down to Älplisee and back to Arosa.

For the Arosa – Medergen – Sapün – Langwies hike, you'll be walking through the small, beautiful villages of Medergen and Sapün. This is an easy hike (not steep), but it's quite a distance. From Langwies, you can take the train back to Arosa.

And for the Schanfigg high hiking trail, there are actually two trails, both ending in Chur. One is from Arosa over Ochsenalp to Tschiertschen and then Chur; the other is through Medergen, Strelapass, Strassberg (Fondei), Nufsch (Pirigen), Hochwang (the small ski region I told you about), and then Chur. Finishing the entire distance takes a lot.

What to Eat & Drink

In autumn, there are lots of deer-based meals to die for, always with spätzle bread and red cabbage. In spring there is asparagus on every menu in large variety.

My favorite local dish is capuns (veggies, dough, and meat rolled in a chard leaf, cooked in bouillon, then baked with cream and cheese). You simply *have to* try that one. Then there's the bündner gerstensuppe (a cream soup with barley, dry meat, and vegetables), which is very tasty. Pizokel (a dough similar to spätzle but better) is a great dish for vegetarians. Maluns (slow-fried potatoes) and plain in pligna (oven-made hash browns) are also very tasty and particular to this region.

Where to Eat & Drink (Favorite Restaurants & Bars)

At Vetter (on Seeblickstrasse), you'll find regional food, good prices, good quality, nice ambiance, and a large assortment of wines. This place is my personal favorite.

Then there's Ahaan Thai (in the Hotel Kulm on Innere Post-strasse). If you like Thai food, that's the place to go! Fancy, original, authentic...it's a little pricey but definitely worth it.

Next, there's Gspan (on Gspanstrasse), which is small, cozy, affordable, and tasty and has good offerings for larger groups, and Taverne (also in the Kulm Hotel) for Mediterranean food, including the best pizza in town. Finally, try Golfhuus (on Maranerstrasse)—a modern, snug place with a large terrace away from the center of town.

For cafes, stop by my parents' places: Widmer's Snackbeck (on Dorfplatz) and Café am See (on Poststrasse).

For bars, try Los (on Haus Madrisa)—the biggest bar in town, playing hard rock and metal music. Halli Galli (on Äussere Poststrasse) is the place to go for après ski (on Wednesdays, all drinks are just 5 francs). And Overtime (on Am Postplatz) is a modern spot with good drinks and nice ambiance. Sadly, it's typically very crowded.

Budget Tips

In Arosa, there is an all-inclusive card, which saves you a lot of money, especially for skiing, local transportation, and some other offerings. As a hotel guest, normally you'll get one of those automatically, but you can also grab one at the tourist office if you aren't in one of the hotels.

EASTERN SWITZERLAND

You'll definitely want to come to Arosa by train. Not only does the road from Chur have 365 turns (which can be a bit daunting and dangerous, especially in winter), but parking is not cheap or easily found. Gasoline is also more expensive here.

How to Fit In
Arosa is a mix of Swiss and international people, so cultural faux pas are rare. What we don't like is what young and drunk people often do—you know, property damage, disturbing the peace (especially at night), barfing and urinating in stairways, etc. The latter is officially prohibited with a fine of 100 francs.

As far as tipping goes, I round up or give around 10%.

How to Meet Locals & Make Friends
The bar, the pub, or a small local event could be good places.

Final Notes & Other Tips
Arosa is basically built on tourism and our tourism has been on the decline. This means that we've seen a lot of changes in town over the past few years—bars and hotels closing or under new ownership—and our economy has been struggling a bit. What this also means is that if you're looking to get away from the hordes of tourists, Arosa is now a good place for that. You might just have that hiking trail all to yourself.

DAVOS
The highest city in the Alps.

FIND WI-FI HERE: Most restaurants.

LANGUAGE: Romansh & German   **CANTON:** Graubünden

Claudi Melber
Ski Instructor. Biker. Hiker. Outdoor Enthusiast.

About Claudi
Originally from Germany, I now live in Davos and work full-time as a sports teacher and occasionally as a ski instructor. In my free time, I love skiing, hiking, biking, and gymnastics.

What to Do In Davos (The Basics)
First, check out the beautiful lake and the great hiking tracks all around us. Klosters—a small town near Davos—has a beautiful walk to the Veraina Valley and another great hike to the Älpeti (Klosters' home mountain). From there, you'll have a great view over the mountains.

It's also nice to take a walk through Davos and go for a coffee in one of the nice cafés in town. If you like ice hockey, you should come in winter to watch a match of the HC-Davos.

Hidden Gems for Seasoned Travelers
For skiing, come in January or early February. The slopes are emptier (because the Swiss holidays are over) and the snow is still amazing most of the time. After a ski day, have a traditional cheese fondue.

In summer, it's always nice to have a swim in the lake after a hike or biking tour. And while you're here, try a plättli (a plate of traditional sausages and cheese from the region).

Day Trips
Take the Glacier Express from Klosters to St. Moritz and back for some beautiful views. St. Moritz itself is also really nice...very high society. And near St. Moritz is Lenzerheide; I love to go skiing there.

I also recommend spending a day in Therme Vals, with its beautiful sauna and pool with a view of the mountains.

Where to Hike
I recommend getting up early and hiking up the Schwarzhorn to watch the sunrise. It's a four-hour hike but absolutely worth it. If you don't want to wake in the dark, it's also great there during the day.

Where to Eat & Drink (Favorite Restaurants & Bars)
For a great cup of coffee and an amazing cake, go to Kaffee-klatsch (at Promenade 72; phone: +41 81 413 3016). Reservations are recommended, as it's always busy.

For a great burger and a chat with the super-nice staff, try Chämi Bar (at Promenade 83). For steak cooked on a hot stone, check out Ochsen (at Talstrasse 10; phone: +41 081 417 6449). For late-night partying, go to Ex Bar (at Promenade 63) or in the Pöstli Club (at Promenade 42).

How to Fit In
When hiking, always greet people as you pass.

Best Places to Take a Photo
The top of the Alps is always a good bet. Take the gondola to Jakobshorn or Parsenn for an amazing view of Davos and the mountains around.

KLOSTERS
A typical Swiss mountain village.

FIND WI-FI HERE: Most hotels & the tourist office.

LANGUAGE: German   **CANTON:** Graubünden

Dumeng Andrist
Family Man. Skier. Ice Hockey Player. Hiker. Hunter.

About Dumeng
I was born in Klosters in 1977 and still live here today. I am married with two children. Work-wise, I am the owner of a sport shop in Klosters (which I run with my wife, my parents, and eight employees). And in my free time, I ski like crazy, play ice hockey, spend time with my family, hike, and hunt.

What to Do In Klosters (The Basics)
In the winter, I recommend skiing. We have so many different possibilities...ski trails for all levels, beautiful off-piste runs. January is a particularly nice time to come, much quieter with better prices and less people on the slopes.

For non-skiers, I recommend taking one of the cable cars up the mountains for a pleasant walk.

In summer, we are a major hiking and biking area, so grab your boots or your cycle and hit the trails.

Hidden Gems for Seasoned Travelers
We have some really beautiful valleys here. I recommend exploring the Schlappin Valley or Monbiel/Vereina.

In town, the Nutli Hüschi Folk Museum, which showcases how locals lived from the 17th to 19th centuries, is pretty special, as is the quirky café Kaffee Klatsch (at Promenade 72) in Davos.

In winter, I'm a big fan of the long ski run from Weissfluhgipfel to the Schieferlodge and our guided tours off-piste from Madrisa to Gargellen and back to St. Antönien.

In summer, there are outdoor concerts once a month. And the Kulturschuppen theater in Klosters is small and fine.

Day Trips
Head to the region's capitol city (Chur), spend a day in neighboring Davos, or make a wonderful and special train trip to the Engadin (where you'll find the well-known city of St. Moritz). There's a wonderful thermal spa in Hotel Vereina in Bad Ragaz (half an hour away by train). And the Bündner Herrschaft wine area is full of places to taste good local wine.

Where to Hike
I recommend the long journey from Klosters to Monbiel, then to Garfun, up to Sardasca, and to the Silvrettalodge. It takes about five hours (though you can shorten the journey by taking a taxi or bus up to Sardasca in the summer and hiking the two hours to Silvrettalodge from there). I also enjoy the trek to the Vereina mountain hut.

What to Eat & Drink
In addition to the classics, try chäsgetschäder (a crispy dish made with cheese and stale bread).

Where to Eat & Drink (Favorite Restaurants & Bars)
The Chesa Bar (at Bahnhofstrasse 12) in our oldest hotel is lovely and old. For a newer style, I recommend Bär's Café (at Alte Bahnhofstrasse 1) or the well-known Casa Antica (at Landstrasse 176).

For food, the Walserhof (at Landstrasse 141) is one of the best restaurants in town. The Vereina Restaurant (at Landstrasse

179), the Alpina (at Bahnhofstrasse 1), or Chesa Grischuna (at Bahnhofstrasse 12) are all highly recommended as well.

How to Fit In
It's always good to read a book about Switzerland or Graubünden. That way you'll know more about it and your stay will be more interesting.

How to Meet Locals & Make Friends
If you're staying a while, try an athletic club or a ski gym to meet locals. For a short stay, go skiing and to the local bars.

Best Places to Take a Photo
Take the cable car to Madrisa where you'll have a marvelous view over the village. Walk up to the Alpenrösli (a mountain hut). Or, by car, take two turns up toward Davos and you'll come to a parking area with a wonderful view over Klosters.

Find Dumeng at andrist-sport.ch.

TSCHIERV

Natural beauty meets a unique sub-culture & language.

FIND WI-FI HERE: At most hotels & holiday apartments.

LANGUAGE: Romansh & German   **CANTON:** Graubünden

Katherine & Marco Gilly
Walkers. Gardeners. Retirees.

About Katherine & Marco
Katherine is English and has been in Switzerland since 1969. Marco is Swiss. We've lived in Tschierv since 1981. And we are both retired—Marco from being a geologist, Katherine from being an English teacher and EFL examiner.

In our free time, we enjoy walking, gardening, listening to music, amateur dramatics, singing, and spending time with our family (three grown-up children).

What to Do In Tschierv (The Basics)
Take in the scenery. Enjoy the unspoiled natural surroundings. Visit the local museums and restaurants.

In the winter, we have really excellent skiing, cross-country skiing, snowshoeing, ski touring, and tobogganing. The Minschuns ski area is ideal for families with young children, with an excellent ski school and classes for all ages and abilities. You can rent skis and other equipment at outlets in the valley.

Hidden Gems for Seasoned Travelers
Visit the Convent of St. John in Müstair for its Carolingian frescoes and convent museum, the Chasa Jaura (a museum of local traditions and artifacts), the Muglin Mall (a 17th-century

343

mill), the Museum Grenzbetzung 1914-18 (the border occupation museum), and the Distilleria Antica (a local family-run distillery). Explore the source of River Rom, the pretty Alpine lake, Lai da Rims, and the Swiss National Park (where you'll find excellent walks and an information center).

Where to Stay

There are hotels and holiday apartments in all six charming villages in Val Müstair (our valley). Guests will find a warm welcome wherever they go.

Day Trips

We like the upper and lower Engadin—a long valley with high mountains on either side. It's home of the Engadin Ski Marathon every March and is beautiful in every season, with picturesque villages, beautifully decorated houses decked out with flowers all summer long, and excellent walking, hiking, and mountain biking. The golden larch forests of autumn are a particularly amazing sight.

Another favorite is St. Moritz, which is very chic with plenty of expensive boutiques and interesting museums (the Segantini Museum and Engadiner Museum, to name two). In winter, there's a lot going on, from horse racing to polo to cricket on the frozen surface of the lake. Just outside town in Pontresina, the Museum Alpin is also worth seeing.

Scuol, with its spa bath, is a great place to go for a relaxing day after some intense skiing or hiking in the region. Guarda is very picturesque and is well known as the place that inspired the famous Ursin books written by Selina Chönz and beautifully illustrated by Alois Carigiet.

Then there's Merano (South Tirol), which is a totally different world from our small mountain villages. They have wonderful shopping areas, delightful municipal gardens, and a very beautiful botanical garden called Trautmannsdorff. There's also a great market where you can endulge in fresh fruit, vegetables, cheeses, salamis, air-dried bacon, etc. It's right by the station and held every Friday all summer.

In the summer months (July to October), Bormio (in Italy) is an excellent day trip. The bus trip to Bormio takes you over the Umbrail Pass—the highest road pass in Switzerland—with commentary. Once you're there, the old thermal baths, dating back to Roman times, are the must-see. And if you like, you can continue on the bus from Bormio to Tirano (on the Swiss/Italian border) and take a train through the valley of Poschiavo, over the Bernina Pass, to Pontresina, and then back down the Engadin to Zernez (and from there you can catch a bus back to Val Müstair). We haven't done this yet, but we've heard good things and intend to do it this summer. For bus schedules and info, visit *postauto.ch* or ask at the tourist office.

And finally, Livigno is an interesting place to visit and a duty-free zone.

Where to Hike
Swiss National Park, Val Müstair, the S-charl Valley via Pass da Costainas, the Umbrail Pass, Lai da Rims, and the path along-side River Rom, which runs the length of the valley, are all excellent choices.

What to Eat & Drink
We enjoy local specialties like charn crua (air-dried beef), salsiz (dry-cured sausage), local cheese (from the dairy in Müstair, as well as from the mountain huts), and hirsch or gemspfeffer (venison stew, mainly available in autumn).

As for wines, the county of Grisons has some excellent choices, like Maienfelder, Jeninser, and Malanser, as do the Venosta and Vinschgau valleys just south of us in Italy.

Where to Eat & Drink (Favorite Restaurants & Bars)
Our top choices are Hotel Staila (at Via Maistra 20 in Fuldera), Hotel Central (on Buorcha in Valchava), and Hotel Helvetia (at Via Maistra 62 in Müstair).

Budget Tips

The Gasthaus Alpenrose and Plattatschas at the Umbrail Pass and Restaurant Hirschen (at Via Maistra 30 in Lü) are more affordable than most.

How to Meet Locals & Make Friends

Not many people in Val Müstair speak English, but they are always ready to be helpful and enjoy meeting visitors from elsewhere. The local language is Romansh (which is interesting in itself), but all inhabitants also speak Swiss German/German and probably Italian. Some might also speak French.

Best Places to Take a Photo

For visitors arriving via the Pass dal Fuorn, on reaching the summit (Süsom Givé), the view sweeps over the whole of the valley looking toward Mount Ortler, which stands majestically above the other mountains and which was, prior to World War I, the highest mountain in Austria. (Why isn't it still the highest in Austria, you ask? The borders shifted and it's now in Italy).

There is also an excellent view from the terrace of the Gasthaus Alpenrose. And Lai da Rims is stunning!

Find Katherine & Marco at chasagallas.ch.

CHUR

Beautiful scenery, good gastronomy, & a great vibe.

FIND WI-FI HERE: Most hotels, bars, & restaurants.

LANGUAGE: Romansh & German   **CANTON:** Graubünden

Stefanie Schmid
Traveler. Hostel Front-Office Manager.

About Stefanie

I'm originally from the Rheinfelden area but started traveling when I was 21. I went to Australia first and when I came back I worked in hospitality in many different places. Then I moved to Geneva, worked at a city hostel, and discovered that this is my dream job. From then on, I've been working for hostels anywhere I've lived.

In between jobs, I travel long-term through places like Southeast Asia, Central America, Australia, India, and Canada.

These days, I'm at another dream job, working as the Hostel Manager in the JBN Hostel in Chur.

What to Do In Chur (The Basics)

First, walk around Chur's old town. Then go up to Brambrüesch (our home mountain) to hike, bike, or ski.

Hidden Gems for Seasoned Travelers

You'll find the nicest sunset/sunrise above the vineyards and past the canton school. Just walk through old town Chur toward Arosa up to the canton school and sit on the steps with the whole town spread out below you. This is my favorite spot in Chur.

347

EASTERN SWITZERLAND

Where to Stay
Chur is quite small, so if you stay in town, you can walk everywhere in 10 minutes or less. Welschdörfli is the area where all the good bars and nightlife are, so if you are a party animal, stay there.

Day Trips
Lenzerheide (a mountain resort about an hour away by bus) is really nice.

In the summertime, you can hike or bike to Arosa, returning in the evening. In the winter, you can do the same with skis or a snowboard (the slopes of the two resorts are connected as of winter 2014).

Flims/Laax is also cool for skiing in the wintertime and biking in the summer.

But the really nice things to see are Caumasee (Lake Cauma) and Crestasee (Lake Cresta), which dazzle with blues and greens that change with the light.

In that same direction, you'll find the Rinaulta—one of the nicest canyons in Switzerland.

Where to Hike
The nicest place to go hiking nearby is Dreibündenstein. Our gondola goes up from Chur to Brambrüesch and from there you can walk to Dreibündenstein (or even to Lenzererheide) or just hike around Brambrüesch itself.

Mittenberg and Fürstenwald are also nice if you want to go for a short bike ride or hike.

Where to Eat & Drink (Favorite Restaurants & Bars)
To start, I like Tom's Beer Box (at Untere Gasse 11), where you've got 100 beers to choose from. Then there's Werkstatt (at Untere Gasse 9), which has a relaxed vibe and live music.

For more live music, Selig Tanzbar (at Welschdörfli 19) is good. In the winter, they have a cool live band almost every Friday.

Last but not least, I like Schall und Rauch (on Welschdörfli), which is a nightclub with excellent cocktails.

How to Meet Locals & Make Friends
Go to a quieter, less crowded bar in the old town and talk to somebody. If you buy someone a braulio (traditional herbal liquor), you're in.

Best Places to Take a Photo
Both in the old town and up at my favorite sunset/sunrise place at the canton school (described above).

Find Stefanie at justbenice.ch.

ABOUT THE AUTHOR

Gigi Griffis is a world-traveling entrepreneur and writer with a special love for inspiring stories, new places, and living in the moment. In May 2012, she sold her stuff and became a digital nomad. These days, she's living in Switzerland and exploring and writing about Europe with her pint-sized pooch, Luna.

Gigi is the author of six books, including 100 Locals travel guides for Italy, Paris, Prague, Barcelona, and (now) Switzerland. Her next guide (for France) will launch in late summer 2015 followed by a New York City guide in the winter.

Love what you read here? Find more at *gigigriffis.com*.

ACKNOWLEDGEMENTS

Special thanks to the 100 wonderful people who gave interviews about their homes and expertise for this guide. You are the heart and soul of this work. And it is your passion for your towns that inspired the entire 100 Locals series.

Also, to my designer, Björn Musyal, who is one of the best design professionals I've ever worked with in my life. To my lovely editors—Jessica Trivizas, Jessica Ballou, Jacklyn Lee, Danielle Perrin, Alison Garland, Lakeisha Roberts, and Nichole Faina. And to everyone who helped me install computer programs, work out formatting, make decisions about what to include and how to present things, and deal with all the other tiny details that go into book creation, including Brett, Emily, Georgette, Annette, and my fabulous Facebook community. Without you this book wouldn't be possible.

Finally, thank you to Bobbi Taylor, whose entrepreneurial example is an ongoing inspiration to me, to Valerie, who keeps me sane, and to Lucia, whose support is invaluable.

TRAVELING AROUND EUROPE?

More 100 Locals books are available at gigigriffis.com:

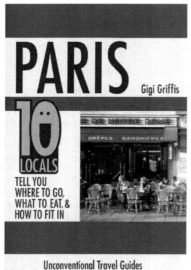

26518908R00197

Made in the USA
Middletown, DE
30 November 2015